Peter Quennell

is one of England's most highly respected literary critics and a versatile and distinguished author in his own right. At Oxford he established his name as a poet, and, since then, has written a novel, *The Phoenix-Kind;* a work of critical acumen, *Baudelaire and the Symbolists;* a book of short stories, *Sympathy;* and has translated *The Memoirs of the Comte de Gramont.* In 1930 he accepted a professorship at a Japanese college, and upon his return to London published an account of this visit in *A Superficial Journey through Tokyo and Peking.*

Best known of his works thus far has been *Byron: The Years of Fame.* Recently, since the completion of *Caroline of England,* he has been traveling on the Continent in search of original records of the poet's life in Italy, which will be the subject of his next book.

CAROLINE
OF ENGLAND

When gruff George of Hanover came to London to be crowned George I of England, he brought with him from the Continent a troublesome son, George Augustus, and the son's wife, Caroline of Anspach. Thus Caroline, the high-bosomed, high-colored German princess, became Queen of England by one of the coincidences of international royalty. She bore George II's many children, chose his mistresses, made his state decisions, and continued to appear in his eyes the simple little mädchen he thought he had married.

For the last time, English life was the life of the court: hence this book about Caroline and the Augustan age is a book about everything that mattered in England from 1700 to 1750. With the bluff Robert Walpole at her one side and the sinuous Lord Hervey at the other, Caroline fought her father-in-law, fought her eldest son, handled the delicate English courtiers with rough German humor, and contrived to make the English people forget that the eyes of their king were forever looking wistfully toward the little principality of Hanover.

It is Peter Quennell's particular genius as a biographer that he transports the reader into the period he has chosen, makes him think in the idiom of that distant day. To sup with Pope and Voltaire, to chat at a reception with Lord Chesterfield, to keep an assignation with Hervey, to escape with George I for a holiday of slippered ease in Germany, one needs but open these pages.

The Augustan age was brief and it was something less than heroic. But it was sparkling, subtle, and unique, and Peter Quennell has caught its full flavor in this distinguished biography.

By Peter Quennell

BYRON: THE YEARS OF FAME

THE PHOENIX-KIND
(A NOVEL)

Caroline of England

AN AUGUSTAN PORTRAIT

By Peter Quennell

"Il ne faut point d'esprit pour s'occuper des vieux événemens."—VOLTAIRE TO MADAME DU DEFFAND.

"A King is to be such a distinct Creature from a Man, that their thoughts are to be put in quite a differing shape . . . "—HALIFAX'S "CHARACTER OF CHARLES II."

THE VIKING PRESS

NEW YORK

1940

COPYRIGHT 1940 BY THE VIKING PRESS, INC.

PRINTED IN THE UNITED STATES OF AMERICA

PUBLISHED IN JANUARY 1940

SECOND PRINTING JANUARY 1940

TO CYRIL CONNOLLY

Foreword

It may be as well to include a few lines on the intention of this book. My study of Caroline of Anspach and England does not profess to be a work of intensive historical research or an essay in the interpretation of political motives. What I have attempted to do is to compose the portrait of a remarkable woman in the setting of one of the least known periods of English history and to examine the effect of her position on her private character. A number of critics have assisted me with good advice, but I wish to record a special debt of gratitude to my friend Sir Edward Marsh, who has been kind enough to read through and correct the proof sheets. The greater part of the section devoted to Pope has appeared in the *Cornhill Magazine* and is reprinted by permission of the Editor.

P. Q.

Illustrations

CAROLINE
OF ENGLAND

GENEALOGICAL TABLE

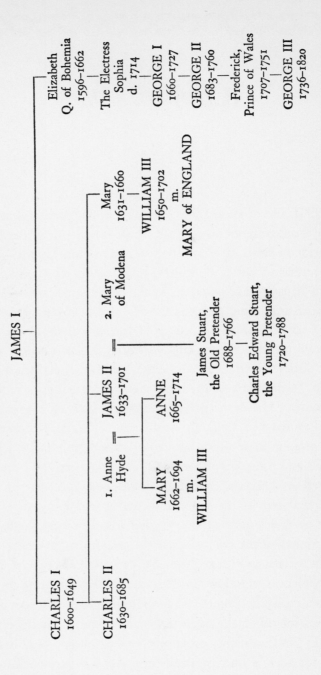

JAMES I

CHARLES I
1600–1649

Elizabeth
Q. of Bohemia
1596–1662

CHARLES II
1630–1685

The Electress
Sophia
d. 1714

JAMES II
1633–1701

1. Anne
Hyde

2. Mary
of Modena

Mary
1631–1660

GEORGE I
1660–1727

MARY
1662–1694
m.
WILLIAM III

ANNE
1665–1714

James Stuart,
the Old Pretender
1688–1766

WILLIAM III
1650–1702
m.
MARY of ENGLAND

GEORGE II
1683–1760

Charles Edward Stuart,
the Young Pretender
1720–1788

Frederick,
Prince of Wales
1707–1751

GEORGE III
1736–1820

Chapter One

1

*I*F THE life of every family is difficult, the problems of a royal family are sometimes insuperable. Pride is endemic in royal blood; and pride of birth gives an edge to natures that might otherwise have remained mild, underlines and emphasizes minor faults, lends a haughty exaggeration to the stolidest temperament. It is not surprising, then, that the history of any royal family should be very often a history of quarrels, and that royal personages remarkable for the patient and self-effacing performance of their public duties should be equally remarkable for their lack of private reserve. In domestic disputatiousness, few families have outdone the House of Hanover, and when, after a period of uneasy expectation, they reached England in the year 1714, they brought with them among their other hereditary baggage a large legacy of quarrels and ill-feeling. Three years later, in 1717, their differences achieved a scandalous and dramatic climax. Incensed by the unfilial behaviour of his son and heir, the old King first put the Prince of Wales under arrest—yeomen with lowered halberds being stationed at the door of the Princess's bedroom—next ordered his immediate expulsion from St. James's Palace. The Princess bravely elected to follow her husband. Still weak after childbirth, she rose, rallied her Maids of Honour and prepared to set out. Her children, including the latest little prince, she was obliged to leave behind. The hour was inopportune. No preparations had been made for such a hurried departure. All was wretchedness, confusion and despair, and in the gloom that enveloped the royal party the only relief was provided by Miss Bellenden, a pretty and irrepressible Maid of Honour, who was heard humming the words of an old tune—"Over the Hills and Far Away"—as she bounded downstairs to join the fugitives.

That night they rested at a house in Albemarle Street which belonged to Lord Grantham, the Prince's Chamberlain. George Augustus, who thus found himself under the humiliating necessity of seeking shelter, at a moment's notice, beneath a servant's and a subject's roof, was now a man of thirty-three; his wife, Wilhelmina Caroline, was seven months older; and though it was the Prince who always appeared to assume the command, who spoke loudest and longest and seemed to fling his authority and dignity in the faces of his hearers at every word, there were some who realized that the Princess was a power to be reckoned with. But experience had taught her to conceal her gifts. Born Princess of Brandenburg-Anspach, she had passed her earliest years in the singularly dangerous and uncomfortable atmosphere of late seventeenth-century German courts, where an elaborate ceremonial, borrowed from Versailles and St. Cloud, overlay the primitive savagery of their petty rulers. Her father had died when she was three, and the Margravine thereupon quitted the enormous and splendid palace in which her daughter had been born, with its florid frescoes representing the turbulent apotheoses of past Margraves, its porcelain galleries and gilded Baroque chambers, and made her way to the court of her friends, the Elector and Electress of Brandenburg, who presently saw to it that she should marry again. Their motives were judicious, but their choice unfortunate. The Elector of Saxony, being violently attached to his mistress, had no desire to contract the political alliance for which he was intended, and, having submitted, was at no pains to conceal his aversion. Notwithstanding all that his courtiers could do, he had determined to make a bigamous second marriage, and

pamphlets in defence of polygamy, written on the Elector's behalf, had already been circulated through his dominions, when
smallpox—that *deus ex machina* of so many early tragedies—
claimed the mistress, who had just then succeeded in driving her
lover's consort into humiliated retirement. The Elector had refused to leave her sick-room. Watching the hideous progress of a
disease that destroys the last traces of beauty before it extinguishes
the final spark of life, he, too, fell its victim and died less than a
fortnight later, in the year 1694. His widow expired in 1696, leaving her daughter alone and helpless at the age of twelve.

The years that followed, however, were comparatively peace-
ful. The Elector and Electress of Brandenburg (afterwards first
King and Queen of Prussia) were her guardians, and at the court
of Berlin, under the eye of the Electress Sophie Charlotte, daughter
of the Electress Sophia of Hanover and sister to the future George I
of England, Caroline was bred up to play her part in the great
matrimonial game, to form a further link in the intricate system
of family alliances. It was the ordinary destiny a royal virgin must
expect; but very far from ordinary was the education that she
received; for her guardian, Sophie Charlotte, was an exceedingly
remarkable woman, and the court that she assembled at her palace
of Charlottenburg just outside Berlin suggested the philosophic
court of Akbar rather than an establishment kept by a Christian
and German princess during the last decade of the seventeenth
century. Here came metaphysicians, scientists, free-thinkers, Jesuits
and Protestant divines; and, just as some monarchs have arranged
spectacular combats between strange animals fetched from the
farthest corners of the earth, so the Electress would dispose of her
theological monsters, setting the Jesuit against the Huguenot, the
priestly controversialist against the sceptic, herself egging them
on to battle with an occasional sally. These contests, which were
impassioned and earnest, though (one cannot help suspecting)
generally a little heavy-handed, sometimes lasted till the small

hours of the morning; and since the King, a more typically Teutonic personage, got up very early, while the Queen retired to bed very late, their courtiers were often obliged to move on from the Queen's evening assembly to the King's morning levee without pausing to snatch an hour of repose.

It was at Charlottenburg that Caroline met Leibniz, who continued to advise and flatter her to the end of his life, as he had advised and flattered Sophie Charlotte and her mother, the Electress Sophia. But more important was the influence of her own sex. Towards her guardian she felt an attraction, deeper, perhaps, and more disinterested than she was ever to feel again, and, besides imitating her tricks of speaking and moving, Caroline acquired the same tastes, interests and habits of thought—Sophie Charlotte's love of theological argument, and a certain speculative laxity in questions of dogma. Meanwhile she was emerging from adolescence. Large, plump, firm-bodied, Caroline was generally esteemed a beauty—but a beauty in the German style, fit to satisfy the huge, wholesome appetite of a contemporary German prince, with her beautifully modelled hands and arms, and a bosom so smooth and so expansive that even in advanced middle age it could still command from her husband an almost doting admiration. Soon she was to receive a splendid proposal of marriage. In 1704 the Archduke Charles, heir to the Holy Roman Empire, made an offer which was conveyed through the Elector Palatine; but the Princess, though she professed herself much gratified, hung back, seemed to be on the point of consenting, then decided that she must refuse, alleging that she could not change her religion. It was in vain that the King of Prussia bullied his ward, in vain that a Jesuit priest, employing all the skill of his brilliant Order, unfolded before the young woman's obstinate eyes all the spiritual seductions of the Roman Church. She was ready to argue, but she would not be persuaded. Sitting down with a Bible between them, the priest and his intended proselyte would dispute at great length, but when the priest, being the more experienced, managed to break through her defences, the Princess's only answer was to burst into tears. Long afterwards Caroline's refusal to join the Catholic Church was made a subject of solemn panegyric by English court-poetasters. They declared that she had "scorned an Empire for religion's sake"; but it seems more probable that it was not her religion so much as the speculative and irreligious tendencies she had imbibed from the Queen of Prussia that stood her in good stead—that what she feared to lose was less her Protestantism than her independence.

Next year was to present a more serious trial. In January 1705, the Queen of Prussia, who was visiting her mother at the court of Hanover, fell ill and learned from her doctors that she must die. Her death-bed—prototype of many sceptical eighteenth-century death-beds—has been described in some detail by her celebrated grandson, Frederick the Great. The French chaplain at Hanover tendered his services, but they were politely declined, for, as the Queen remarked, she had devoted twenty years of study to religious questions, and he could tell her nothing that she did not already know. She was dying in peace, she added. Death had come to crown her curiosity. At last she would be able to satisfy her inquisitiveness about the origin of things, "which even Leibniz could never explain to me—to understand space, infinity, being and nothingness"; while, as for the King, her husband, "I shall afford him the opportunity of giving me a magnificent funeral." . . . Somewhat nonplussed, no doubt, by her display of fortitude, the priest took refuge in pious commonplace, and ventured to observe that even kings and queens were mortal and must expect to die like other men. *"Je le sais bien,"* replied the Queen, and, soon afterwards, giving a deep sigh—a sigh of impatience at the priest's dullness, or of satisfaction that she was at length setting forth on such an eminently philosophic journey—Sophie Charlotte closed her eyes for the last time. Confined to her room by a serious illness, the Electress Sophia was unable to be present at her daughter's death-bed. Caroline was at Anspach with her half-brother, and to Leibniz, who wrote a long letter of commiseration, she replied that, "Heaven, jealous of our happiness, has taken away from us our adored and adorable Queen. The calamity has overwhelmed me. . . ." It was only the thought that she herself might soon follow that gave her some consolation.

Yet, although she had lost friend, guardian and adviser, Caroline's existence showed no signs of coming to a premature and tragic finale. She was still a marriageable princess, of uncommon personal attractions; and the Elector Palatine now returned to the attack, making a second and even more determined attempt to marry her off to the Archduke Charles. So difficult did the situation soon become that Caroline again retired to Anspach, to her half-brother's palace; and it was here, among the mild diversions and humdrum ceremonial of a small German court, that she passed the summer months of 1705. In the meantime, the Electress Sophia was nursing her plans. For her daughter's protégée she had long felt the greatest affection and admiration; and she considered that her favourite grandson, George Augustus, could have no better wife, since Caroline united great sweetness of disposition and charm of appearance to a firm, masculine and managing temper not unlike her own. But she was not allowed to put her scheme into execution; and when the moment came to make a decisive move, the Elector, instead of confiding in his mother, entrusted negotiations to an experienced private emissary. The preliminary steps, then, were undertaken by the Elector—and undertaken with a delicacy and romantic circumspection that royal courtships of the period very often lacked. The young Prince went to Anspach, but he travelled *incognito* as an ordinary Hanoverian nobleman, and in this disguise joined the royal circle after supper and was able to observe the Princess without embarrassment. His response was immediate and uncomplicated. A simple, hot-blooded young man, whose character was innocent of the smallest taint of intellectualism, he saw in the plump, high-bosomed, fresh-coloured young woman to whom he was presented the almost perfect type of desirable feminine beauty—a princess into the bargain, endowed with the qualities and quarterings that befitted his rank. Still disguised, he returned to Hanover; and during June, the Elector's emissary, carrying secret instructions, made his way to the court of Anspach. "Whereas" (read these instructions) ". . . our son, the Electoral Prince, has seen the Princess of Anspach, and is seized with such an affection and desire for her that he is most eager to marry her without delay: We therefore should gladly rejoice to see such a union take place, and hope that the Princess may be equally favourably disposed." The emissary was to begin by seeking a private interview: he was to inform the Princess that the young friend who accompanied him on his last visit to the court of Anspach was, in reality, the Electoral Prince of Hanover, who had been attracted by reports "of the Princess's incomparable beauty and mental attributes" and who was now so captivated that he had asked, and obtained, the Elector's fatherly permission to seek her as his wife. The emissary executed his task faithfully. He requested an interview, was admitted, told his tale and received from the Princess the agreeable intelligence that she was entirely free. Next, she consulted her half-brother. He assented; a contract of marriage was drawn up; and though preparations were temporarily suspended by the death of the bridegroom's maternal grandfather, the marriage finally took place at Hanover on September 2nd, 1705.

Thus Caroline joined the Electoral family, contracting an alliance which, though a few years earlier it might have seemed only moderately distinguished, now carried with it prospects of the most brilliant kind. Her husband's grandmother was heiress to the throne of England. Born in 1630, the granddaughter of James I, this indefatigable old lady had entered her seventy-sixth year,

yet maintained a lively—almost a greedy—interest in the dominions she soon expected to inherit. There was every chance that she
would out-live their ailing sovereign. Anne was sickly, dropsical,
self-indulgent; the Electress Sophia, on the other hand, enjoyed
excellent health and possessed a fund of energy and spirits that
many of her courtiers found extremely exhausting. Day by day,
between the clipped hedges, down the long formal walks, among
the fountains and statues of Herrenhausen, she would pace for two
or three hours, keeping up an incessant rattle of conversation as
she stumped briskly forward, while her attendants tagged dutifully a step behind. An engraved portrait published in England,
after her claims to the English throne had been ratified by Anne's
recognition of the Act of Settlement in the year 1702, gives us an
exceedingly vivid impression of the Electress Sophia as she must
have appeared at the time of Caroline's wedding. Her face has all
the craftiness of shrewd old age. Plump, slightly porcine, framed
in a large dark frill and surmounted by a cluster of thick white
curls, which emerge from beneath one of the high-peaked head-
dresses of the period, it is the face of a clever, autocratic, but not
unkindly dowager, though her eyes are inquisitive and the pursed
mouth has a sardonic smile. The sort of matriarch whom her
family vote "difficult." . . . Certainly, both George Augustus and
his father, the Elector, are said to have treated her on occasions
with rather less deference than she felt she deserved; and the
Elector, knowing that she was a gossip and a great letter-writer,
excluded her, as far as might be, from affairs of state.

After the death of her daughter, the Queen of Prussia, the
Electress's closest intimate was her niece, the Duchesse d'Orléans,
who had made an unlucky marriage with the brother of Louis
Quatorze and lived a life of embittered exile at the French court.
Temperamentally, the two women had much in common. More
intelligent than their brothers, sons and husbands, they combined
a deep love of genealogy—of that mystic family tree whose

branches stretched into the farthest courts of Europe, whose bole was rooted in Germany and France, and whose uttermost boughs bore a petty crop of minor princes, marquis, barons—with a genuine liking for the society of learned men. Their interests and pursuits were nearly identical. They enjoyed fresh air, at a time when most ladies lived behind sealed casements or, like Madame de Maintenon, in a chair so carefully protected from draughts that it resembled a padded and windowed coffin. They were frank and free of speech—sometimes to the point of brutality—and each of them was a tireless and voluminous letter-writer. Now the Duchesse d'Orléans was writing home. A lapdog—one of the many little dogs with which she was always surrounded—perched on her massive knees, a pen grasped in her fat shapeless hand, she would cover five, ten, sometimes twenty or twenty-five sheets with the intrigues, scandals, anecdotes of the French court, varying her narrative with an occasional acid—though never self-pitying— reference to the difficult position that she occupied. Useless to pretend that she liked the French! Gallic characters and Gallic manners were equally antipathetic to the brusque, sanguine, sharptongued German lady whose sense of fun overflowed into outrageous scatological jokes, and whose pride of birth did not require the support of ceremony. Her brother-in-law, Louis Quatorze, she accepted as a celestial phenomenon, impossible not to acknowledge though hard to esteem; but Madame de Maintenon she regarded with a loathing that grew more and more intense, usually designating her in her correspondence (which was often intercepted and occasionally perused by Madame de Maintenon herself) as *die alte Zote*—the old trollop!

Monsieur, however, was her chief trial. One of the most fantastic —at moments it would seem one of the most pathetic—figures of the *Grand Siècle,* Monsieur at a very early age had been taught the love of feminine finery and feminine avocations—such as embroidery and *maquillage*—that remained with him to the end of his existence. It has been suggested that Monsieur's effeminacy was cultivated and encouraged so as to remove any danger of his setting himself up as an ambitious rival to his more masculine brother. The plan, if plan there was, had succeeded beyond expectation. Monsieur had grown up sensitive, affectionate, courageous, yet doomed by the difficulties of his temperament to unhappiness, ridicule and misunderstanding.

In 1701, Monsieur had died. Madame, however, was still at the French court; and her example, and the vast letters in which she described the wrongs, humiliations and petty annoyances to which she was perpetually being exposed, must have strengthened Caroline's view of family life—her conviction that it was a difficult and explosive business. The history of her husband's family was far from comforting. The Elector disliked his mother; the Electress had abominated her son's wife, and even now, when Sophia Dorothea of Celle had been imprisoned in the Castle of Ahlden for more than ten years, she would not admit a word in the young woman's favour. The uneasy ghost of Königsmark had not yet been exorcized. That good-looking military adventurer had made the mistake of laying simultaneous and successful siege to two women as important as the Electoral Prince's wife and the Elector's mistress, Countess Platen, a member of the unscrupulous family which had provided the Hanoverian court with ministers and mistresses for many years. Whatever the fate that had overtaken him on the threshold of the Princess's apartments, late one night during the summer of 1694, it had been conclusive; and, whether or not it was true that Countess Platen had personally assisted at his murder and had appeared to trample him underfoot with her high-heeled shoes as he expired, he had entered the Leine Schloss and had there vanished beyond recovery. Apologists have suggested that the Elector's treatment of his wife was much resented by his son; but there is very little evidence for this belief, and it seems improbable that (except, of course, to vex his father) a young man as conventional as George Augustus would have rallied to the support of a woman who had broken the strict hereditary code and had allowed herself to be caught in secret infidelity with an officer of her husband's private bodyguard.[1]

Since Sophia Dorothea's disgrace, George Louis's mistresses, three in number, and all of Hanoverian extraction, had held open court. These ladies have often been described; and across the interval of the centuries they loom up as monstrous and fantastic figures, the flaming red wig of the one, the black wig affected by the other; Schulenburg, who was tall and thin as a rake, Kielmansegge—daughter to Countess Platen, wife of the Prime Minister—who was exceedingly corpulent and had been nicknamed by the Electress Sophia "the fat hen." Another Countess Platen stands at their side. She was better-looking than her companions, but she was also more promiscuous, and, when the younger Craggs, son of the Whig politician, came to Hanover, he had the distinction of being picked out as her *amant de cœur*. All three were self-seeking and avaricious—business women of the period who had adopted the only profession then open to hard-headed members of the submissive sex; none of them had the smallest pretension to intelligence or charm; but among them they set the tone of court society. The Elector was devoted to them in combination, and, observing her father-in-law, Caroline deduced various lessons which were to prove extremely useful when she was dealing with her husband, who, though he hated his father, shared many of his tastes and preferences. Both father and son were exceedingly conventional in matters of love. A prince owed it to him-

---

[1] According to Horace Walpole (who had the story from Lady Suffolk), after George I's death there appeared in his son's dressing-room a portrait thought to represent Sophia Dorothea; it was also said that, had the Princess survived, George II intended to bring her over to England. Lord Hervey, on the other hand, asserts that when George II talked of his early life—which he did, at times, very freely and in great detail—he never referred, directly or indirectly, to his mother's existence.

self to appear as a man of gallantry, and a mistress was as important a part of his household as a valet, coachman or page of the back-stairs. Neither was by instinct an accomplished amorist. Their needs were simple; their approach was correspondingly direct; while both would have revolted against any passion that threatened to upset the punctual and ceremonious ordering of their daily lives. Both were keenly aware of their dignity as masculine beings. It would have been fatal to interpose obstinate feminine resistance once masculine desires had been aroused; and Caroline, though she might have preferred fidelity, soon reconciled herself to the virtues of compromise and conciliation. Moreover, it was plain that her husband loved her; and on the 5th of February 1707, at seven o'clock at night, her lady of the bedchamber had the satisfaction of informing the English envoy that the Princess Electoral had given birth to a son, Frederick Louis, great-grandson of the heiress of England, a large, strong baby much admired by the women of the court.

The flourishing condition of the Electoral family must have added yet another item to the burden of woes and grievances already supported by Queen Anne, who had borne seventeen children only to furnish material for seventeen royal epitaphs. Then the old Electress was a constant source of anxiety. She was intriguing with the Whigs, and had several times suggested that either she or the Electoral Prince should be allowed to visit England—a suggestion that moved the poor Queen to distraction; for she declared that it would affect her as disagreeably as being shown her own coffin while she was still alive. She consented, nevertheless, to confer titles and honours on George Augustus after the birth of his heir, making him Baron Tewkesbury, Viscount Northallerton, Earl of Milford-Haven, Marquess and Duke of Cambridge, and giving him precedence over all other English peers. The Elector, for his part, determined to show his independence and, not displeased, perhaps, at an opportunity of annoying his irrepressibly meddlesome parent, treated the representatives of England with considerable rudeness, thus increasing the air of tension on both sides. Life at Hanover, meanwhile, was growing feverish. From the great Duke of Marlborough downwards, many ambitious Englishmen had visited the Hanoverian court, reputable and disreputable, secret agents bearing important messages, politicians with an eye open to the future, accredited emissaries of the Queen, adventurers with their way to make in the world. Among the last, none were more prominent or, ultimately, more successful than Mr. and Mrs. Howard, who came to Hanover because their credit and fortune in England were exhausted and Hanover seemed a likely place to repair them. Mr. Howard was an extravagant younger son, Mrs. Howard, born Henrietta Hobart, the daughter of a Norfolk baronet. The first years of married life had eaten up their resources. On their way to Hanover (Horace Walpole tells us) they travelled "in the common wagon," and there is a story that, when they had arrived and wished to ingratiate themselves with the ministerial faction by giving a dinner-party, the wife was obliged to sell her fine head of hair to a periwig-maker in order to settle the account. The impression that they made was satisfactory; Electress and Princess declared themselves delighted with the pretty young Englishwoman; and it was decided that she should become one of Caroline's personal attendants—a post that she retained till her retirement from public life many years later.

An even more important consequence followed. Though there was something in her disposition that made Henrietta Howard the best-loved woman of her time—a blend of gravity and sensibility, allied to sound good sense, that captivated men as dissimilar as Pope, Swift and Horace Walpole—she began life as an adventuress, married to an adventurer. Her capital was her intelligence and her good looks. George Augustus was a professed man of gallantry; he noticed Mrs. Howard, was observed to pay her court in the abrupt, downright strutting manner that was especially his own, and before long had enrolled her as *maîtresse en titre*. This arrangement, which was both satisfactory to the Prince's vanity and helpful to the Howards' financial circumstances, took no account of Mrs. Howard's inclinations. At most she may have liked, or felt a sort of indulgent, almost maternal affection for the choleric, dapper, pink-faced little man; but it would not appear that she ever loved him, while she must have realized that her so-called "lover" was in love with his wife. But Mrs. Howard was a philosopher, if not a cynic; and in Caroline, luckily, she discovered a woman of equally heroic mould, who practised the art of subjugating by giving way. Caroline was not pleased, but she did not permit herself to show resentment; while the old Electress, whose own married life had been a long tale of husbandly infidelities and in whose thoughts the succession always came uppermost, regarded the affair as eminently suitable, since her grandson would now have a chance of improving his English.

Nor could Caroline complain that her husband neglected her. His visits to his mistress, far from being romantic escapades, were part of a ceremonial time-table which he followed to the second; and during their private hours he gave demonstrative proof that his passion for his wife was still undiminished. Between 1707 and 1713, three daughters were added to their family, the Princess Anne, Princess Amelia and Princess Caroline. Unlike George Augustus, who made no pretence of wishing to have young children about him, Caroline was an attentive and kindly, if not particularly indulgent, mother whom her daughters learned to respect at an early age. But her interests transcended nursery routine. She had set herself to learn English, acquired some fluency in that difficult tongue, though her pronunciation always remained thick and guttural, and generally did her best to prepare for the future. George and Caroline had been married nine years when an unexpected event—from their point of view, at least, it could scarcely be termed a calamity—suddenly occurred to increase their importance in the dynastic scale, bringing them a step closer to the throne of England. The old Electress had seemed as brisk and hearty as ever; but the intrigues in which she was engaged with her grandson and the English Whigs had entailed much anxiety; and the failure of their last effort—which had as its object that George Augustus should be allowed to take his seat in the English House of Lords—was a severe shock both to her ambition and to her self-esteem. Queen Anne wrote that no member of the Electoral family should set foot in her kingdom as long as she lived. Electress, George Augustus, Caroline—all were greatly chagrined; and having received the Queen's letter, the Electress rose from the card-table and spent some three hours pacing distractedly to and fro in the gardens of Herrenhausen. Next day, during the afternoon—it was June 1714—she set out for her usual exercise. She was accompanied by Caroline and her attendants and, while she walked, she talked of the communication she had received, beginning, as she grew more excited, to walk faster and faster. Then her colour changed, and she suddenly stumbled and fell forward. Caroline, a *dame de compagnie* and her Chamberlain caught her in their arms. They cried for help; and the Elector, who was strolling near by, ran up and "put some *poudre d'or* in her mouth." She was carried to her apartments and bled; but the blood had already congealed and only a few drops could be drawn off. The Electress Sophia, Heiress of England, granddaughter of James I, great-granddaughter of Mary Queen of Scots, had died of apoplexy and thwarted ambition— or, some declared, of a broken heart—"in the eighty-fourth year of her age."

Two months later, on August 1st, she was followed by the ailing, unhappy woman, so much younger than herself, whom she had confidently expected to out-live. It had been Anne's dearest wish to secure the succession for her brother, the Old Pretender; and the difficulty of reconciling this secret hope to the professions of friendship that she was obliged to make towards Elector and Electress—a difficulty that grew more acute as the emissaries of the Electress Sophia grew more and more insistent—undermined the little strength that she yet retained. The Tories, helped into power by the influence of Lady Masham, were now divided among themselves. Oxford and Bolingbroke had fallen out, and the recriminations of their partisans gave every council the character of a civil war. Caught between the two armies, the Queen suffered intensely in body and spirit. She wept, fainted and was carried from the room. It was plain that she was very infirm; still the Tories continued to enjoy all the fierce satisfactions of internecine party strife. Another council, she wailed, would certainly kill her; and, as she trembled at the thought of the approaching ordeal, an epileptic seizure struck her down. "My brother! Oh! My poor brother, what will become of you?" she was heard to murmur before she lapsed into unconsciousness.

2

LADY MASHAM broke the news to the assembled Tories; and the Tories, who had behaved with callous indifference to the Queen's sufferings while she was still alive, were now confounded by the information that their mistress was past any help and that, in Lady Masham's words, they were "undone, entirely ruined." As usual, they had wasted their opportunity. The high-minded, wrong-headed ghost of Charles I, the sceptical indolent spirit of his elder son—some emanation of hereditary weakness seems to have perplexed the counsels and muddled the decisions of statesmen and soldiers who have taken up arms in defence of the House of Stuart, making them do the right thing when the occasion was least opportune and the wrong thing—or nothing at all—when the advantage was theirs. In 1714 Jacobite prospects throughout

England appeared extremely hopeful. The Stuarts, as too many apologists have reminded us, though they possessed the knack of arousing furious antipathy, had also the gift of awakening loyalty; while the House of Hanover could claim no real loyalty and had already succeeded in arousing some prejudice among Englishmen who had observed its members on their native ground. Oxford and many other cities were devoutly Jacobite. A little promptness on the part of the Tory leaders might have saved them the day; for it was evident that the Elector of Hanover, whose heart remained at home and who regarded the English succession as a flattering, but burdensome and possibly dangerous inheritance, was not prepared to take any desperate risk. Yet no—just as Englishmen have found it easy to die for the Stuarts, but exceedingly difficult to live with them on comfortable terms, so their service has never conduced to prompt and intelligent action when action was needed; and the Tory leaders hesitated, fumbled and lost the initiative.

Bold proposals were made, only to be passed over. There was the Duke of Ormonde, who promised the support of the army if the Queen could be induced to nominate her brother to the throne, and Atterbury, Bishop of Rochester, who announced that he was ready, if his friends gave the word, to proclaim James King of England *in pontificalibus* at the Royal Exchange and Charing Cross. Next day, when the council had begun its session, the Duke of Somerset, who represented the English Whigs, and the Duke of Argyll, who spoke for the Whigs of Scotland, suddenly entered the council chamber. They had not been summoned, they said, but, having heard of the Queen's state, they came as by duty bound.[1] At once the Duke of Shrewsbury rose to welcome them and invited them to take seats. The Tories, who had been uncertain what to do, now realized that they had fallen into a trap neatly

---

[1] *Wentworth Papers,* p. 408.

laid by Argyll, Somerset and Shrewsbury; and almost at her last gasp Anne was persuaded to name Shrewsbury Lord Treasurer. On August 1st, early in the morning, the Queen died at Kensington Palace, and "the high and mighty Prince, George, Elector of Brunswick and Lüneburg," was proclaimed King of Great Britain, France and Ireland in her stead. The agitation of the previous days immediately subsided. Troops had been massed round London; there were illuminations in the metropolis to honour the new reign; and "Lord Bullingbrook sunday" (wrote Peter Wentworth to his brother Lord Strafford) "made a Bonfire and the finest illumination in town at his house in Golden Square, but that might be out of Policy fearing the mob, but there was no occasion for this precaution, for King George was proclaimed very Peaceably and everything has continued ever since."

In short the Jacobites had decided that their battle was lost. "I can't say I am sorry I have little news to writ to you" (continued Peter Wentworth, to the same correspondent, seventeen days later) "because that happens from having everything going on so peaceably and quietly. At present the striff is who shall show themselves the most Zealous for the Present King George, wch is some disappointment to the leading Whigs, for they did expect some opposition in the manner of granting the Civil List, wch the less experienced Tories were ready to give, but they were better advised by the wiser, who are proposing everything that's for the honour and dignity of the Crown, so much that some people out of doors of both Partys begin to fear that we shall have the rights and libertys of Englishmen complymented away, but those reflections are made by people that are of opinion that we have a Prince that's ready to catch at them." Meanwhile the Elector had been informed of the Queen's death—first, by Bothmar, his representative in London, whose messenger reached Herrenhausen on the evening of August 5th; secondly, by Lord Clarendon, the English envoy, who burst into his liege lord's bedroom at two o'clock the following morning. When the news arrived, the envoy had been keeping an assignation. Hence his late arrival; the King was not very well pleased at being woken up. His manner was stoical and frigid. He did not like Clarendon; and, on being asked for his commands, he replied in his blunt, uningratiating style that "I had best stay till he goes . . ."

He went at the beginning of September, accompanied by his son, whom he distrusted but preferred to keep under his own personal supervision, and one of the most curious escorts that have ever arrived to celebrate the opening of a new reign; for besides a large Hanoverian suite, designed to protect him from the society of a people whom he neither loved nor understood, and Mustapha and Mahomet, the Turks whom he employed as body servants, his two favourite mistresses, Schulenburg and Kielmansegge, embarked with George Louis at the Hague. Kielmansegge, whose creditors were troublesome, had been obliged to leave Hanover surreptitiously, after the King had set forth. But both were present when he landed at Greenwich on September 18th; and the oddity of their appearance caused much diversion in England, where since 1660 the standard of looks demanded of royal mistresses had been exceptionally high. The King had landed on a Saturday evening; and the next day he held his first levee, in the magnificent apartments of Greenwich Palace, looking out over a broad stretch of the river. A crowd of great personages were presented to him; but, whereas the Whigs were received with condescension, the Tories (the Whigs were glad to see) were treated with coldness, or, at least, with a very marked reserve. Later, King and Prince "were graciously pleased to exhibit themselves some time at the windows of the palace"; and, on Monday, an enormous train of coaches took the road that led to London and St. James's, pausing at Southwark to hear a long congratulatory speech rehearsed by the Lord Mayor. A gigantic glass coach had been reserved for the King and the Prince of Wales; and, as they swayed side by side in their moving showcase, dragged by eight horses between the ranks of cheering subjects who lined the way from Greenwich to St. James's Palace, it was possible to observe them with some exactitude. The Prince smiled broadly; but he had been instructed by his father that he must not bow. The King bowed repeatedly, placing his hand on his heart, but he did not smile. Indeed, from start to finish, the stolid dignity of George Louis's demeanour was never once relaxed.

Yet, of the two, impartial observers preferred the King. Stolid he might be; but there was something straightforward and downright about the sovereign that suggested that he knew his place and was very well pleased that other people should know theirs. He had little charm; but the most engaging English monarchs had hitherto proved themselves the most undependable. "An honest blockhead" (wrote Lady Mary Wortley Montagu, in her celebrated *Account of the Court of George I*). ". . . Fortune, that made him a king, added nothing to his happiness, only prejudiced his honesty and shortened his days. No man was ever more free from ambition. He was more properly dull than lazy, and would have been so well contented to have remained in his little town of Hanover, that if the ambition of those about him had not been greater than his own, we should never have seen him in England; and the natural honesty of his temper, joined with the narrow notions of a low education, made him look upon his acceptance of the crown as an act of usurpation, which was always uneasy to him. . . . He was passively good-natured, and wished all mankind enjoyed quiet, if they would let him do so." To this it must be added that George I appears to have possessed in a very high degree that kingly presence of mind which often makes up for the lack of any real intelligence, and that he had shown his valour and resource on numerous battlefields.

Less reassuring was the impression left by his son. Inevitably the Prince's position was somewhat awkward; and the uneasiness that

GEORGE I

Engraving by Picart

ST. JAMES'S PALACE

Engraving by Stewart after Burnet

he felt was revealed in the vehemence and irritability that he displayed on many different occasions, particularly when he was in the near neighbourhood of his hated father. He had never acquired the art of hiding his feelings; "the fire of his temper" (continues Lady Mary) "appeared in every look and gesture; which, being unhappily under the direction of a small understanding, was every day throwing him upon some indiscretion. He was naturally sincere, and his pride told him that he was placed above constraint; not reflecting that a high rank carries along with it a necessity of a more decent and regular behaviour than is expected from those who are not set in so conspicuous a light. He was so far from being of that opinion that he looked on all the men and women he saw as creatures he might kick or kiss for his diversion; and, whenever he met with any opposition in those designs, he thought his opposers impudent rebels to the will of God, who created them for his use, and judged of the merit of all people by their ready submission to his orders, or the relation they had to his person."

By temperament father and son were absolute monarchs; but their absolutism had very little in common with that almost mystical gospel of the absolute ruler which, at the beginning of the next century, crystallized in the formation of the Holy Alliance. Their point of view might perhaps be more accurately compared to the attitude of some hot-headed contradictious rural landowner who, on succeeding to a new estate, suddenly finds himself confronted with an entirely new set of rules and restrictions, who, for the first time in his life, comes face to face with a pettifogging rural district council and is goaded to fury by their intolerable interference. Of what advantage to reign if one did not rule? But between the English sovereign and the free exercise of his function all manner of obstacles had been built up. An extraordinary country!—and to illustrate his complete bewilderment at British customs, George I (who did not lack a certain matter-of-fact German humour) used to tell the story of how, the morning after his instalment in St. James's Palace, he had looked out of the window across the pleasant landscape of St. James's Park, with its walks, its boscage and its clear waters, and had been told that it was his. He was well satisfied, but "the next day Lord Chetwynd, the Ranger of *my* park, sent me a fine brace of carp out of *my* Canal; and I was told I must give five guineas to Lord Chetwynd's servant for bringing me *my own* carp out of *my own* canal in *my own* Park!"

With so acute a feeling for the royal *thine* and *mine,* George Louis may well have considered that his position in England was as anomalous as it threatened to be precarious; while, to make that position even more difficult, he was indebted for his throne to the support of a party whose principles he detested, whose record inspired him with the utmost repugnance, and whom in private conversation he often styled "the king-killers." Luckily, these king-killers were on his side. For the time being, at any rate. . . . And, anxious to save himself both labour and danger, George determined that he would leave the direction of internal affairs entirely in their hands. Unlike his mother, the Electress, who had prided herself on her knowledge of the English tongue and —perhaps unjustifiably—on her understanding of the English constitution, George knew no English and admitted that the constitution, to which his subjects attached such an exaggerated importance, presented problems utterly beyond his grasp. He announced, therefore, that his presence at Council must be dispensed with. Previous monarchs had presided in person over the meetings of their ministers; and George I's abstention made it possible for the English Cabinet and English party government to develop along present-day lines. His first ministry was composed entirely of Whigs, headed by Lord Townshend, the brother-in-law of Sir Robert Walpole. Sir Robert himself received the comparatively unimportant post of Paymaster-General to the Forces; and it was not until 1715 that he became First Lord of the Treasury and Chancellor of the Exchequer, thus assuming a leadership that (except for one brief period of retirement) he was to retain through the better part of three decades.

Gradually, the bustle and excitement died away. The Tories knew their fate, and had fared, on the whole, no worse than they might have expected. The Whig place-hunters, who had been so busy at Greenwich and St. James's during the early days of the reign, when hordes of loyal gentlemen (Peter Wentworth among the rest) had been eager to hand the King from his barge or caracole at the side of his equipage as he rode up to London, had either received the appointments for which they asked or had resigned themselves to some second-best post and salary. The King had looked over his palaces and gardens, and, though he said little, had intimated that he was not displeased; while the ordinary social round had begun again. We learn that George Louis, in spite of his aversion from English manners and the English standard of good looks, proved "very obliging." He and the Prince (noted Peter Wentworth) "have been at several places in town at supper"; and the King, who loved cards, had consented to take part in a game of "sixpenny Ombre at the Dutchess of Shrewsbury's." Then, on October 15th, the Princess of Wales reached England. Here was a fresh subject for speculation and intrigue; and, when she entered the drawing-room one evening at seven o'clock and sat down to piquet, "all the company flock't about to that table," and the basset and ombre tables were deserted. Caroline, who had enjoyed a triumphal progress from Hanover, unhampered by the presence of father-in-law or husband, was exceedingly gracious. She smiled, gave her hand to be kissed, repeated the names of those who were presented, and next day went out walking in the Park accompanied by a huge crowd.

Five days later came the Coronation. A single characteristic Caroline had not inherited from her beloved Sophie Charlotte—the Queen's dislike of ceremony in all its forms. For Caroline,

it was an important part of her existence; easy and familiar among her friends, she appreciated nevertheless that cumbrous and splendid ceremonial which, on great occasions, puts royal personages beyond the reach of ordinary men and women and relegates them to a special world of their own, where every word and every gesture is charged with meaning. Still strange to England, she attended the long and elaborate service at Westminster Abbey, saw her father-in-law solemnly invested with all the appurtenances of English royalty, heard him swear to defend the Protestant Faith and afterwards walked in the procession to Westminster Hall. The Abbey had been packed with loyal subjects—some more sincerely loyal than others; for in the crowd were a large number of professed Jacobites; and, when the Archbishop "went round the throne, demanding the Consent of the People," the aged Lady Dorchester, who had been the mistress of James II, turned angrily to Lady Cowper, a fervent Whig and future Lady of the Bedchamber, and demanded if the old fool thought anybody there would say no, while there were so many drawn swords about! A diversion of a different kind had been caused by Lady Nottingham, who, "when the Litany was to be sung" (reports Lady Cowper), "broke from behind the Rest of the Company, where she was placed, and kneeled down before them all (though none of the Rest did), facing the King, and repeating the Litany. Everybody stared at her. . . ." And Lady Cowper, though it had brought tears to her eyes to see "our holy Religion thus preserved, as well as our Liberties and Properties," considered that such a display of High Church enthusiasm was somewhat excessive.

Otherwise, the Coronation passed off smoothly. It is true that, here and there in London, seditious murmurs were heard and shouts from the mob of "Damn King George"; but, in high political circles, the Tories were more concerned to make their peace with the new order—and, if possible, climb back into power and office—than to waste sentiment and regrets upon the old.

New royal households were being recruited. Lady Cowper (whose journal is our chief authority for the court doings of this period) had petitioned for the post of Lady of the Bedchamber to the Princess; and soon after the Coronation she learned that her hopes had been gratified, and attended Caroline at the Palace to kiss her hand. Once her homage had been paid, Caroline raised her, embraced her "three or four times, and said the kindest things . . . far beyond the value of any Riches." Among her colleagues, Lady Cowper had four duchesses—the Duchess of Bolton, an amusing and garrulous person, being the most noteworthy—two countesses, besides herself, as Ladies of the Bedchamber, and four untitled ladies who occupied the subordinate position of Bedchamber Women—Mrs. Howard (already mentioned), Mrs. Clayton (better known under her subsequent style of Lady Sundon), Mrs. Selwyn (mother of Horace Walpole's great friend) and Mrs. Pollexfen. The Princess's entourage also included five Maids of Honour; but this last addition to her household must be described elsewhere, for each of the Maids seems to deserve a separate portrait. It was their function to attend the Princess and talk to her husband, to join them at cards, run errands and go out hunting.

They accompanied their mistress to public solemnities. On October 29th, the Princess and her suite travelled down to the City to view the Lord Mayor's Show; and the whole of the previous day (according to Lady Cowper) "was passed in Disputes amongst us servants" as to whether the Princess ought or ought not to receive the Lady Mayoress with a kiss. Precedents were quoted on both sides; and not until it had been discovered that Queen Anne had refrained from kissing the Lady Mayoress of the period when she visited the City was the problem finally settled against osculation. Much disconcerted by this veto, which cut her pride to the quick, "my poor Lady Humphreys made a sad Figure in her black Velvet, and did make a most violent Bawling to her Page to hold up her Train before the Princess, being loath to lose the Privilege of her Mayoralty." Though she admitted, a little shamefacedly, that Lady Humphreys was, in fact, some kind of relation of her husband's through his first marriage, Lady Cowper could not help being amused; and she was even more diverted to learn that an ill-natured person had assured the King and Princess that the alleged Lady Humphreys was no true wife but "that my Lord Mayor had borrowed her for that Day only." She had much ado to convince them that the story was false; and "at last they did agree that if he had borrowed a Wife, it would have been another Sort of One than she was."

That evening the Prince's birthday was celebrated. There was a ball, at which the Prince danced "better than Anybody" and the Princess acquitted herself with grace and distinction, wearing slippers instead of the ordinary high-heeled shoes. Next day—it was the 1st of November—the King and his attendants supped at Lady Bristol's. George Louis, who always relaxed in agreeable feminine company, displayed great good humour and "said a World of sprightly things." The Duchess of Shrewsbury—she was half-Italian and very talkative—did her best to amuse him; and the Duchess of Bolton, who was equally vivacious, chattered in her usual indiscreet and lively style. It was this lady who, being asked by the King to translate the title of an English play, *Love's Last Shift,* rendered it "La Dernière Chemise de l'Amour"; and on the present occasion, she upset Lady Cowper by the "Repetition of some words in French . . . which convinced me that the two foreign ladies"—Kielmansegge and Schulenburg—"were no better than they should be." She soon learned that Caroline detested them both. Madame Kielmansegge had entrusted Lady Cowper with a book to give to the Princess; and, when she had discharged the commission, Mrs. Howard (who knew the ways of the Hanoverian court) took her aside and "told her that there was a mortal Hatred between them, and that the Princess thought her a wicked Woman." She added that Kielmansegge had undoubtedly sent the book through her "to persuade the Princess that she was very well with me" and thus ruin Lady Cowper's credit. If it had not been so, she would have employed one of her friends, the Duchess of Bolton or the Duchess of Shrewsbury. "But" (observed Mrs. Howard) "she never stuck a Pin into her Gown without a Design."

These animosities, however—the hatred of the father for the son, and of the daughter-in-law for the two grasping and suspicious concubines—were not at once allowed to appear on the surface. For a time the life of the court and the country was smooth. The Princess continued to go out walking—an exercise she loved—and "showed our English Ladies that she could walk as well as ever the Princess Sophia had done," received learned divines—another favourite amusement—and revealed her literary tastes by demanding the collected works of Francis Bacon. King and Prince were often seen at the theatre and opera. Drawing-rooms were packed, and play—much to Lady Cowper's annoyance, for she could not afford to lose—was exceedingly high. On Twelfth Night 1715, Caroline and the Duchess of Montagu "went halves at Hazard" and won six hundred pounds. No one sat down to the tables with less than two hundred guineas, and, while the more important members of the royal entourage played at cards, around them seethed "a world of shouldering and hunching People," who trampled confusedly on toes and trains. The Venetian Ambassadress was particularly unfortunate. Signor Tron, her husband, was extremely jealous; and it was said that when he beat her—which he did very often—she used to beg him, whatever happened, to take care of her face. That plea she now repeated at St. James's in her thick Italian accent; "and 'Prenez garde à mon Vizaze!' was her Cry all Night long." So loud were Signora Tron's complaints that they reached the sovereign's ears; and, turning to somebody who stood behind him, *"Entendez-vous l'Ambassadrice?"* he remarked with hearty Hanoverian humour. *"Elle vous abandonne tout le reste du corps, pourvu que vous ayez soin du visage."*

The year 1714 had ended cheerfully; if not popular, the new King was at least tolerated; then, little by little, the balance began to change. Much resentment had been stirred up by the King's favourites. From Schulenburg and Kielmansegge, who dealt openly in sinecures, to Mustapha and Mahomet, who made the most of their position near the King, the whole Hanoverian assemblage seemed determined that, since their stay in England was likely to be cut short, they would do well to squeeze out the uttermost farthing as long as it lasted. Thus a certain Mr. Chetwynd had procured an appointment with the Board of Trade by paying Madame Kielmansegge five hundred guineas down, promising her a pension of two hundred per annum while he continued to hold the place, and throwing in (rumour added) a pair of fine brilliant earrings. Peculation was not a vice that critics of the early eighteenth century regarded as particularly serious, but that it should be practised by foreigners at the English expense—by designing Hanoverian statesmen, Bothmar, Bernstorff, Robethon and the others, and by mistresses who were neither British nor beautiful—inspired disappointed Tory patriots to transports of rage. Libels poured daily from the printing press, finding an easy target in the two grotesque female adventurers who personified all the worst and most indefensible points of the new dispensation; and "nothing could be grosser" (writes Horace Walpole, jotting down his reminiscences for the amusement of the Misses Berry) "than the ribaldry that was vomited out in lampoons, libels, & every channel of abuse against the Sovereign and the new court, & chanted even in their hearing about the public streets."

The attitude of the government became more oppressive. During the early months of 1715 it was decided to force through a General Election; and in March, thanks to a wholesale campaign of bribery carried out with the public funds, the Ministers secured a powerful Whig majority. One of their first moves was to threaten the Tory lords. There was talk of impeachment; and, towards the end of March, Bolingbroke, whose behaviour, ever since the proclamation of the new King, which he had celebrated with a magnificent illumination at his Golden Square house, had been diplomatic and conciliatory, left London in disguise and crossed the Channel. Ormonde soon followed Bolingbroke's lead. Only Oxford remained to face his accusers. He was impeached, committed to the Tower and drove to prison, accompanied by an indignant cheering crowd.[1] The same crowd gathered to hoot at the King and his satellites. Let George (advised the ballad-mongers) return to the "slaves and German boobies," over whom he would still be reigning if Queen Anne had "done justice." Away with the "Hanover rats," his friends and advisers! Nor was this agitation confined to the mob. White roses—the Jacobite emblem—were worn and flaunted about the streets by a great many English ladies, and sentimental toasts to the Pretender, and to James, Ormonde and Bolingbroke in conjunction, were proposed and loudly acclaimed at country banquets.

All this was reported to the Pretender, who, unluckily for himself and for the cause that he represented, had very little understanding of the English mind. Discontent he interpreted as the shadow of rebellion—a willingness to revile the House of Hanover as a readiness to take up arms on behalf of the Stuarts. Bolingbroke, who had joined his court in Lorraine, advised him to proceed gradually; but James, supported by Ormonde, was determined to act; and in Scotland the clansmen were already moving. During the first days of September, news reached London that James's standard had been raised over the Highlands; and, at the beginning of October, a small body of Northumbrian Jacobites proclaimed James King of England in the town of Warkworth. It

---

[1] See Pope, *Letters to Several Ladies*. Letter XI: "The Earl of Oxford has behaved so bravely, that in this act at least he might seem above man, if he had not just now voided a stone to prove him subject to human infirmities. The utmost weight of affliction from ministerial power and popular hatred, were almost worth bearing for the glory of such a dauntless conduct as he has shewn under it."

is hardly necessary to recapitulate the events that followed. For some weeks, at least, the position of the government and of the Hanoverian dynasty seemed extremely precarious, but both the King and his Ministers acted with unusual firmness and good sense. A large camp was established in Hyde Park; and Pope, writing to Lady Mary Wortley Montagu, speaks of the excitement caused by new regiments, new uniforms, new guns and "the sight of so many gallant fellows, with all the pomp and glare of war, yet undeformed by battles. . . ." Meantime, troops of horse and foot, sent to Oxford, Bristol and Plymouth, helped to damp down the Jacobite ardour of the South and West; and comforting intelligence soon arrived from the North that, although the Northumbrian Jacobites had invaded Lancashire, they had been rounded up and had surrendered their arms at Preston. The Scottish contingent, under the Earl of Mar, much more formidable in numbers, would appear to have been no less feebly led. Again one thinks of that curious state of bemused indecision that had overcome the adherents of the Pretender while Queen Anne lay dying; for Mar, who had the advantage, declined to move, and not until the middle of November could he be prevailed on to try a general engagement. The result was indecisive; and from Sheriffmuir Mar retired to his former headquarters at Perth, and there dallied and allowed his opponents to gather strength. James himself landed in Scotland on the 22nd of December, but his presence did nothing to improve his prospects; and Jacobite partisans, who had expected a dashing and energetic leader, were dismayed to meet a prince in whom the dullness and apathy of the elder James were combined with the habitual sloth of Charles II. They saw in him, they complained, not a trace of spirit. "His countenance"—a typical Stuart mask, with full protruding lower lip, large sensual nose and small thick-lidded eyes—"looked extremely heavy," and well it might, since he set foot in Scotland only to discover that his fortunes were waning; to enjoy the empty satisfaction of being crowned King and at last slip off in a French boat to renewed exile.

James fled from Scotland on the 4th of February, Mar's troops broke up and disappeared into their Northern fastnesses by twos and threes, and all semblance of peril was at an end. It remained to make an example of the ringleaders. During December, London turned out to see the insurgents who had capitulated at Preston brought through the city. Lady Cowper, who had many Roman Catholic relations among the rebels, did not attend the show; but "almost Everybody went to see them," and as they rode past, their arms pinioned and soldiers leading their horses, "the Mob insulted them terribly . . . saying a thousand barbarous Things, which some of the Prisoners returned with Spirit"; while a warming-pan was carried in the procession—a reference to the old story that the Pretender was not the true-born son of James II and Mary of Modena, but had been smuggled into the palace under a warming-pan's lid. On February 9th, the prisoners were put on trial. It was an occasion of great ceremony, which Lady Cowper, whose husband had been named High Steward, thought very wrong; and she reports that the Prince himself "was there, and came home much touched with compassion." Caroline was equally disturbed. To say that the Princess had a warm heart would be to do less than justice to the complexity of her temperament; but there is no doubt that she was capable of feeling sympathy, and that she proved disinterested at least as often as she seemed ungenerous. Certainly, she was touched by the fate of the prisoners; but Caroline had not yet achieved a position in which she could afford to meddle with questions of high public policy. Several Jacobites escaped; others were reprieved and granted a pardon; but Lord Kenmure and young Lord Derwentwater both mounted the scaffold.

Thus, amid petitions, confessions, the jeers of the mob that a few months earlier had shown itself just as ready to shout for King

James and damn King George, and dying speeches from the block
on Tower Hill, the Jacobite rising of 1715 came to an ignominious
close. Throughout the worst period of danger George Louis had
evinced considerable courage and good sense; courage was perhaps his greatest virtue; and, although after the collapse of the
rising, he had allowed Walpole and the other Whig ministers to
have their way, and had refrained from interfering on the side of
clemency, there is no evidence that his attitude had been vindictive. But now his thoughts had begun to turn towards Hanover. He
had approached his English inheritance with some alarm; and,
while it was true that the "king-killers" were still his friends, and
had recently passed the Septennial Act, which would enable them
to stay in power seven years instead of three, the events of the last
few months had been very far from reassuring. He endured England, but Hanover was his real love. Back he must go to that sane
ordered existence, where life ran as smoothly as a well-oiled Dutch
clock, where ministers, like the sentinels in the courtyard, kept
their proper stations. No English minister should be allowed to
thwart him. Did the Act of Settlement prevent his leaving England—then that clause of the Act must be repealed! Next, there
was the question of a regency. George Louis understood how much
the prospect of becoming Regent must appeal to his undutiful and
ill-tempered son; and he was determined that the Prince's importance should be strictly curtailed. A fierce quarrel, involving
King, ministers, son and daughter-in-law, immediately broke out,
and during the latter part of June and the first week of July Lady
Cowper's diary bristles with agitated jottings, which tell how the
King had declared that he would put off his journey; how he
threatened to send to Hanover for his brother Ernest Augustus
and make *him* guardian of the realm and Duke of York; how he
"insisted upon humbling the Prince" and demanded the dismissal
from the Prince's household of his friends the Duke of Argyll and

Lord Islay; how the Prince was "in an Agony" and the exasperated Princess "all in flame."

"They are all mad" (wrote Lady Cowper despondently) "and, for their own private Ends, will destroy all." From one passage, it would seem that George Louis had announced that, unless his wishes were respected, he would not return to England; and it may have been this suggestion that induced the Prince to come to terms, volunteering to dismiss the obnoxious Argyll and declaring that he was "resolved to sacrifice Everything to please and live well with the King. . . ." Though he was not appointed Regent, he received the ancient title of Guardian of the Realm and Lieutenant. For six months he would be virtual sovereign of the kingdom, a position that was satisfactory enough; while his father delighted to reflect that within a very short time he would again be setting foot on Hanoverian soil, forgot his acrimony and appeared at his final Drawing Room of the year "in mighty good Humour." When Lady Cowper wished him "a good Journey and a quick Return, he looked as if the last Part of my speech was needless, and that he did not think of it." He sailed for Hanover on July 9th, leaving Caroline and George Augustus to make the most of the first considerable share of sovereignty they had yet enjoyed.

3

*T*HE FIRST taste of power is always emollient, and "the King was no sooner gone" (observes Lady Cowper) "than the Prince took a Turn of being civil and kind to Everybody, and applied himself to be well with the King's Ministers, and to understand the State of the Nation." During July, Prince, Princess and their combined households moved to Hampton Court, where they resided "with great splendour" through the summer months. Every day the

Prince and Princess dined in public. Wren's magnificent modern additions to Cardinal Wolsey's rambling red-brick palace were at this time less than twenty years old; and Caroline, accustomed to the regularity and formality of Herrenhausen, must have appreciated the spacious and dignified proportions of her new residence —the imposing south front and the fine range of state apartments, looking out on the gardens and down the long tree-bordered canal or inwards to the arcaded Fountain Courtyard. Both Queen Anne and Queen Mary had left behind them much elaborate and precious equipment—Queen Anne her crystal chandeliers; Queen Mary the large collection of the blue and white china that now stands ranged in the cupboard and on the many-tiered mantelpieces of almost every state room. The bedchamber where the Prince and Princess slept had been expensively refurbished during the previous year; and Sir John Thornhill, the newly appointed court painter, had made up in exuberance for what he lacked in genuine creative ability and had frescoed the ceiling with a huge and highly coloured composition of prancing and sprawling divinities—Aurora rising from the waves in a golden chariot, amid a flourish of gesticulating allegorical figures; while around the cornice he had placed portrait medallions of George I, George Augustus and Princess Caroline, and over the window little Prince Frederick Louis, whom his mother and father had not seen since they reached England.

To complete their room the Princess and Prince had ordered a state bed of crimson damask, surmounted by an enormous and richly scalloped frieze. But more significant was the red damask canopy—evidently ordered at the same time—which they caused to be erected in the Queen's Audience Chamber. It was here that they held their state receptions; for no pains were spared to emphasize the truly royal character of the new court and, by the splendour and liberality of the Prince and Princess, to provoke a comparison subtly unfavourable to the absent King. Caroline had already begun the work. During the winter of 1715, which had been so exceptionally severe that the Thames was locked in ice from the beginning of December to the third week of January,[1] she had contributed to the relief of the unemployed watermen out of her own private funds; and her well-considered generosity had had its reward. George Augustus, on the other hand, who was nearly as parsimonious as his father, had adopted a different but equally effective method of acquiring popularity. Whenever an occasion offered, he would announce in his guttural Westphalian accent that for his part he was British through and through—that he adored England and thought his father's subjects "the best, the handsomest, the best shaped, the best natured and lovingest People in the World and that if Anybody would make their Court to him, it must be by telling him he was like an Englishman."

An agreeable change, this, from the attitude of stolid suspicion maintained by the less expansive and, incidentally, less calculating sovereign! After the spectacle of King George, surrounded and guarded by his tiny Hanoverian clique, it was pleasant to see his daughter-in-law, large, majestic and self-assured, talking and walking with her English attendants, conferring with learned English divines, surrounded by English Maids of Honour, who included some of the prettiest, cleverest and most spirited young women of the day. In her Maids the Princess was particularly fortunate. Mary Lepel and Mary Bellenden were both beauties; and to the possession of good looks each seems to have added a subtler and more special attribute—the kind of charm that is often described but never defined. Perhaps of its nature it was indefinable. Through the verses of Pope, Gay, Peterborough, Chesterfield, creeps an accent very seldom found in conventional poetic flattery of that or of any other period—a mixture of friendship and adoration, of desire and

---

[1] During March 1716, the Northern Lights appeared in the sky above London, causing much alarm and many superstitious forebodings. See the entry in Lady Cowper's Diary for March 6th.

of something not unlike regret. The epithets that they evoked would fill a page. Mary Bellenden, in Gay's celebrated *Welcome to Pope from Greece,* becomes "Smiling Mary, soft and fair as down"; and in the same poem, her friend appears as the very personification of youth and freshness—"Youth's youngest daughter, sweet Lepel." Miss Bellenden was noted for her abounding spirits. "Her face and person" (writes Horace Walpole in his *Reminiscences*) "were charming; lively she was almost to étourderie, &, so agreeable and engaging she was, that I never heard her mentioned afterwards by one of her contemporaries who did not prefer her as the most perfect creature they ever knew." Though they were neither of them in the smallest degree prudish, both Marys with youth, liveliness and brio combined a not inconsiderable measure of worldly good sense. Sophia Howe, on the other hand, was helplessly volatile. Gay represents her, among the friends gathered to welcome Pope home, as having joined the deputation quite by mistake: "Nor knows with whom, or why she comes along." And the whole of her character and the explanation of her subsequent misfortunes seem to be epitomized in her remark (quoted by Walpole) when the Duchess of St. Albans scolded her for giggling at Chapel and added that she "could not do a worse thing." "I beg your Grace's pardon," retorted Miss Howe, still giggling, "I can do a great many worse things!"

It is indicative of the cheerful and unconventional atmosphere that prevailed at the Princess's court that the behaviour of her Maids of Honour as often as they attended the Chapel Royal should have caused some disturbance. The early eighteenth century was by no means strict in its notions of religious decorum, for the King himself regularly slept or discussed politics through the service; and in 1705 we find old Lady Wentworth writing to her son that her favourite lapdog, Fubs, has just been to church with an admiring niece, "and, I will assure you, Fubs satt very orderly." But the conduct of the Maids of Honour passed all bounds. Such was

GEORGE II

From a painting by Hudson

HAMPTON COURT

Engraving by Shury after Neale

the upheaval they created that Bishop Burnet petitioned the Princess to have the gallery in which they sat screened off from the rest of the building; and Lord Peterborough, one of the many admirers who had gathered to ogle at a distance, commemorated the occasion in doggerel verse:

> Bishop Burnet perceived that the beautiful dames
> Who flocked to the chapel of hilly St. James
> On their lovers alone their kind looks did bestow,
> And smiled not on him while he bellowed below.
> To the Princess he went, with pious intent,
> This dangerous ill to the Church to prevent.
> "Oh, Madam," he said, "our religion is lost
> If the ladies thus ogle the knights of the toast."

Caroline had laughed, but she had given way:

> The Princess by rude importunity press'd,
> Though she laugh'd at his reasons, allow'd his request:
> And now Britain's nymphs in a Protestant reign
> Are box'd up at Prayers like the virgins of Spain.

Besides Mary Lepel, Mary Bellenden and Sophia Howe, Mary Bellenden's sister and Bridget Carteret were also numbered among Caroline's "virgin band," and added to the interest and gallantry of the Prince's court. A sixth Maid—Miss Meadows—was renowned less for her beauty or for her wit than for her exemplary prudence; and the name Meadows became synonymous with all that was least like Bellenden or Howe, most impeccable in conduct and most unexhilarating.[1] The others had a whole vocabulary of slang and

---

[1] See Pope's *Answer to the Following Question of Mrs. How,* printed in his *Miscellanies:*

> What is Prudery?
> 'Tis a beldam,
> Seen with wit and beauty seldom.
> 'Tis a fear that starts at shadows;
> 'Tis (no, 'tisn't) like Miss *Meadows.*

nicknames. Thus Mary Lepel was known to her friends as "the Schatz"; Mrs. Howard as "the Swiss" and her rooms in the Palace as "the Swiss Cantons"—it has been suggested because her behaviour was always carefully neutral; while "frizelation" and "dangleation" stood for flirtation and the business of pursuing, or dangling after, a member of the opposite sex. In later years, Lepel and Bellenden agreed that they had never been so happy as during the period when they were together at Hampton Court. "I wish we were all in the Swiss Cantons again," lamented Mary Bellenden, a year after she had married and left London, writing to her "dearest of Swisses" from Knole; and seven years later Mary Lepel, also married and also an exile in the country, took up the same complaint, replying to the same correspondent: "The place your letter was dated from recalled a thousand agreeable things to my remembrance which I flatter myself you do not quite forget. I wish I could persuade myself that you regret them, or that you could think the tea-table more welcome in the morning if attended (as formerly) by the *Schatz*. . . . I really believe a *frizelation* would be a surer means of restoring my spirits than the exercise and hartshorn I now make use of. I do not suppose that name still subsists, but pray, let me know if the thing itself does, and if they meet in the same cheerful manner to sup as formerly. Are ballads or epigrams the consequences of those meetings? Is good sense in the morning, and wit in the evening, the subject or rather the foundation of the conversation? . . . I pass my mornings at present as much like those at Hampton Court as I can, for I divide them between walking and the people of the best sense of their time; but

---

'Tis a virgin hard of feature,
Old and void of all good nature;
Lean and fretful, would seem wise;
Yet plays the fool before she dies.
'Tis an ugly envious shrew.
That rails at dear *Lepell* and You.

the difference is, my present companions are dead, and the others were quite alive."

A Maid's career, nevertheless, had its tedious moments: and Pope, whose affection for Mrs. Howard was only second to the idolatrous adoration that he professed for the Misses Blount and Lady Mary Wortley Montagu, records its *ennuis* in a characteristic and famous letter. Always at his happiest when he was surrounded by the delicate solicitude of one or two admiring feminine friends, Pope had had himself rowed over to Hampton Court, and there "met the Prince with all his ladies on horseback, coming from hunting." Bellenden and Lepel had immediately taken him "into protection (contrary to the laws against harbouring Papists) and gave me a dinner, with something I liked better, an opportunity of conversation with Mrs. H. We all agreed that the life of a Maid of Honour was of all things the most miserable; and wished that every woman who envied it, had a specimen of it. To eat Westphalia ham in a morning, ride over hedges and ditches on borrowed hacks, come home in the heat of the day with a fever, and (what is worse a hundred times) with a red mark on the forehead from an uneasy hat; all this may qualify them to make excellent wives for foxhunters and bear abundance of ruddy complexioned children. As soon as they can wipe off the sweat of the day, they must simper an hour and catch cold in the Princess's apartment: from thence . . . *to dinner with what appetite they may*—and after that, till midnight, walk, work, or think, which they please."

Though not a severe task-mistress, Caroline, like the Electress Sophia, had an energy that very often wore down her attendants; and at Hampton Court, when she had dined in public and received company, or read and written in her cabinet all the afternoon, she would leave the Palace and walk in the gardens, "sometimes two or three hours together," then go to the pavilion at the end of the bowling green, where card-tables had been set. Here she would play while night was falling. "This" (notes Lady Cowper) "she did very frequently"; till, one dark and rainy night, Madame de Buckenburg, who was extremely corpulent,[1] slipped and twisted her ankle; "and I think, after that Accident, the Princess went there no more, but used to play in the Green Gallery from Nine to about half an hour past Ten. The Duchess of Monmouth used to be often there: the Princess loved her mightily, and certainly no Woman of her years ever deserved it so well. She had all the Life and Fire of Youth, and it was marvellous to see that the many afflictions she had suffered had not touched her Wit and good Nature, but at upwards of Threescore she had both in their full Perfection."

Such was the social background of those summer months; but behind the scenes, in the private apartments of the Prince and Princess, there was little respite from anxiety and agitation. The English courtiers hated and despised their German colleagues; George and Caroline were exasperated by the presence of Count Bothmar, George Louis's agent and spy, who had been "left by the King to keep all Things in order, and to give an Account of Everything that was doing." Every move the Prince made was reported to Hanover; and George Louis soon heard of his son's growing popularity and learned that both George Augustus and Caroline were receiving representatives of the different political parties and interviewing *his* ministers, and seemed in a fair way to building up a parliamentary interest independent of his own. Though Argyll had received a nominal *congé,* his influence was still strong; and Townshend had found it necessary to endeavour to win over the Prince and Princess to the ministerial side. Caroline had no liking for Lord Townshend, whom she had described to Lady Cowper as "the sneeringest, fawningest knave that ever was"; and when

---

[1] Alas! like Schatz I cannot pun,
  Like Grafton court the Germans;
  Tell Pickenbourg how slim she's grown,
  Like Meadows run to sermons. . . .
    POPE. *The Challenge: A Court Ballad.*

he first undertook to placate the husband he was ill-advised enough to neglect the wife, "even to the showing her all the Contempt in the World. He made his Court to Mrs. Howard and Mrs. Ballandine" (adds Lady Cowper) "so that when I came to Hampton Court, I was never so surprised in my Life as to see that so little Respect was shown to the Princess. She had too much Quickness not to feel this as much as was possible." Lady Cowper, who realized that Caroline was not a woman to be trifled with, persuaded a third person to point out to Lord Townshend the error of his ways; and the minister was sufficiently sensible to take the hint. Henceforward, he treated Caroline with the utmost regard; and "this brought the Princess into perfect Tranquillity."

The Princess's political importance grew with her husband's. During the summer, a difficult situation arose between the absent King and his ministers; for the King envisaged all problems of foreign policy in terms of the Hanoverian interest, while Townshend and Walpole represented the hatred to which he would expose himself if he attempted to drag England into a European war. The Prince and Princess supported Townshend's view, and about the middle of August Lord Sunderland was dispatched to Hanover on a conciliatory mission. It is significant that, when he visited Hampton Court to take his leave, he should have had an interview with the Princess alone in the Queen's Gallery. The trend of their discussion we do not know, but both became so excited as they paced up and down that the Princess begged him to lower his voice, or the people in the garden below would hear what he was saying. "Let them hear!" cried Lord Sunderland in a rage. "Well, if you have a mind, let 'em," retorted the Princess, with a good-humoured forbearance which may have been diplomatic rather than absolutely natural. "But you shall walk next the windows, for in the humour we both are, one of us must certainly jump out at the window, and I'm resolved it shan't be me!"

At the end of October, the Court returned to St. James's. They returned, as they had come, by water, in a gilded state barge, accompanied at a distance by boatfuls of musicians. It was an exceptionally fine day. "No scenes of Paradise" (Pope had told Martha Blount), "no happy bowers" were "equal to those on the banks of the Thames"; and "Nothing in the World" (declared Lady Cowper) "could be pleasanter than the Passage nor give One a better Idea of the Riches and Happiness of this Kingdom." Then on November 4th, the Princess fell ill. She had known that she was pregnant at Hampton Court; and, as soon as the symptoms of labour began to declare themselves, the Council was summoned to the Palace, and courtiers packed the ante-room of her apartments, clamouring for news. A royal *accouchement* is always a nervous business. The German midwife—"whose Countenance prognosticated ill, she being the very Picture of the French Resident"—had been engaged by Caroline herself; but the English ladies were anxious that a Scottish physician, Sir David Hamilton, should be allowed to officiate in her stead. During Monday night, the Council and the royal family sat up waiting to hear that the Princess had given birth, but there were no signs of a delivery. And, when, next day, the Princess had a long and violent fit of shivering, the whole assembly fell into a sudden panic, and the Council sent off Madame de Buckenburg to beg the Prince that he would authorize Sir David Hamilton to take the German midwife's place. By Wednesday morning, the entire court was in an uproar. Sir David Hamilton's services had been refused, but the midwife declared that she would not lay a finger on the Princess unless she and the Prince would promise to support her against the English ladies, who were "high dames," she averred—*hohe Damen*—and had threatened to hang her if the patient miscarried. George Augustus's temper had never been good; and, so immoderate was the passion that now overcame him, that he swore he would throw anyone who presumed to meddle out of the window —thus effectively restoring peace and quiet. There was no further talk of Sir David Hamilton; the courtiers surrounded the angry midwife with all kinds of flattering and soothing attentions; and Lord Townshend, meeting her in an outer room, "ran and shook and squeezed her by the Hand, and made kind Faces at her; for she understood no Language but German. This" (commented Lady Cowper) "I think the Tip-top of all Policy and making One's Court." Yet Caroline's state did not improve; and "the poor Princess continued in a languishing condition till Friday night, when she was delivered of a dead prince."

It was some while before Caroline recovered her strength; and George Augustus, who feared that at any moment now his father might decide to return to England, was obliged to leave her behind when he set out on a quasi-royal progress through the southern counties. No move could have been better calculated to dislodge the King. Since July he had enjoyed a life of almost uninterrupted felicity at his Electoral court; and so unruffled was his good humour that there were those who imagined that he had completely forgotten "the accident which happened to him and his family on the 1st August 1714." Every night the court was entertained by his Majesty's own company of French comedians; and Lady Mary Wortley Montagu (who reached Hanover on her celebrated journey to Constantinople towards the end of the autumn) spoke in enthusiastic terms of the King's "affability and goodness," but in terms slightly more disparaging of the Hanoverian beauties by whom he was perpetually surrounded. "All the women" (she informed a correspondent) "have literally rosy cheeks, snowy foreheads and bosoms, jet eyebrows and scarlet lips, to which they generally add coal-black hair. These perfections never leave them till the hour of their deaths, and have a very fine effect by candlelight. But I could wish they were handsome with a little more variety. They resemble one another as much as Mrs. Salmon's [1]

---

[1] Mrs. Salmon kept a famous waxwork show.

Court of Great Britain, and are in as much danger of melting away, by too near approaching the fire, which they for that reason carefully avoid, though it is now such excessive cold weather, that I believe they suffer extremely by that piece of self-denial."

From his seraglio of high-coloured, high-bosomed beauties, from his large luxurious palace and small homely German town, George Louis extricated himself with the greatest unwillingness. But the moment had come to put a stop to his son's pretensions; while his ministers—supported by his son—seemed determined to hold up a scheme of Hanoverian aggrandizement on which he had long set his heart. In return for the two provinces of Bremen and Verden, which would make a sizable addition to his Electoral domains, England was to join Denmark against Sweden and Russia. Townshend objected to the danger and, as far as England itself was concerned, the uselessness of such a policy, whereat the King promptly dismissed Townshend and promoted Stanhope to fill his vacant post. Plainly it was time to leave for England and there reassert his paternal and royal authority. During the closing days of November he landed at Margate, and drove to London in an unusually difficult and aggressive mood.

Some immediate explosion was apprehended; and it is remarkable, considering the characters of the adversaries and the bitterness accumulated on both sides, that an open and scandalous crisis should have been so long in materializing. But the Prince and Princess could be compliant if it suited their book, while the King, as soon as he reached England, was distracted first by the discovery of a fresh Jacobite conspiracy, next by the resignation of Walpole, who—much against George Louis's wishes—followed Townshend into private life, shortly after the opening of Parliament in February 1717. The King was exceedingly reluctant to let him go: according to the elder Horace Walpole, Sir Robert's brother, when the Chancellor waited upon the King to give up his seal of office, "his Majesty seemed extremely surprised, and absolutely refused to accept it, expressing himself in the kindest and strongest terms. . . ." As often as Walpole laid his seal upon the table George Louis took it up again and dropped it into the Minister's hat. It was not until the tenth repetition of this comedy that the King finally gave it, "expressing great concern, as well as resentment at my brother's perseverance." Sir Robert was not usually an emotional man, but he left the King's presence flushed and upset, with tears standing in his eyes; and it was said that those who entered the closet noticed that the King was himself "no less disordered."

A whole year had elapsed since the King's return when the earthquake, which had long threatened, suddenly heaved up beneath the foundations of the British court, dividing the courtiers into two separate and hostile companies. During November the Princess was brought to bed of her third son. The King, on hearing the news, sent formal congratulations; but when the Prince dutifully proposed that his father and his uncle, the Duke of York, should act as godparents, George Louis decided that the Duke of Newcastle—a man for whom both Prince and Princess felt a peculiar detestation—must replace the Duke of York at the infant's christening. This was more than the irascible Prince could bear. The christening took place in Caroline's bedchamber, and throughout the ceremony, while the Archbishop of Canterbury officiated at the foot of the bed, George Augustus's prominent eyes were observed to flash fire, his thick lips to be quivering with passion. Thus far he had managed to control himself. The service came to an end. George Louis was at one side of the couch talking to the Princess, the Prince at the other. Then, abruptly brushing past Mrs. Howard and Mrs. Selwyn, his face contorted with rage, George Augustus advanced upon the Duke of Newcastle, who was standing near the King, and in a guttural half-whisper, holding up and shaking his finger under the Duke's nose as he spoke, ejaculated, "You are a rascal, but I shall find you!"

The Duke of Newcastle turned pale and left the room. George
Louis "saw the bustle but did not hear the words distinctly"; and,
as soon as he had gone, the Prince asked Mrs. Howard to meet
him in Miss Bellenden's apartment. Thither Mrs. Howard immediately hastened. She found Mary Bellenden dressed and ready to
leave; "and she who was all life and spirits & did not care a straw
about politics, said 'Oh! Lord, it is Pettecum's first Assembly, I
must go to it,' and away she went." When the Prince arrived (Mrs.
Howard told Horace Walpole) he abused the Duke of Newcastle
with the utmost violence. And meanwhile, in another quarter of
St. James's, those who were ill-disposed to the Prince and Princess took the opportunity of working on the King's mind, assuring
him that what the Prince had said was not "I will find you" (by
which he meant, apparently, that he would find means to be re-
venged) but "I will *fight* you"—a challenge to personal combat
levelled at a subject by the heir to the throne of Great Britain! So
unprecedented an emergency demanded extreme measures. Next
morning the Princess sent for Mrs. Howard; but, as she entered
an outer chamber, Yeomen of the Guard stepped forward and presented their halberds at her breast. She could not pass, they said;
they had their orders. Mrs. Howard then asked for a message to
be sent up by the back-stairs to explain to the Princess why she
had not come; at this moment an officer emerged, who said that it
was a mistake and that anybody belonging to the household of
the Prince and Princess might go through. Within she found the
Prince loudly demanding who dared to imagine that he would
waste his swordsmanship on so rascally an opponent as the Duke
of Newcastle. Nor was his temper much improved by the arrival,
somewhat later in the day, of an embassy, consisting of the Dukes
of Kingston and Roxburghe, charged with a weighty message of
reproof and expostulation. Next morning, when the Prince had
been under arrest for more than twenty-four hours, Thomas Coke,
the King's Vice-Chamberlain, was announced in the ante-room.

The Prince hurried forth, immediately came back again, summoned Coke and, turning to the Princess, told her that the Vice-Chamberlain had a message to which she must listen. Caroline wept; but George Augustus commanded the emissary to read his instructions; and poor Mr. Coke, trembling so violently that he could scarcely bring out the words, stumbled through the sentences of the King's command. It was a solemn order of expulsion from St. James's Palace. The Prince and his household were to vacate their apartments by seven that evening.

Chapter Two

1

THE retreat was neither orderly nor dignified. Abandoning at the King's command their children, but scrambling together such luggage as they could assemble in the very short space of time allowed them for the arrangement of their affairs, Prince and Princess departed up St. James's Street and took refuge in Albemarle Street at the house of the Prince's Chamberlain, where, according to a contemporary ballad:

> Higledy-pigledy they lay
> And all went rantum scantum.

From this uncomfortable lodging, the Prince (evidently, at the instigation of his wife) wrote the King an apologetic letter. But the King demanded nothing less than complete submission. He detested and despised his son; but for his daughter-in-law he felt a repugnance not untempered by a shade of respect—Caroline was a she-devil, he used to declare: she was *"cette diablesse Madame la Princesse"*—and he had no intention of giving way to their combined cajolery. He had had enough of their pretended dutifulness "to make him vomit"; now they must return as penitents, or not at all.

Meanwhile, the new-born prince was in serious danger. As a great concession, Caroline was allowed to tend her child in St. James's Palace; but, when the King ordered his removal to Kensington, he sickened, developed convulsions and (in the unsentimental phrase of the *Proper New Ballad*) "kick'd up his heels and died." Luckily, Augustan parents were inured to such losses; it was Caroline's strength that she had learned to put her husband's interests far above any other consideration; and these interests were now threatened on every quarter. Though the King could not actually cut off his son—though, that is to say, he could not deprive the Prince of the very large income fixed by Parliament—he could, and did, deprive him of all the public honours due to his rank. He could forbid him access to the Chapel Royal. He could give formal notice that persons who visited the Prince and Princess would not be received at St. James's Palace, and could direct that all courtiers who held appointments both with the Prince and with the King must instantly leave the Prince or be dismissed by the monarch.

It was an awkward predicament for nervous place-servers. Wavering miserably between present advantage and hopes of future gain—the King was not young, but he was vigorous: the Prince's fortunes were low, but his prospects were well assured and he possessed an extremely long memory—the courtiers are described as "amazed" and "thunderstruck," confounding themselves in their attempts to act with discretion. Little by little, two parties began to emerge. On the one hand, there was the King, supported by his personal attendants—"His Turks and Germans all," as the Jacobite ballad scornfully designates them—and ladies and gentlemen of the ministerial faction; on the other, an opposition court composed of the Prince and Princess's original household and a great many clever and fashionable opportunists who, with nothing to lose in royal favour, had decided to earn their future sovereign's gratitude. The scene of their operations was Leicester House. Here, in a big seventeenth-century mansion, set back behind an imposing courtyard, on the north side of Leicester Fields—then a pleasant garden, with trees, flower-beds and formal walks—Prince and Princess had finally taken up their residence. Here Caroline revived the splendours of their summer of sovereignty. In a less ambitious and somewhat more English manner, she emulated at Leicester House the gatherings she had once studied at Charlottenburg; for not only did politicians pay their respects, but writers, too, were received and even encouraged, while the greatest of English scientists was a favoured visitor.

Newton came from his house in neighbouring St. Martin's Street. Rather more unsure of his welcome (since Caroline preferred scientific and theological debate to questions of pure literature) was Pope, the devoted friend of Mrs. Howard and a keen careerist, in spite of his professed liking for detachment and solitude. Gay fluttered on the fringes of the royal circle. But George Augustus did not care for elegant poetasters; and Gay, after a lifetime of fluttering and compliment-turning, of gossiping with maids of honour and inditing fables, was to die unrewarded, or rewarded only by Pope's epitaph. Among politicians and men of fashion came Chesterfield and Hervey. Neither of these extraordinary beings had yet assumed his final and fully formed character; but the outlines of both personalities were already evident. Each was a professional courtier and a professional dandy; and it was their common misfortune to expend upon trivial ends and small interested ambitions a strength of feeling that demanded some larger issue. Their worldliness was as earnest as other men's saintliness. Their frivolity had about it something of the terrible concentration of an arduous, physically exacting game, played for its own sake, yet in an atmosphere of intense antagonism. Philip Stanhope was hampered by his lack of beauty. He was short, ungraceful, had an enormous ugly head and blackened teeth.[1] Women were seldom disposed to love or admire him; but in his role of man of the world he spoke much, though lightly, of his amorous successes, hinting at a vast variety of dissipations. Hervey, in contrast, was improbably handsome. His portrait, painted during youth,

---

[1] He was described by George II, in later life, as a "dwarf baboon."

shows us a long oval face, delicate, decidedly effeminate features, fine hands and a general air of languid elegance. He understood women and was an accomplished flatterer. The fact that he rarely desired to possess them made it all the easier to turn women the way he pleased; for he had feminine delicacy and feminine insight. Sensitive and not devoid of tender feelings, like many bisexual natures he was exceedingly perfidious.

Such were two of the "promising young gentlemen" who frequented Leicester House. Belonging to an older generation, Lord Peterborough takes a less important part in the story, but he may be mentioned as an example of aristocratic individualism carried to an almost poetic extreme—a figure not perhaps quite at his ease in this or in any other period, though the Elizabethan age might have suited him better. To the Augustans he seemed the relic of a world that was passing. It was Lord Peterborough's boast that before he was twenty-one he had been guilty of three separate capital offences, of which high treason was apparently the first and murder the second; and, in later life, he had distinguished himself both by his remarkable skill as a strategist and by his unflinching courage as a commander, when he had stormed Spanish citadels in the face of tremendous odds. Physically he bore a strong resemblance to Don Quixote. Tall, thin, cadaverous, he disregarded convention, often did his own household marketing, and at Bath was sometimes seen wearing his blue ribbon and star, but with a chicken and a cabbage tucked under his arm. He was a dilettante and a pleasant occasional versifier; and, at the age of sixty-five, his reputation as one of Europe's most accomplished amorists was further increased by the assiduous and highly romantic siege he laid to Mrs. Howard, who received his protestations with her usual gravity and calm good sense. Their correspondence has been preserved among her archives; and it is a curious tribute to Mrs. Howard's charm that, besides dedicating to his imaginary mistress a remarkably pretty lyric:

I said to my heart betwixt sleeping and waking . . .

Lord Peterborough should have written her a long series of effusive letters, which illustrate (as their editor observes) all "the sad intricacy of a metaphysical chase." But Mrs. Howard was proof against literary pleadings; she had chosen the path of duty and quietly adhered to it.

That duty was to figure as the Prince's mistress. George Augustus was not a constant lover. He had recently been paying an impassioned court to the beautiful Miss Bellenden; but Miss Bellenden's heart was engaged, and when the Prince, sitting by her one evening, after all kinds of oglings and heavy gallantries, pulled forth his purse—a bad habit he had—and began to count his money, "the giddy Bellenden lost her patience" and, jumping up, exclaimed, "Sir, I cannot bear it! If you count your money any more, I will go out of the room." This rebuff sent the Prince back to Mrs. Howard. She, at least, never snubbed his royal advances; while the "steady decorum" of her bearing, her mild and well-bred acceptance of the world as it was, soothed his vanity and gratified his love of order. Unfortunately her husband was less decorous. Mr. Howard had ceded his wife to the Prince, but he did not propose to lose the benefit of her earnings. He had previously created a violent and noisy scene in the courtyard of St. James's Palace; and now, at the King's instigation—for he was a Groom of the Bedchamber—he demanded that the Princess should hand over the runaway and obliged Caroline to grant him a personal interview. Of its upshot we are informed in Hervey's *Memoirs*. She had been "horribly afraid of him" (Caroline told Lord Hervey) ". . . as I knew him to be *so brutal,* as well as a little mad, and seldom quite sober, so I did not think it impossible that he might throw me out of the window." Mr. Howard ranted and threatened, declared that he would drag his wife from the Princess's coach by main force. The Princess edged gradually towards the door and, when she had reached a place of comparative safety, *"je pris mon grand ton de Reine, et je disois,* 'I would be glad to see who should dare to open my coach door and take out one of my servants'; *sachant tout le temps qu'il le pouvoit faire s'il le vouloit.* . . . Then I told him my resolution was positively neither to force his wife to go to him if she had no mind to it, nor to keep her if she had." Caroline, on her royal high horse, could be exceedingly formidable; but Mr. Howard, backed up by the authority of his master the King, who applauded any attempt to harass his daughter-in-law, declined to be intimidated by this display of dignity. And, when summer came and the Prince and Princess moved down to Richmond, Mrs. Howard needed the protection of an armed escort.

The affair of Mrs. Howard was inconclusive. Neither the King nor the Prince had won; for, though the Prince had kept his favourite, he eventually found it necessary to conciliate her husband by paying him a pension of twelve hundred pounds a year; and George Augustus was naturally parsimonious. There were occasions, nevertheless, when he spent with a will. Since the King was himself mean, and considered that the royal park under his windows would be better devoted to some useful agricultural object such as growing turnips, his son and daughter-in-law, after maintaining a splendid state at Leicester House, had no sooner removed to Richmond [1] than they set about reviving the grandeurs and gaieties of Hampton Court, with hunting parties, horse-races, balls and music. Once again, the Maids of Honour appeared on horseback. Once again, mounted on borrowed hacks, suffering agonies from uneasy headgear, Lepel, Bellenden, Carteret, Howe (the latter presently to vanish in deep disgrace) were to be seen flying across hedges and ditches, thundering down interminable green rides, jogging home, flushed and dishevelled, as evening descended. Horse-races were run beneath the terrace; and, while the Court

---

[1] They inhabited Richmond Lodge, recently confiscated from the Jacobite Duke of Ormonde.

looked on from above, boats thronged the river filled with sight-seers who "all stayed, until it was late, upon the water to hear the Prince's music which sounded much sweeter than from the shore."

If the King had hoped for penitence, he was disappointed. With brazen equanimity, in a long and stately procession of entertainments, receptions, galas, the Prince and Princess continued to go their way; while the King meditated severer methods of discipline. It was at this period, apparently, that he received, though he did not entertain, a proposal, outlined by Lord Berkeley, to seize the Prince, hurry him on shipboard and transport him to the American plantations, whence he would never reappear. The King's vengeance fell short of such extremities; but he had other plans; and, besides separating the Prince and Princess from their children —a measure in which he was supported by the Lord Chief Justice —he himself prepared the rough draft of an Act of Parliament, according to which the Prince, as soon as he ascended the throne of England, would be deprived automatically of his claims to Hanover. But quarrels—even family quarrels—must have an end. With filial impertinences and fatherly reprisals, the contestants had manœuvred themselves into a position beyond which they could not advance; and the prospects of a patched-up peace grew a little brighter.

Here Walpole steps solidly back into the limelight. Since his retirement from politics he had passed most of his time amid a round of country amusements, hunting and drinking with East Anglian neighbours or adding to the magnificence of Houghton's picture gallery. But ambition still worked in that massive frame. Beneath the bluff sanguine features of the country gentleman lurked a mind that was quick and subtle and penetrative, an intelligence that demanded vigorous exercise. In May 1719, the King announced his intention of leaving England on one of those prolonged Hanoverian holidays that were almost as necessary to his well-being as food and sleep; and, when he returned, in November

of the same year, the government, weakened by the incessant guer-
rilla warfare waged between St. James's Palace and Leicester
House, attempted to enlist Robert Walpole. Walpole, however, declined the suggestion. He refused, at least, to range himself against
the Prince, and declared that only a reconciliation in the royal
family would induce him to accept office—a condition to which
the government gladly agreed. They too—like the contestants
themselves—were tired of the struggle; and Robert Walpole was
deputed to act as peacemaker.

Walpole set to work with his usual energy, and one of his first
steps was to gain the support of the Princess. Only through Caroline could George Augustus be brought to reason. We do not know
exactly what part Caroline may have taken in the protracted negotiations that dragged out through the winter and spring months,
but it seems probable that the Princess, though deeply incensed
against her father-in-law, was consistently on the side of peace;
while, from our knowledge of her subsequent proceedings, we may
infer that such influence as she exerted was exerted indirectly. It
had never been her way to thrust herself forward. She obeyed; she
subsided; she agreed; and yet, by some mysterious process of matrimonial legerdemain, in the end *her* judgment was often decisive.
Walpole, then, invited her assistance. She saw him constantly; he
consulted her on every point; and after a time Lady Cowper (who
did not love Walpole) was able to report that he had "engrossed
and monopolised the Princess to a Degree of making her deaf to
Everything that did not come from him." Under their combined
pressure, the Prince grew uncommonly docile. The King, it is
true, continued restive. "Can't the Whigs come back without
him?" he grumbled, when his ministers explained to him the expediency of a reconciliation. And, "Did you not always promise
to bring me the Prince bound hand and foot? . . . What's become
of all the money you promised me?" But, in the end, he, too, grew
more conciliatory. The Prince signed a letter that Walpole had

drafted; and a messenger returned, summoning him to attend at St. James's.

It was St. George's Day, Saturday, April 23rd. The Prince immediately entered his chair and was carried to St. James's Palace, where he was received by the King in his private cabinet. George Augustus began with a set speech. He expressed the grief he had felt at being so long under his father's displeasure, declared that he was "infinitely obliged to H.M. for this permission of waiting upon him," and gave vague but adequate promises of future good conduct. The King, for his part, was almost speechless. *"Votre conduite, votre conduite,"* he muttered thickly several times; and, after the interview had lasted some five minutes, George Augustus bowed himself out and took his leave. He emerged, apparently restored to favour. At once the news flew round the waiting court; and Stanhope, the perfect court-intelligencer, rushed up to Bothmar and Bernstorff, the two German ministers, who were standing in the outer room, announcing "in his shrill scream," *"Eh bien! Messieurs, la paix est faite . . . la paix est faite."* Back at Leicester House Caroline heard a distant hubbub. It was the Prince's triumph; escorted (for the first time since his disgrace in 1717) by a royal guard of beefeaters and surrounded by an enthusiastic mob, George Augustus was returning with suitable ceremony. But his eyes (Lady Cowper noticed) were "red and swelled, as One has seen him upon other Occasions when he is mightily ruffled"; and he promptly dismissed the courtiers and retired from view.

The court reassembled at five o'clock that afternoon, and in the meantime Leicester House had changed its aspect. Royal guards were posted in the courtyard; the square was "full of coaches; the Rooms full of Company; Everything gay and laughing; Nothing but Kissing and wishing of Joy." The Prince himself had quite recovered his equanimity; and, when Lady Cowper was summoned into the Princess's closet to seal a letter to the Archbishop of Canterbury, the Prince clasped her in his arms and administered half a dozen jubilant kisses "with his usual Heartiness when he means sincerely"; at which the Princess burst out into one of her loud good-natured German laughs, exclaiming, "So! I think you two always kiss upon great occasions." "All the Town" (noted Lady Cowper) "feignedly or unfeignedly, transported." Next day the King received the Princess. They met in the apartments of the little Princesses at St. James's Palace, where Princess Anne, the eldest, was lying ill. George Louis and Caroline withdrew into an inner room and remained in secret conference for an hour and ten minutes; while the attendant courtiers, obliged to kick their heels outside, were entertained by Mahomet, the King's Turkish servant, who described in macabre detail the death of his master's sister, the late Queen of Prussia. This unfortunate lady was thought to have been poisoned by diamond-powder mixed in her food, "for when she was opened her Stomach was so worn, that you could put your Fingers through at any Place, as did Mahomet." Her brother, the King, said Mahomet, was so affected by his loss that he went five days without eating, drinking or sleeping, but continued to pace up and down his chamber, banging his toes against the wainscot ("which he ever does when he walks") till he had worn out his shoes and his "Toes came out two Inches at the Foot."

Then, finally, the Princess reappeared. Diplomatic and self-restrained as always, she professed herself enchanted with the "King's mighty kind reception, and told the Doctors and Everybody how mighty kind he had been to her"; when, in fact (she confided to Walpole), he had treated her with the utmost roughness, had upbraided her violently and at considerable length, "adding that she might say what she pleased to excuse herself; that she could have made the Prince better if she would, and that he expected from henceforward she would use all her Power to make him behave well." Next day the two courts were formally reconciled. It was an uncomfortable occasion; for though the King had invited the Prince to his Drawing Room he refused to speak to him or any of his associates, and "the whole Thing" (decided Lady Cowper) looked "like two Armies drawn up in Battle Array." The King's court stood in mass-formation behind their leader at one end of the apartment, the Prince's suite behind theirs at the farther extremity. The Prince looked down, and preserved a modest and respectful attitude, but the King kept glancing furiously in his direction, "and One could not help thinking" (observes Lady Cowper) " 'twas like a little Dog and a Cat—whenever the Dog stirs a foot, the Cat sets up her Back, and is ready to fly at him. Such a Crowd was never seen, for not only Curiosity but Interest had brought it together."

Caroline, magnificently, ignored these snubs. At the Chapel Royal, at the theatre (where the two courts heard *"Radamistus, a fine Opera of Handel's making"*), at the next Drawing Room and amid the celebrations that marked the monarch's birthday, George Louis still declined to speak to his son; but no degree of coldness or rudeness could discourage his daughter-in-law. Not for nothing had she studied the arts of submission. In Germany they had called her a *"grandissime Comédienne";* she had fretted at the enforced inaction of the last three years, and now relished the opportunity of playing a difficult and delicate part, conciliating some enemies and scoring off others. At times she was diplomatic; at times she was brutal; and it was in the latter strain—one suited admirably to her bold fresh-coloured German countenance and loud guttural German voice—that she took the younger Craggs to task for his share in the quarrel. Craggs was for waving away responsibility. The trouble, he protested, had been caused by tattling underservants, "who had reported abundance of things, which they said were true; that for the Ministers, he would answer they had never done any such things. . . ." Their only complaint against the Prince was that his friends formed a parliamentary opposition which "broke through all their Measures: 'And perhaps,' says he, 'I myself have been one of the Foremost to say it, it being true.' "

Here the Princess caught him up with remarkable vehemence. "I was told," she exclaimed, "you had condescended so low as to call me a Bitch"; at which Mr. Craggs let fly a "Volley of Oaths and Curses," protesting that he was horrified by the accusation, and continuing till the Princess checked his harangue. "Fie! Mr. Craggs," she observed sardonically. "You renounce God like a woman that's caught in the fact!"

There could be no doubt that she was enjoying her return to court; and her attendants—Lady Cowper among others—began to notice that their mistress, in whom up to the moment of the reconciliation they had seen only good, courageous and endearing qualities, had a side that was more devious and far less amiable: that she was a woman to be feared and, perhaps, distrusted. What were they to make of her alliance with Walpole? That politician, they began to believe, had "possessed her Mind"; and the loyal, high-spirited Princess, whom they had followed into exile, was now "in Transports of Joy" at the "new Accession of Flatterers"; while her character changed under the hardening influence of ambition and artifice. Robert Walpole, certainly, was a redoubtable friend. But Walpole, as it happened, was not to be left very long in quiet enjoyment of his diplomatic triumph, for a fresh crisis— of far greater magnitude—was now preparing; and even Walpole would be hard put to it to repair the damage. Much more ominous than any differences in the royal family was the rapid growth, the terrifying expansion, of the South Sea Bubble.

2

THE FIRST puff had been given by Robert Harley. Several years back, in 1713—two years before the advent of the House of Hanover—faced with a Treasury that was almost empty and a Civil List that was heavily in debt, he had conceived an ingenious plan of paying off some nine million pounds of the public obligations by distributing to the government's creditors the stock of a new company which he proposed to form for that especial purpose and which would enjoy the monopoly of South American trade. The company was to receive interest and management charges. In a speech so brilliant and so plausible that it was afterwards described as the "Earl of Oxford's masterpiece," Harley contrived to push the measure through Parliament. Unfortunately, what he had failed to take into account was the extreme difficulty of establishing the company itself upon any genuine or solid commercial basis. The King of Spain distrusted English enterprise. Under the terms of the Peace of Utrecht the company was allowed to send a single ship every year to the ports from which they had promised themselves unbounded wealth; and when war broke out that privilege was at once withdrawn. George I was elected Governor of the struggling company, but the value of South Seas stock showed a steady decline.

At this stage the human factor begins to predominate. Since systems of chronology are artificial, it is curious that human affairs —changes of mood experienced by an entire race, the gradual and mysterious shift of human impulses—should correspond so very often to changes of century. Thus every century seems to begin with a period of unrest. A feeling of gathering oppression concludes the epoch; and Dryden in his lovely *Centennial Masque,* with its burden of remembered griefs and faint forecasting of better things:

> 'Tis well an old age is out
> And time to begin a new

had ushered forth the seventeenth century to noble music. But the new age had proved equally distracting. Anne's brief reign had been characterized by violent religious controversies and savage party strife; and, though George had come peacefully to the throne of England, he had not held it amid conditions of peace and order. Nor in France had the course of history been very smooth. The Regent (who had succeeded to power on the death of Louis Quatorze in 1715) found the country reduced by the ravages of Marlborough's campaigns to a practically bankrupt condition; and it was in this predicament that he received the proposals of that enterprising Scottish adventurer, John Law, who had first insinuated himself into his company by his skill at backgammon. Gambler, man of pleasure, adroit courtier, Law was one of those odd eighteenth-century personages (ranging in type from Casanova to the hermaphroditic Chevalier d'Éon) who constantly disappear and reappear in the pages of history, expelled from one capital in utter disgrace, sighted again in the best society of another metropolis (where they seduce the most beautiful ladies of the court, win or lose enormous sums at the card-tables), only to vanish with the same mysterious and fated air. Law himself had been a wanderer for several decades. His schemes and theories, which he had attempted to market in Scotland as early as 1700, had never received a favourable reception until, happening to return to Paris just after the death of Louis Quatorze, he was able to submit them to the Regent, who thought that he had recognized in Law his financial saviour. Soon Law had conquered a position of supreme importance. His plans developed with dazzling richness, at incredible speed.

His rise, which carried him to the post of Controller-General of French finances, his fall—which occurred suddenly and ludicrously, when the Regent, rising in rage from the close stool, his breeches still dangling around his legs, publicly threatened to commit him to the Bastille—have no direct connexion with the present narrative. Indirectly, though, he had left his mark; for Law's example excited English financiers, and the hysterical hubbub of the Rue Quincampoix (Parisian centre of Law's Mississippi Boom) soon re-echoed between the house-fronts of Change Alley. The

South Sea directors were notably stirred; and John Blount, who considered that Law's operations had been modelled on a study of some of his own earlier financial schemes, decided that the time had come to improve on his imitator. Similar in their ambitions and their interests, Law and Blount were exceedingly unlike in both appearance and temperament, Law being handsome, courtly, dissipated, John Blount a clever middle-class tradesman whose pinched features suggest the severe background of a London counting house. But Blount's plans were almost equally ambitious. With the growth of the Mississippi company to provide an intoxicating example for enterprising modern financiers, Blount's mind (which had been "wonderfully affected" by his knowledge of events across the Channel) "could brook no longer the narrow thoughts he had entertained before," and hatched a project that aimed at nothing less than the transference to the company of the entire National Debt, then calculated to have reached a figure of more than fifty-one million pounds. To enable the company to support this colossal burden, Blount meditated the formation of an enormous financial combine that would include both the South Sea and East India Companies; while, to be allowed to shoulder it, he needed the interest of the existing government. The latter he obtained through Aislabie, Chancellor of the Exchequer in Sunderland and Stanhope's administration, a weak and colourless man, gifted with no grasp of financial affairs and undistinguished by any particular degree of honesty. Towards the end of January 1720, Aislabie rose to sponsor Blount's scheme before the House of Commons. In spite of staunch opposition on the part of the Bank of England (which had been frightened into making a competitive bid) and certain necessary reductions and alterations, the Bill was eventually passed by a large majority. Huge bribes had been distributed to prominent persons; a sufficiency of speculators was now needed to defray expenses.

Rapidly the bubble was lifting and filling. It is unfortunate that no great novelist should yet have appeared to explain in literary terms the evolution of some gigantic financial hoax and analyse the mental processes that have contributed to its development. Between financial acumen and ordinary common sense a very definite division should perhaps be made: for, plainly, they do not always co-exist, and one might argue that they are often irreconcilable. Common sense would have suggested that, whatever the spirit in which Blount and his fellow-directors had embarked on their scheme, they must eventually be overwhelmed or resort to trickery, since not otherwise could they hope to discharge their obligations. If the company was to make money, its stock must rise. When their stock had risen beyond a certain point, the directors would be able to redeem the public indebtedness at a profit to themselves, for individual claimants were to be paid off—largely though not entirely—in South Sea stock assessed at its market value. As the company had, at that moment, few real commercial assets, and their golden trafficking in the southern hemisphere remained a dream, stock would only rise under artificial stimulus; and that encouragement the South Sea directors set out to supply. Fabulous reports were put into circulation. It was rumoured that Spain and England were on the point of concluding a new and important commercial treaty. Tales were told of the prodigious wealth of Peru and Mexico—of inexhaustible silver mines, of the lucrative slave trade. Commercial cupidity was invested with romantic trimmings; the ghosts of Drake and Raleigh seemed to hover round the Royal Exchange.

The stock rose. It rose steadily for several months. On January 1st, some time before the Bill had passed through the House of Commons, it stood at 128, and during March it out-did the directors' most enthusiastic expectations by mounting to 380. April saw it quoted at 500—this further rise having been engineered by Blount and his agents, who were making regular and heavy purchases behind the scenes. Nothing could now arrest the growth of the boom. . . . But booms and their concomitant depressions are interesting not only to students of economic cause and effect (who might observe in the development of the South Sea Bubble the first adult excesses of a new capitalism); they are interesting also to students of human nature. Their occurrence is typical of certain periods. They coincide with a wave of general unrest, with a feeling of nervous excitement throughout the community, which may express itself by a dozen different manifestations. This mood had already become perceptible. Moralists of the early eighteenth century agree in deploring the restless, unbalanced, sensation-greedy temper of the times. They comment, for example, on the spread of gambling; they remark the predominance of Woman; they note how feminine pursuits have coloured society, and how the two sexes are now confused in the pursuit of excitement, with infinite damage to the old-fashioned domestic virtues. Plainness and economy had fallen from favour. Coffee and chocolate—expensive, new-fangled beverages—now fumed in every fashionable woman's drawing-room; liqueurs were secretly tippled by ladies of quality who met, in the intervals of gossiping and card-playing, at the China houses which (besides being popular places of assignation) carried large stocks of costly and delicate Oriental porcelain, newly imported from the factories of Canton and Yedo.

Now a fresh vice was to be added to the English repertory. Robert Walpole, not in his own life a captious moralist, but a man of the world blessed with unusual common sense, had prophesied the spread of this social evil when he inveighed against the proposals of the South Sea directors. Their scheme (he told the House of Commons) "countenanced the pernicious practice of stockjobbing, by diverting the genius of the nation from trade and industry; it held out a dangerous lure for decoying the unwary to their ruin by a false prospect of gain." And he urged that, if the proposals of the South Sea Company were accepted, some limitation should be put on the rise of their stock, adding that "the great principle

THE SOUTH SEA BUBBLE

Hogarth

SIR ROBERT WALPOLE

Engraving by Robinson after Jarvis

of the project was an evil of the first magnitude; it was to raise artificially the value of the stock, by exciting and keeping up a general infatuation and by promising dividends out of funds which would not be adequate to the purpose." Walpole, however, had been over-ruled; and it is characteristic of the man that, deeply and honestly though he deplored the scheme, he did not hesitate to profit by its execution; to have abstained, no doubt, would have struck him as the rankest hypocrisy. He bought stock when it was still possible to buy with advantage, and was "fully satisfied" to sell out "at 1000 per cent."

Others were not so fortunate or not so cynical. Stock-jobbing, as Walpole foretold, soon became a mania, a frenzy, a sort of hysterical preoccupation to which ordinary occupations gave right of precedence. The industrious City of London was swamped by speculators; and these speculators were recruited from every class, every age, every quarter of the country, all shouldering in the direction of the South Sea Building. The Prince and Princess were both purchasers of South Sea stock; and during the next eight months of financial hurly-burly there was probably not a single eminent and ambitious man—for that matter, there were very few eminent women—who failed to risk something in the absorbing enterprise. Women proved specially avaricious. Deserting basset and ombre tables, forgetful of lapdogs and blue-and-white porcelain:

> The Court, the Park, the foreign Song
> And Harlequin's grimace

—"young tender virgins" were to be seen pushing their way amid Jews and Gentiles, unalarmed by Hebraic beards and whiskers. Emblazoned coaches choked the narrow lanes of the city:

> Here Stars and Garters do appear
> Among our lords the Rabble,

To buy and sell, to see and hear
The Jews and Gentiles squabble . . .
Our greatest ladies hither come
And ply in chariots daily;
Oft pawn their jewels for a sum
To venture in the Alley.
Young harlots, too, from Drury Lane
Approach the Change in Coaches,
To fool away the gold they gain
By their impure debauches.

It was calculated that since the spread of the stock-jobbing fever, two hundred new and splendid equipages had appeared in the streets of London and that as many more were on the stocks in the coachbuilders' yards. Add to this "above 4000 embroider'd Coats" together with "about 3000 gold watches at the sides of whores and wives," and the glory of the Grand Bubble becomes apparent as it sailed skywards into the regions of Cloud-Cuckoo-Land. Smaller bubbles, in a crowd, attended its progress—ventures as fantastic as a proposal to raise two million pounds "for effecting the Transmutation of Fluid Mercury or Quicksilver, into a solid and malleable body, so that 'twill spread under the Hammer, and be of equal Use, Beauty and Value with the purest Standard Silver" (which promised subscribers 800 per cent) or a Swiftian apparatus called Puckle's Machine Gun, designed to discharge "round and square cannon balls and bullets . . . making a total revolution in the Art of War."

Among the more reputable of these minor projects was the English Copper Company (formed to mine copper in the mountains of Wales), of which the Prince, against the advice of Walpole and the Speaker of the House of Commons, Sir Spencer Compton, had graciously permitted himself to be elected Governor. That copper might not exist in Wales, or not in sufficient quantity to make its exploitation possible, seems scarcely to have entered the subscribers' heads. Indeed so over-heated was the state of public feeling that the very remoteness and unreality of any project, far from deterring subscribers, appear to have inflamed their imaginations as if profit-gathering and real commerce were natural enemies. The public asked for no guarantees and, certainly, received none. No ocular evidence that these numerous high-sounding ventures had emerged beyond the stage of the prospectus-sheet was ever produced or ever demanded. If square cannon-balls were cast, they remained hidden; while the operations of the scientists who proposed to transmute quicksilver into a solid and malleable substance, to extract butter from beech-nuts or oil from sunflower seeds, to turn salt water into fresh or launch a nostrum for syphilis, were circumscribed by the four walls of some secret laboratory. But the South Sea Company was still the main bubble; and the South Sea junto were exceedingly indignant at the success of their imitators, who threatened to divert revenue from their central scheme. Measures were concerted between Company and Government which aimed at the elimination of all lesser adventurers.

During June a royal proclamation was issued defining certain "extravagant and unwarrantable Practices" which had lately become common and deploring the harm they had already done "by taking off the minds of many of our Subjects from attending their lawful employments, and by introducing a General Neglect of Trade and Commerce." There followed a clause warning the small fry of projectors and stock-pedlars that, after the lapse of a fortnight, they would be regarded as a Common Nuisance and, as such, liable to rigorous punishment by law. Apparently this Proclamation had the hoped-for effect. By June 24th South Sea stock achieved its peak price, touching the unexampled figure of 1050; and Blount, who had recently received a baronetcy, left London to take the waters at Tunbridge Wells. Here he comported himself with an almost royal ostentation. The suite with which he drove down had been large and sumptuous; his behaviour at the Wells (where "he and his family, when they spoke of the scheme, called it 'Our Scheme'") was so arrogant as to suggest his prototype, Law; but, all the time, he was busily engaged in selling his holdings. "Certain it is" (declares a journalist) "that he wrote every Post to his Brokers, and no sooner was one parcel of Stock disposed of than he ordered another to be sold."

In the same month the King had departed for Hanover, leaving behind him a Council of Regency which he had drawn up to act as a check on his son. When he sailed, London was at the height of its stock-jobbing mania—

> So Oddly rich, so madly great
> Since bubbles came in fashion

—that every day provided some new story of wealth suddenly acquired, obscurity hoisted to dazzling altitudes; but during the first few weeks of his absence a change was felt. As the result of secret selling the market weakened. Then the directors of the company, having persuaded the Government to prick a number of lesser bubbles, obtained from the Lords Justices writs against four larger and slightly more respectable concerns, including the Welsh copper company already mentioned.[1] Three of these rival companies were put out of action; and the shareholders, who, in many instances, had borrowed on their holdings money with which to gamble in South Sea stock, were now obliged to sell out that stock to repay their bankers. South Sea stock declined seriously at the end of August: the Grand Bubble had begun to descend like an extinguished fire-balloon.

Panic fear succeeded unreasonable exaltation. In the last days of August, Lord Berkeley of Stratton reports to Lord Strafford that

---

[1] The Prince of Wales thereupon resigned his position and retired from the field with a handsome profit.

"some of the Directors have been playing the Rogue" and "have putt people in a fright" from which "itt is not so easy to bring them out again," but adds that he expects "a considerable alteration in a few days." That alteration, however, was much for the worse. Within a month, South Sea stock had dropped to 135; and, in a final attempt to restore public confidence, George Louis, happily established in his Hanoverian dominions, was summoned back to reassure the English stock-market. He returned in November— with no good effect. "A great many" (wrote Lord Berkeley) "flatter themselves with the King's coming . . . and the meeting of Parliament, but I wish it is not past their power to cure the fright that has seized everybody." The situation was, indeed, past any amendment. Outrageous in its prosperity during the spring and early summer, London had now subsided into the depths of gloom. Stories of ruin and suicide were as common as tales of sudden accessions to wealth and extravagant *parvenu* luxury only a few weeks earlier. Numerous speculators cut their throats or blew out their brains; once-mighty noblemen were reduced to accepting office as mere colonial governors; while the proprietors of private madhouses had their hands so full that they were obliged to shut their doors against further patients.

"So many undone people" (observed Lord Berkeley) "will make London a very melancholy place this winter. . . ." "All falling; the Directors are curst; the top adventurers broke; four goldsmiths walked off. . . . Every man with a face as long as Godolphin's" (wrote Matthew Prior, who had just seen the disappearance of a comfortable paper fortune) *"vogue la galère;* I must fare like the rest"; Pope, somewhat less unlucky since he had been able to secure a part of his profits, contented himself with a letter of philosophic reflections to Atterbury, the Jacobite Bishop of Rochester; and the ballad-makers of the moment took up the refrain. "The Town," they declared, had become "desart," peopled only by images of horror or despair:

Some hang, some drown,
And some distracted run.

Its streets were devoted to dullness and solitude:

All things are hushed,
As law itself were dead;
Poor pensive Fleet Street
Droops its mournful head. . . .

But angry crowds gathered near the South Sea Building; and at Westminster the Commons assembled in a buzz of fury.

At St. James's, too, the consternation was universal. It was an open secret that both ministers and mistresses had accepted bribes, and certain members of the Hanoverian faction so far lost their balance as to suggest to George Augustus, before the King's return, that he and his family should flee the kingdom, that some form of dictatorship should be proclaimed, or that he should apply for the assistance of foreign troops. Could the dynasty, already unpopular, survive this blow? No doubt it was as well for the royal family that the directors of the South Sea Company were all of English origin and that the project had been encouraged by an English government: since, otherwise, a revolution might have been unavoidable. Luckily for them this was a domestic catastrophe. Parliament met at the beginning of December, and members (most of whom had lost heavily by the South Sea slump) sank their differences in a grand chorus of recrimination. The King's Speech had counselled mildness tempered by firmness. But Shippen, that intransigent and incorruptible Jacobite, who could always be relied upon to constitute himself a lively one-man opposition, proposed an amendment to the effect that it was the duty of the House to manifest "the highest resentment" against men who had abused the public confidence and enriched themselves by the plunder of the nation. Comparatively Shippen's speech was moderate; any vehemence or animosity he displayed was completely eclipsed by that of Lord Molesworth, who, in the stormy debate which followed, gave it as his opinion that, although there was said to be no law by which the directors of the South Sea Company could be punished, modern England should follow the example of ancient Rome, where parricides were stitched up in sacks and cast, still alive, into the Tiber; for the "Parricides of their Country" were equally culpable.

In other circumstances this fury would have been more impressive. It was unfortunate, no doubt, that the assemblage of indignant legislators should also represent, for the most part, a gathering of injured and disappointed speculators, and that several pillars of the government (now anxious to placate the public by penalizing the company) should have accepted large gifts of stock to promote the scheme. But indignation, when self-interested, has an especial fervour; amid the hubbub only Walpole preserved his balance, and Walpole spoke for moderation with double authority, since he had both opposed the scheme and had made a profit out of it. Remedy, he suggested, must precede revenge; "he therefore desired that the House should proceed calmly and regularly, lest by running precipitately into odious inquiries, they should exasperate the distemper to such a degree as to render all remedies ineffectual." Thanks to Walpole's moderating influence, tempers began to grow calmer, brains to grow clearer; the first bloodthirsty and senseless uproar showed signs of diminishing. His own bill for the restoration of the public credit was passed on January 3rd by a large majority.

Though Walpole's bill (which sought to divide a part of the South Sea Company's accumulated obligations between the East India Company and the Bank of England) had passed into law, it was eventually superseded by other measures; but its immediate effect was beneficial. Throughout the winter months he laboured in the cause of peace, attempting on the one hand to safeguard such elements in the original scheme as appeared to him deserving of preservation, on the other hand to limit the extent of the damage. His efforts were at least partially successful. But victims there must be; and the House, having addressed itself to the extremely congenial task of hunting out offenders, now plunged deep into the "odious inquiries" that Walpole had deprecated. January was given over to these researches. On January 12th the sub-governors of the company, the Deputy Governor and some two dozen of the directors were submitted to a close examination and afterwards pronounced to have been "guilty of a Notorious Breach of Trust," at which Knight, the cashier, fled the country. Blount and other directors were at once arrested and committed to the Tower; the books of the company were investigated; and it was established that bribes, in the form of fictitious stock, had been distributed to a great many prominent and influential persons, including Sunderland, who had received £50,000; the elder Craggs, whose support had been enlisted at the cost of £30,000; the Duchess of Kendal (formerly Schulenburg, *doyenne* of the King's mistresses), who had accepted £10,000; the Countess Platen, who had been purchased at the same figure; and two of her "nieces" (believed the bastard daughters of the King), who had divided £10,000 between them. Aislabie was also dipped in the scandal. The Commons, now warming to its work, thereupon passed a confiscatory bill "for raising money on the estates of the sub- and deputy-governors, directors, cashier, deputy-cashier, and accountant of the South Sea Company, and of Mr. Aislabie and Mr. Craggs, towards making good the damage sustained by the company; and for disabling such of those persons as were living, to hold any place, or sit in parliament for the future."

The spoilers were ceremoniously despoiled by Parliament; and Sir John Blount, who had amassed £183,334 during the last twelve months, was stripped to his last thousand pounds. The elder Craggs escaped with the help of an overdose. During February his son, the Secretary of State, had died—it was thought of smallpox, though his decease may have been due to fatigue and excitement, or (as was hinted by some journalists) to a "Merry Meeting . . . in which 'twas said there was too great use made of Burgundy, Champagne and Tokay wines"; and, in March, his progenitor expired, of a "lethargick fit, after having (as is supposed) taken too large a composition of a composing Draught." By the early summer, Commons and Lords (though not the great body of South Sea creditors, who, in April, created a serious disturbance outside the House) were tired of the once-absorbing subject, and the affairs of the delinquent company were at last wound up, with a loss to the public far less considerable than had at first been feared. Sunderland owed his acquittal to Walpole's eloquence; but he judged it prudent to retire precipitately from the administration.

Thus Walpole and Townshend returned to power. That is to say, Walpole, by virtue of his particular combination of tact, executive ability and shrewd common sense, was able to reassume his former leadership. Naturally, his line of conduct was criticized. Walpole had a realistic view of political life; it was not his function to reform the existing machinery; but it was his strength, given that machinery, to make the wheels revolve to the greatest possible advantage and to see, at a glance, where the greatest advantage lay. Nothing was to be gained by crisis or scandal. His position, nevertheless, made him an easy target; and in the *Craftsman* and other Tory papers, all "the sophistry of Bolingbroke, and the wit of Pulteney" were directed against the part that he had played, particularly stigmatizing his efforts to "screen" Sunderland. But the general consensus was on Walpole's side. At the darkest moments of the collapse, and during its aftermath, the knowledge that Walpole had been called in raised the spirits of the public from utter despondency, and his return to office encouraged the process of convalescence. The nation rallied, sick and shaken, from its financial frenzy, to find Robert Walpole in quiet command of the sick-room.

O<small>NCE</small> installed, he was not easily to be dislodged. The King, in other relationships with his English subjects cold, lethargic and mistrustful, had a real affection for *ce gros homme,* whose financial capabilities he professed to regard with an almost superstitious reverence. Walpole (he informed the Princess, during one of the political conversations that they used to keep up during the service at the Chapel Royal) could turn stones to gold. Walpole, moreover, had a knack of amusing him. The minister's eldest son was the Ranger of Richmond Park; Walpole shot or hunted there once or twice a week and, after shooting, he frequently entertained the King at a small house he had taken on Richmond Hill. George Louis was "fond of private joviality." He loved punch; Walpole, a hard and experienced drinker, took the opportunity these friendly meetings offered, till the Duchess of Kendal (who hated Walpole) became much alarmed. Her spies and agents accompanied the King to Richmond; but when, acting on her instructions, they did their best to prevent his drinking too heavily or sitting up too late, the King flew into a towering Teutonic passion and silenced them "by the coarsest epithets in the German language."

To make their odd intimacy yet more remarkable, the King spoke no English, the minister neither German nor French, and Latin was their ordinary medium of communication. Yet, notwithstanding differences of language and outlook—the King sank deeper and deeper into the bosom of his Hanoverian entourage; and the Germans, headed by the Duchess of Kendal, had recognized in Walpole their arch enemy—for the next six years the minister maintained his predominance. The King liked and esteemed him; the Princess respected him; though it is true that her respect and admiration were no longer so unqualified as in days gone by. The results of the reconciliation had been disappointing. To secure peace Walpole had promised more than it lay within his power to perform; and the Princess realized that she and her husband had gained little, for they were still not allowed the management of the three elder princesses (who continued to reside with their grandfather at St. James's Palace) while the King still suspected and rebuffed the Prince. And then, Walpole, as it happened, was an incautious talker. His references to the Princess (now growing corpulent with the advance of maturity) were not always charitable or strictly decent, and his broad pleasantries were often repeated to Caroline. The Princess had an absorbing sense of her personal dignity; and it was only her acute sense of political expediency that prevented a breach.

For the interests of Walpole and Caroline were yet closely identified. What was dignity—what, indeed, were the tenderest private feelings—when compared with that complete devotion to her husband's cause which had provided the motive power of her conduct since 1714? Thus she assisted Walpole to counter the plans of Bolingbroke. A pagan philosopher whose philosophy did not protect him against the constant goading of ambition, Bolingbroke had grown tired of his foreign solitude and dispatched his newly married but unacknowledged second wife, the Marquise de Villette, to make his peace with the directors of English policy. She arrived in England and hastened to Leicester House. There she interviewed the Princess; but, when she attempted to explain that her husband had merely entered the Pretender's service in the hope that he might be useful to the King, Caroline cut her short with a blunt dismissal. Her speech (related the Princess afterwards) "had so much villainy and impudence mixed in it that I could never bear him nor her from that hour." . . . Madame de Villette next resorted to the Duchess of Kendal; but, although the Duchess, loving money and hating Walpole, accepted a substantial bribe to promote the exile's return and though the minister, coerced by the

King, was obliged to give way, Bolingbroke's recall brought him
none of the results he had hoped for: Walpole's influence encircled
him like an invisible rampart. He obtained a dearly bought interview at St. James's Palace; but the King received his attack on
Walpole with contemptuous coldness.

That same year saw the elimination of another enemy. Atterbury, Bishop of Rochester, who, in 1714, had offered to proclaim
James King of England in full pontifical splendour at the Royal
Exchange and Charing Cross, and who had since been a secret
agent for the Stuart cause, was betrayed to the English ambassador
by the French Government. His arrest in August 1722, his banish-
ment in 1723, aroused much indignation; Pope, who numbered
both Bolingbroke and Atterbury among his closest friends and
most intelligent literary patrons, wrote of the "unconquered soul"
he displayed during his imprisonment in the Tower; he was publicly prayed for in London churches and described by enthusiasts
as "a second Laud"; but these protests were rather noisy than effective. They did nothing to shake Walpole's ascendancy. The country, as a whole, remained undisturbed; and, during the summer of
1723, George Louis set out on his customary expedition to Hanover, accompanied by the usual troop of ministers and mistresses.
Like his son, the King was a creature of habit. Interrupted first by
his quarrel with the Prince, secondly by the explosion of the South
Sea Bubble, he soon fell back into his previous round of pleasures
and ceremonies, and once again the rhythm of court life became
dully regular. At stated intervals he left for Herrenhausen or returned to St. James's, stolid, dignified and precise as a clockwork
effigy.

Mistresses were to be visited, marriages settled. His daughter,
the Queen of Prussia, pressed for a double marriage between the
King's elder grandson Frederick Louis (who still remained in
Hanover) and her eldest daughter Wilhelmina, and between her

eldest son Frederick William (who afterwards achieved fame as Frederick the Great) and Caroline's second daughter, the Princess Amelia. George Louis loved the Queen, but he detested his son-in-law. A martinet of the most ferociously sadistic type, whose chief amusement was the collection of gigantic grenadiers, kidnapped or specially bred to embellish his army, the King of Prussia terrorized his entire household, thrashing and imprisoning his children on the slightest pretext and sentencing his officers to the salt mines for trivial offences. At this gloomy court, George appeared in 1723. "She is very tall, how old is she?" was his only comment, when his granddaughter, the prospective bride, was presented to him by her parents. His attitude was phlegmatic and unaffectionate; and, after entering the Queen's private apartments, his first action was to seize a candle, hold it close to the trembling Princess's face, and examine her closely and silently from top to toe. The results of this inspection were inconclusive; the plan of a double marriage was not abandoned but no steps were taken to advance the project; and the King returned to Hanover and thence to England. His grandson, Frederick, was only sixteen at the time of the visit; and there would be no need to marry him off for several years.

The succession was in no immediate peril. The King himself, it is true, had suffered from some kind of seizure during his stay at the Prussian court, collapsing at the end of a state banquet, losing hat and wig, and spending a whole hour stretched unconscious on the floor of the banqueting room; but for an elderly man and a hard-liver he seemed healthy enough. He was sixty-three; he might last out another decade. With tight-lipped patience the Prince and Princess at Leicester House sat down to await the processes of nature, meanwhile consolidating their position as far as they could. Caroline continued to bear children with admirable fortitude; in 1721 she had produced William Augustus, Duke of Cumberland, subsequently her favourite child; and the little boy, her second surviving son, was soon followed by a fourth and fifth daughter: Mary, born in 1723, and Louisa, in 1724. But the driving force of her vast vitality was unimpaired. Still immensely ambitious for herself and her husband, she was careful to appear in public at every opportunity and to extend her influence by every means within her power, paying particular attention to the City of London. Deputations were received and festivities patronized. Thus, on the Princess's birthday in 1724, stewards of the Society of Ancient Britons were allowed to present their loyal congratulations in the drawing room of Leicester House. On another occasion Prince and Princess presided at a concert in the Inner Temple and a ball at Lincoln's Inn. They appeared on the terrace at Somerset House to witness a Lord Mayor's Day pageant along the river; and, when livery-men rowed up to the river wall and offered them wine, they drank a tactful toast amid tumultuous acclamations.

There was little communication between the two courts; but, on his return from one of his later Hanoverian visits, George Louis so far relaxed his disapproval as to present the Princess with a novel plaything; though whether his intention was ironic or kindly it is hard to decide. His gift was nothing less than a "Wild Boy." This strange and pathetic being, captured in the obscure depths of a forest near Hamelin, where he had run on all fours, scaled trees like a squirrel and nourished himself by devouring twigs and moss, was thought to be twelve or thirteen years old; but he could not speak and appeared to have few glimmerings of intelligence above the animal. Dressed in a new blue suit lined with red and red stockings (in which, it was noted, he looked "extremely uneasy") the Wild Boy was first exhibited at St. James's, then handed over to the care of the Princess, who entrusted him, as an interesting subject for experiment, to Pope's friend, the humane and learned Dr. Arbuthnot. But all the Doctor's experiments were unsuccessful; the darkness of some German primeval forest seemed to occupy the interior of that brutish head, and the changeling was eventually farmed out in Hertfordshire. There he grew old and there he lies buried, under a simple inscription: PETER THE WILD BOY.

Another, and even stranger, personage followed him—though the strangeness of this second apparition proceeded not from the absence of intelligence, but from its excess, not from the lack of thought but from a complexity of tortured feelings, in which ambition was perpetually struggling with self-disgust and tender emotions with a consuming hatred for the whole of humanity. Now that she had seen a wild German boy, said Dr. Swift on being introduced, at the Princess's often repeated request, by his old friend Mrs. Howard, no doubt her Royal Highness was curious to see a wild Irish Dean. Burly, black-browed, fierce-eyed, Swift carried within him all the resentment accumulated during years of tedious exile—an exile that had lasted since he had watched his hopes of high ecclesiastical preferment, founded on a close friendship with Oxford and Bolingbroke, collapse so tragically in 1714. The triumph of *The Drapier's Letters* had not consoled him. When Swift returned to London twelve years later he was making a last throw for the power he desired—perhaps he felt the premonition of his future breakdown—and exploiting his last resources of hope and energy. He made a further visit, in 1727; and it was during this same year that the reading public first received Swift's account of the fabulous journeys, on which his imagination had been engaged between 1720 and 1725, among the islands of Laputa and Blefuscu, Lilliput and Brobdingnag. *Gulliver's Travels* proved immediately and enormously popular. Recent critics have gibed at Swift's infantilism; in the *Journal to Stella* they have pretended to distinguish a deliberate escape from the difficulties of mature life into the fantasies of a wilfully prolonged childhood; but if Swift's nature had its deliberately childish side—and if that side is not always very pleasing—his inventive faculty had a childlike concision and a childlike directness. Adult imaginings are often sketchy. Swift's fancy combines the precision and simplicity of a talented child—a child's passion for detail and neatness of view —with the sustained energy and imaginative strength of an adult writer. Other satires by comparison seem harsh and clumsy, other fantasies the merest vapourings of a moon-struck intelligence.

The authorship of the work was at once discovered. And among its most attentive readers was Caroline, who, although she may not have been capable of gauging its more abstruse literary merits, was quick to appreciate its satirical background. Again she received Swift at Leicester House; and when the patriotic Dean presented her with a sample of Irish poplins, she promised to reward him with a portrait-medallion. Unfortunately that promise was never honoured. The Princess was too busy to be very punctilious, and the Dean, though a distinguished addition to her literary circle, was not the only man of letters who frequented her drawing room. For example, there was a brilliant French adventurer. Fresh from his imprisonment in the Bastille, with the memory of his ignominious fustigation by the Chevalier de Rohan still sharp in his mind, Voltaire had landed in England on Whit Monday, May 30th, 1726,[1] and with his usual vivacity had plunged headlong into English life. He had lived through the first days in a kind of enchantment. It was a warm and sunny day when he landed at Greenwich; a soft wind, breathing from the west, rippled the surface of the broad, fast-flowing river, and stirred the majestic foliage of huge trees that fledged the banks of the Thames for many miles in either direction. A fair was being held in Greenwich Park; moreover, it was the birthday of the monarch, and the river was lined with shipping as far as the eye could reach, drawn up to salute the royal barge. Every anchored vessel had crowded on all its canvas; and between two ranks of flapping and bellying sails crawled the state barge like some gilded water-insect, preceded by several boatloads

---

[1] For a discussion of the exact date of Voltaire's arrival, see Churton Collins: *Voltaire in England*.

of fiddlers and trumpeters, who discoursed music as the oar-blades threshed slowly forward. A roar of cheering echoed along the river banks; and Voltaire listened in amazement to such evidence of loyalty.

Perhaps he failed to understand the English temperament. But of the various Frenchmen who at one time or another have made it their business to investigate the mysteries of England, none has set to work with a greater enthusiasm. Every turn of the spectacle increased his excitement. Now it was the dexterity and beauty of young Englishwomen managing their horses under the trees of Greenwich Park; now the cultured hospitality of English merchants, as evidenced particularly in the person of a certain Mr. Falkener of Wandsworth; now the respect shown to writers and men of science. Bolingbroke welcomed him; Dodington patronized him. Pope invited him to stay to dinner at Twickenham; but it was at this dinner-party that a somewhat unfortunate domestic incident occurred to mar the friendship of two great satirists. Pope, as all the world knew, was a devoted son; and when old Mrs. Pope, over the dinner table, inquired of the young Frenchman how he came to be so thin and to have so poor an appetite, Voltaire replied with such appalling frankness and gave her "so indelicate and brutal an account of the occasion of his disorder, contracted in Italy," that she was obliged to rise and totter off to her own room. But the association, nevertheless, was not unproductive. Pope excused Voltaire's lapse from decorum by saying that he supposed he had come to England, as most foreigners did, "on a prepossession that not only all religion, but all common decency of morals, was lost among us"; while Voltaire praised his eloquence and wit, declaring that "no man ever pleased him so much in serious conversation." Both were members of that favoured literary circle which had assembled round Bolingbroke in his retirement at Dawley. Here Voltaire met Swift, Gay and Arbuthnot; here he extended those researches into the philosophy of Newton which were to exert so profound an effect on his later writings; and it was here that he polished and revised the *Henriade*. But, at the same time, he coquetted with the government party and was careful to pay his court to the Prince and Princess. He was even privileged to attend at St. James's Palace, where his reception by the King was extremely flattering.

Their encounter took place in 1727. George Louis received Voltaire towards the end of January; and, as summer approached, he made ready for Herrenhausen, to enjoy his regular holiday from English affairs. His spirits were good, and his health seemed excellent. Indeed, before he set out, the rather fusty personnel of his established harem was increased by the addition of a young, dashing and not unattractive English mistress, Anne Brett, the daughter of Lady Macclesfield.[1] We catch a last glimpse of him in the dusk of his private apartments. Sir Robert's youngest son, Horace, was now ten years old, a clever sickly little boy in whom gossips of the period pointed out a strong resemblance to Lord Hervey's short-lived brother—Carr, Lord Hervey—once Lady Walpole's *cicisbeo*. Certainly Horace had many Hervey characteristics; he was quick, sensitive, effeminate, somewhat spoiled; and when he expressed a vehement desire *"to see the King,"* his mother, who loved him with a doting affection, and Sir Robert, whose "infinite good nature . . . never thwarted any of his children," decided to gratify the childish caprice. The King's junior mistress he had already seen, and he remembered having been terrified by her "enormous figure," her "two fierce black eyes, large and rolling beneath two lofty arched eyebrows, two acres of cheeks spread with crimson" and her "ocean of neck that overflowed and was not distinguished from the lower part of her body . . ." But now he was to be granted a greater privilege. Lady Walpole begged

---

[1] Mother, by her earlier connexion with Lord Rivers, of the poet Savage. Miss Brett is described by Horace Walpole as "very handsome, but dark enough . . . for a Spanish Beauty."

the Duchess of Kendal to obtain for her son the favour of kissing his Majesty's hand before he left England; and accordingly, two nights before the King's departure, the little boy was carried to St. James's Palace and introduced into the rooms of Lady Walsingham, the King's daughter who passed off at court as the Duchess's niece. Next he was led into the Schulenburg's ante-room. There stood the King and, just behind him, his venerable mistress,[1] "a very tall, lean, ill-favoured old lady." Short, pale, elderly, of an "aspect rather good than august," George Louis wore "a dark tye wig" and coat, waistcoat and even stockings of a plain, inconspicuous, snuff-coloured brown only relieved by the azure ribbon across his chest. He picked up the child, kissed him and said a word or two. Then Horace was led back to his waiting mother.

On June 3rd, 1727, the King embarked. The Duchess of Kendal, as always, accompanied him; but, since the sea-voyage never failed to make her ill, she stayed behind at the Hague to recover her energies. The King himself was a remorseless and tireless traveller. Surrounded by a large and cumbrous suite, he hurried ahead of his mistress through the Low Countries, and on the 9th had reached the Dutch frontier at the town of Delden, where he consumed a heavy supper at the house of a certain Count Twittel, devouring several watermelons to round off the meal. His attendants humbly advised that he should remain the night; but George Louis, punctual, imperious and obstinate, yearning for Hanover and hating delay, took the road again during the small hours of the following morning. It was not long before the courtiers noticed a change. The King collapsed; but no sooner had he rallied than his obstinacy reasserted itself with double vehemence—nothing would induce him to rest till they arrived at Osnabrück! Half-conscious, he still issued that single command. From the depth

---

[1] Sophia Dorothea of Celle had died in imprisonment the previous year; and it was generally believed that George I had thereupon married the Duchess of Kendal with the left hand.

of his floundering and jolting carriage, through what remained of the night and the whole of the next day, "To Osnabrück, to Osnabrück!" he continued to vociferate, urging postilions and escort to breakneck speed, driving them on with a final outburst of royal will-power. They halted at the castle of Osnabrück when night had fallen; but the King was lifted down a dying man.

Attended by his brother, Duke of York and Prince Bishop of Osnabrück, George Louis expired at Osnabrück on June 10th, 1727, in the room that had originally been his birth-chamber. Four days of furious riding brought the news to London. Sir Robert received it at his Chelsea villa and immediately mounted a horse and set off for Richmond, where Prince and Princess were spending the summer months. When he arrived, the Prince was taking his afternoon sleep. Thirteen years earlier his father had been roused by Lord Clarendon with the information that he was King of England, and had received the news with a singularly bad grace; and George Augustus now conformed to the paternal pattern. Hot and dishevelled, grasping his breeches in one hand, he first declared bluntly that the news was false, then—on being shown the dispatch from Osnabrück—read it through without a trace of expression or feeling. Caroline, who had also retired, was in another room. Left to his own devices, the King's immediate impulse was to revenge himself upon his father's old minister; and when Walpole asked submissively for the royal instructions, George Augustus directed that he should go to Chiswick, seek out Sir Spencer Compton and take *his* orders. Walpole had no alternative but to accept the dismissal. He bowed, retired from the presence, drove, as he had been directed, to Sir Spencer's house, and there acquainted him with his sudden accession to political supremacy. Walpole's attitude was good-humoured and philosophic. The King, he explained, had sent him "in such a manner as declares he intends you for his minister"; but this was no more than what he and the rest of the world had always anticipated. Sir

Spencer had been the King's Treasurer ever since George Augustus first came to England; and it was only natural that he should receive promotion at the present emergency. "Everything" (added Walpole, not perhaps without a certain touch of malice) "is in your hands; I neither could shake your power if I would, nor would if I could. My time has been, yours is beginning. . . . I put myself under your protection. . . . I desire no share of power or business; one of your white sticks, or any employment of that sort, is all I ask as a mark from the crown that I am not abandoned to the enmity of those whose envy is the only source of their hate. . . ."

Such frankness was not likely to be disingenuous. But Sir Spencer, a worthy, consequential, well-meaning but unimaginative person—described by Lord Hervey as "a plodding, heavy fellow, with great application, but no talents, and vast complaisance for a court without any address"—was scarcely qualified to gauge the feelings of his formidable predecessor. He was delighted but, at the same time, exceedingly flustered. Taking Sir Robert with him, he at once drove up to London and called on the President of the Council, then the Duke of Devonshire, an amiable and dignified *virtuoso* whose knowledge extended to pictures, medals and race-horses rather than to the abstruse chicanery of modern politics. He was of little help to Compton in the present crisis. A speech must be written for the King to deliver at the first meeting of the Council; and Sir Spencer, unable to write it himself, and in the agitation of the moment completely forgetting that he had only to turn up old Gazettes to discover any number of perfectly good models, was so dumbfounded that he buttonholed Sir Robert and implored him, as a personal favour, to step into the next room and prepare a draft. Sir Robert formally declined, then quietly consented; and meanwhile the prospective minister set out to pay his first state visit at Leicester House, where the new King and Queen had just arrived with their court from Richmond. The square was packed with a cheering excited mob; the house itself with a crowd more brilliant but no less excited, all eager to establish their personal loyalty. Sir Spencer was received in private audience and returned, solemn and elated, to his attendant coach, "through a lane of *bowers* . . . shouldering one another to pay adoration . . . and knocking their heads together to whisper compliments and petitions as he passed." At Devonshire House, he found that Sir Robert had concluded his speech-writing, but Compton's embarrassments were not yet over; for, the speech having been read, approved and submitted, the King wished to make alterations, and Compton, again at a loss, was obliged once more to have recourse to the kindness of Walpole, and begged that he would persuade the sovereign to leave it unchanged. Walpole did as he was asked with an air of good nature, allowing the rival to play his cards for him till the game was finished.

He knew that he might still count on the support of Caroline. But that influence, being occult and slow-working, could not immediately declare itself; and, during the first days of the new dispensation, whenever Walpole appeared at Leicester House, he was as carefully shunned as before he had been busily courted; "his presence" (writes Lord Hervey), "that used to make a crowd . . . now emptied every corner he turned to, and the same people who were officiously a week ago clearing the way to flatter his prosperity, were now getting out of it to avoid sharing his disgrace." Lady Walpole was treated with similar harshness. The day following the accession she attended at the royal drawing room and found it quite impossible, hemmed in as she was by "the scornful backs and elbows of her late Devotees," to make her way through the press towards the Queen. But Caroline's plans were already formulated. Glad to have this opportunity of striking a first blow, she immediately singled her out amongst the crowd with the observation: "There I am sure I see a friend!"; at which "the torrent divided and shrank to either side, 'and as I came away' " (said Lady Walpole) " 'I might have walked over their heads, if I had pleased.' "

It was a decisive moment, both for Walpole and for the future of the dynasty. A woman more feminine than Caroline of Anspach, a man more easily perturbed, less worldly and less masculine than Sir Robert Walpole, might have hesitated and failed to recognize their common advantage. Caroline might have been governed by personal resentment—Walpole, distrusting Caroline, have attempted one of those too-ingenious combinations that had proved the undoing of several of his most brilliant and unscrupulous political enemies, in whom lack of scruple was usually counterbalanced by lack of discretion. But their individual gifts made them perfect collaborators. During the first critical and undecided days, while Sir Spencer Compton, delighted yet overwhelmed by his new importance, bustled feverishly and ineffectively to and fro, and while the crowd of vulgar place-hunters continued to treat Walpole to a display of elaborate disregard, Caroline found time to work on her husband, taking her text from the spectacle beneath his eyes. Plainly, poor Sir Spencer was quite incompetent. What they needed was a man with a head for business—a clever financier—a politician who had mastered all the mysteries of the English parliamentary system. . . . If the King maintained Walpole he could count on his gratitude; and Walpole, at the earliest opportunity, allowed it to be understood that he was prepared to repay royal support by every financial complaisance within his power; that they might look to him for a considerable increase in their private revenues.

Nor could his opponents afford to thwart him. It was as much in their interest as it was in his to make a show of lavish generosity towards their new sovereign; and, when Parliament met on June 27th, the question of the Civil List was settled in a manner extremely advantageous to King and Queen; for the King received a larger personal allowance than any English sovereign had yet enjoyed, and the Queen a bigger private income than had fallen to any previous Queen Consort, while provision for the still absent Prince of Wales was left entirely to his father's generosity. Only Shippen arose to voice a protest. Otherwise, all factions vied in their eagerness to please the King, and though malcontents complained that George Augustus had put himself up to auction and had been knocked down to Walpole as the highest bidder, these complaints remained largely surreptitious. The parliamentary pack was re-shuffled soon afterwards; and whereas, up to that time, there had been some critics who believed that Sir Spencer Compton intended to assume power as soon as the Civil List had been disposed of, the composition of the new Parliament proved them wrong, since it was dominated by Walpole and Walpole's followers—all men whom the King had professed to abhor, whom he had described as "rogues," "buffoons" and "choleric blockheads." His opinion of them had changed considerably in the last few weeks. There could be no doubt that the author of that change was Caroline.

Chapter Three

1

THE old autumnal King had disappeared and with him went
the alien troops of spies and favourites. The Duchess of Kendal va-
cated the Palace. She retired to Twickenham and there, as a pious
and elderly dowager, passed the rest of her life among her memories
and her private devotions. George Louis had been a firm believer
in ghosts and vampires, and, on one occasion, had promised his
left-handed consort that, if it were possible, he would return to
her side from the regions of the dead. It was natural, then, that
when a large dusky bird—by some accounts, a raven—alighted on
the window-sill of the Duchess's room, she should have accepted
it as the repository of the King's spirit, housed it in a royally magnificent cage, treated it always with the greatest deference, and
continued to entertain it as long as she lived. But, though mourned
—no doubt sincerely—at the villa in Twickenham and regretted
—from more selfish motives—by his German ministers, George
Louis was unlamented by his British subjects and soon forgotten
by George Augustus and Caroline, now hard at work preparing
their Coronation. It was celebrated on October 11th, 1727. Caroline,
with her love of parade, had gone to especial trouble to make it
an occasion of the very greatest splendour, but George Louis had
dispersed so much ancestral jewellery in presents to his mistresses
that she was obliged to borrow the trinkets she wore, partly from
complaisant noblewomen in St. James's, partly from accommodating Hebrews at the Royal Exchange. Still, the appearance she

achieved was unquestionably sumptuous, in her purple velvet richly furred with ermine and a petticoat so heavily jewel-encrusted that it was found necessary to contrive a sort of pulley that enabled her to raise the hem when she knelt down. She was in some embarrassment, too, over the ritual anointing of her bosom. Only her husband had ever regarded it as an attractive feature; and she arranged that, at this stage of the Coronation, the canopy should be dipped to hide her from view. Lady Mary Wortley Montagu was among the crowd that filled the Abbey; and, though in her letter to her sister, Lady Mar, she has left no account of the royal centrepiece, she gives an entertaining and spiteful account of some minor actors—the aged Lady Orkney, once William III's mistress, described by Swift as the wisest woman he ever knew, who "exposed behind, a mixture of fat and wrinkles; and before a very considerable protuberance"; the "poor Duchess of Montrose," who "crept along with a dozen of black snakes playing round her face"; and Lady Portland (recently ousted from her position as governess to the King's children), who "represented very finely an Egyptian mummy embroidered over with hieroglyphics."

After the Coronation the King and Queen dined in Westminster Hall amid the glow of nearly two thousand wax candles flickering from chandeliers, branches and sconces. This was the outward display of their accession to power. But, in the council chamber, a scene much more extraordinary had already taken place, for at his first council, when the Archbishop of Canterbury produced the late King's will, expecting that his successor, as custom dictated, would read it aloud, George Augustus had thrust it into his pocket, turned on his heel and stalked from the room, leaving the Archbishop and his fellow-councillors in helpless bewilderment. Whether or no the will was burnt, it was never executed.[1] Rumour spoke of legacies to the old King's grandson Fred-

---

[1] For a further discussion of the King's motives, see pp. 203–204.

erick Louis, to his daughter the Queen of Prussia, of forty thousand pounds bequeathed to the Duchess of Kendal; and the King's action, besides exposing him to subsequent blackmail, afforded disquieting evidence of his general attitude. Adversity had done nothing to soften his character. At forty-four he was still the irascible, uncontrolled, pig-headed German princeling who had landed in England with George Louis in 1714, and had smiled broadly—to annoy his father—all the way from Greenwich. Yet with German brutality went German sentiment. A devotion, deep, passionate and disinterested—though the disinterestedness of his feeling was, of course, not unaccompanied by vain and selfish elements—still bound him to the woman who shared his good fortune, as she had shared in every vicissitude for so long a period. Nor was his affection placid and domestic. In Caroline, George Augustus loved not merely the mother of his children, the staunch supporter and invariably patient listener who was the recipient of his confidences and the butt of his rages; he loved the mistress whom, after almost twenty years of close daily association, he continued to find supremely and irresistibly attractive, whom he nagged, scolded and deceived but could never grow tired of. To George Augustus adultery was a duty, marriage a pleasure. In his *liaisons,* he was punctual and prosy; to his wife, a romantic.

Naturally, he imagined that she shared his passion, and with the vanity of a limited and self-centred man—to which fate he added a truly royal lack of reticence—he would speak sometimes of the Queen's absorbing devotion to him. It is possible that he was not entirely misguided. In a nature as dominant as that of Caroline, a character as strongly disciplined by early misfortune, devotion to an individual is not always to be disentangled from devotion to the objective or interest for which that individual stands; and Caroline's ruling interest was her love of power. No doubt she encouraged her husband's complacent belief; but it may be that beneath all considerations of matrimonial and royal politics there did indeed lie an emotion warmer and less impersonal than any she had experienced since the death of her adored Sophie Charlotte—that in the King she loved something more than her own destiny. To realize that one inspires passion is a step towards feeling it; and though George Augustus was regularly unfaithful and though his tempers never spared her when he was in the mood, his brutalities were still the outbursts of an impatient lover. If he was abroad he wrote to her by every post—letters as remarkable for their length as for the extreme minuteness, and often somewhat disconcerting frankness, with which he discussed the smallest details of his daily career. These private chronicles were also full of impassioned love-messages; and Sir Robert Walpole and Lord Hervey once agreed that the King's love-letters (which the Queen frequently showed them) were among the most eloquent and moving productions in that style they had ever read, and that his epistolary gifts might well have made him a dangerous rival.

His admiration, like his infidelity, was undisguised. Caroline had been considered handsome at the time of her marriage; soon afterwards she had suffered a mild attack of smallpox, but her skin had been very little roughened, and in early middle age she is said to have retained a very "pleasing countenance," dignified and authoritative when she chose to make it so, open, friendly and ingratiating if she wished to unbend. "Her penetrating eyes" (adds Walpole) "expressed whatever she had in mind they should. Her voice too was captivating, and her hands beautifully small, plump and graceful." A shade of guile hovers about every portrait. Habits of dissimulation and self-suppression—the self-effacement practised almost since childhood by this *"grandissime Comédienne"* who had threaded her way through the dangers of a small German court and the even greater perils and difficulties of the Court of England—had certainly left their mark on her face and character, till the outward welcome seemed merely to accentuate the inner reserve. She had offered a sacrifice of her personal happiness, and it had been accepted. She could hardly remember a day (she told Lady Cowper) that she had not passed in pain, anxiety and discomfort; but then happiness can take many different forms, and not a few of those forms are acutely painful—at least as regards ordinary peace of spirit. There is a hint of secretiveness beneath the urbanity of Caroline's features and the conscious pride that accompanies a deliberate adherence to policy.

Of ordinary feminine weaknesses she had very few. During the early years of her marriage she had forced herself to determine that as her husband was not likely to be faithful—for that was scarcely in the traditions of royal or Hanoverian wedlock—his escapades should be canalized to her own advantage or at least diverted from any field where they could do her harm. An unfaithful husband would be also a contented husband. Besides, she could console herself with the reflection that George Augustus's adventures were dictated by a full-blooded masculine fatuity—"a silly idea he had entertained of gallantry being becoming"—rather than by a genuine appetite for other conquests. She had no difficulty in controlling his choice of mistresses; and thus every evening at nine o'clock the King was to be observed setting off for Mrs. Howard's apartments—a visit he regulated with such dull exactitude "that he frequently walked about his chamber for ten minutes with his watch in hand," till the appointed hour struck and he could begin the interview. And Mrs. Howard was as exemplary as the King was punctual. Her discretion would have been conspicuous in the married state; in the ungrateful and difficult position that she occupied, it never ceased to astonish critical courtiers who were accustomed to the rapacity and arrogance of the old King's favourites. Mrs. Howard was neither avaricious nor self-seeking. With less vitality and less ambition than Caroline, she had as sound a judgment and her personal feelings were as carefully subordinated; for the role she played was just as exacting and far more invidious. Caroline had some of the advantages that belong to a mistress; her rival many of the drawbacks of the legitimate wife.

At the time of the Coronation, Mrs. Howard was forty. Beautiful she was not and had never been, but she was "of a just higth," symmetrically proportioned, while her face, which reflected gravity, charm and mildness, was framed in "the finest light-brown hair." She "was remarkably genteel" (concludes Horace Walpole, who knew her in her old age, at Marble Hill, the house she had built herself near Twickenham) "and always well drest with taste and simplicity. . . . Her mental qualifications" (he is obliged to admit) "were by no means shining. . . ." Yet, although Mrs. Howard's own intelligence may not have been superlative, she possessed a faculty of pleasing intelligent men, and both Pope and Swift made her the subject of literary "characters." Swift's character, published only after his death, is a poor reward for many years of affection and loyalty—but then Swift's response to affection was always erratic—and it remained for Pope to imprison her qualities in a rhymed impromptu celebrating her grave good-humour and moonlight gentleness.[1] Even the serpent-tongued Hervey allowed her her due. He acknowledged her "good sense, good breeding, and good nature" and that she was "civil to everybody, friendly to many, and unjust to none; in short, she had a good head and a good heart, but had to do with a man who was incapable of tasting the one or valuing the other."

That Mrs. Howard should have remained constant in her at-

---

[1] I know the thing that's most uncommon;
  (Envy be silent, and attend!)
I know a reasonable woman,
  Handsome and witty, yet a friend.

Not warp'd by passion, aw'd by rumour,
  Not grave through pride, or gay through folly,
An equal mixture of good humour,
  And sensible soft melancholy. . . .

On a Certain Lady at Court.

tachment to a man whom, at no time, can she ever have esteemed or loved and who treated her with little generosity, and that the King should have continued to bestow his attention on a woman whom he neither desired nor respected, who was middle-aged and growing extremely deaf, is one of the oddest features of an odd relationship; but the problem becomes less perplexing if we consider Caroline. Evidently it was the Queen who prevented a rupture. A new mistress, she understood, would have been more attractive. Possibly, she would also have been ambitious. The influence she wielded would have been formidable, and Mrs. Howard's influence was so trifling that, after a few preliminary skirmishes (to which she was incited by her friends in the Tory party), she contented herself with the acquisition of a modest settlement and with a peerage and a red riband for her elder brother. At court she was perpetually under Caroline's eye. Every morning, as a Woman of the Queen's Bedchamber, she attended to dress her head; and it was at this time that Caroline found occasion to administer any small snubs, or inflict any minor feminine cruelties, that might be needed to curb a rival's spirit, interspersing them with profuse apologies to "my good Howard." There was a brief struggle over the ceremony of basin-holding. Etiquette demanded that, when the Queen washed, her attendant should proffer the basin on bended knees; and this Mrs. Howard had declined to do, roused to a sudden flurry of self-assertion. Her protests, however, were brushed aside. "Yes, my dear Howard, I am sure you will," remarked the Queen in a tone of indulgent gentleness. "Indeed you will. Go, go! fie for shame! Go, my good Howard; we will talk of this another time." The rebellious servant was given leisure for consideration; and "about a week later" (the Queen informed Lord Hervey) "when . . . she had done everything about the basin that I would have her, I told her I knew we should be good friends again; but could not help adding, in a little more serious voice, that I owned of all my servants I had least expected . . .

such treatment from her, when she knew I had held her up at a time when it was in my power, if I had pleased . . . to let her drop through my fingers—thus——"

Sir Robert had quickly grasped the situation. It was one of his many claims to the Queen's gratitude that, unlike Chesterfield and other injudicious place-seekers, he had always avoided the favourite and courted the wife, thus demonstrating his tact and his native shrewdness. Lady Sundon (the former Mrs. Clayton), who seconded Mrs. Howard in the post of Bedchamber Woman, possessed far more real influence. Described by Horace Walpole, whose father had mistrusted her, as an "absurd and pompous simpleton," she is portrayed in flattering colours by her friend Hervey, who credits her with a "warm, honest, noble, generous, benevolent, friendly heart," "sense enough to perceive what black and dirty company, by living in a Court, she was forced to keep," honour enough to despise that company, and too little hypocrisy to conceal her opinion. "Mrs. Clayton and Mrs. Howard hated one another very civilly and very heartily"; but while "Mrs. Clayton was every moment like Mount Etna, ready to burst when she did not flame, Mrs. Howard was as much mistress of her passions as of her limbs, and could as easily prevent the one from showing she had a mind to strike, as she could the other from giving the blow." With the Queen Mrs. Clayton shared a painful private secret (which concerned the condition of the Queen's health) and an absorbing intellectual preoccupation. Both ladies were engrossed in church affairs. The Queen was of a sceptical and unorthodox turn, but she loved theological disputation and questions of ecclesiastical preferment; and Mrs. Clayton, who was exceedingly Low Church, encouraged her interest in "the less believing clergy."

Mrs. Howard held a few strings and may have pulled at them; Mrs. Clayton had some power which she employed to advantage; but no court favourite could compare in magnitude with Sir Robert Walpole. His bulk overshadows an entire epoch. Nor is he impressive merely as the gifted and unscrupulous statesman who was to retain his office longer than any previous chief minister since the days of Lord Burleigh. He is also a figure-head of the age he lived in—an age that he represented both in his merits and in his shortcomings, in his intellectual ability and his physical gross-ness. Bodily and spiritually his build was opulent. He had an abundance of good and inferior qualities; and these qualities were jumbled together like the personages of one of Hogarth's swarm-ing street scenes, without propriety but, equally, without self-consciousness. Yet a certain magnanimity balanced his attributes —the generosity of a man whose enjoyments are hearty, spontane-ous and uncomplicated and who, to a keen mind, adds a well-functioning bodily organism. He was extraordinarily industrious, but seldom hurried. He had, indeed, that aptitude, peculiar to Englishmen of the governing caste, for seeming to transact busi-ness as an afterthought and never allowing the claims of business to disturb his leisure. The business would get done—and it did get done. But, before he opened the dispatches on his table, he would read a letter from his gamekeeper in Norfolk describing the state of his Houghton coverts. The continental statesman who was a slave to his duty—some plotting cardinal secluded in the depths of his cabinet—would have aroused the good-natured con-tempt of the Norfolk squire.

Yet the country magnate was also an adroit financier. In his broad face, with its deep dewlap, wine-empurpled cheeks, thick commanding eyebrows and piercing eyes, there is a combination of bluffness and astuteness that expresses his temperament.[1] He

---

[1] These were the lively eyes and rosy hue
Of Robin's face when Robin first I knew;
The gay companion and the favourite guest,
Loved without awe, and without views caress'd.
His cheerful smile and honest open look
Added new graces to the truths he spoke . . .

was many different things; but he was nothing by halves. Early instructed in the art of drinking by old Mr. Walpole, who used to declare that no son of his should see his father getting drunk and himself presume to remain sober, he had a capacity for alcohol and a flow of jovial obscenity that were remarkable even at Norfolk dinner-parties. But Sir Robert was, incidentally, a man of taste; and the gallery of pictures he had assembled at Houghton (which included a magnificent Rubens portrait) was considered one of the finest collections in England.[1] Houghton, the house and the furnishings, was his especial pride; and from London he would send minute directions for its interior embellishment—with a "vast quantity of mahogani," "finest chimneys of statuary" and "cielings in the modern taste by Italians, painted by Mr. Kent, and finely gilt." It is true that he found little time to enjoy his library, but this was a deprivation he deeply regretted; and no sketch of his character could be more misleading than one that portrayed him as a cynical and uncultured opportunist and ignored the complexity of his mental attributes, cynical and coarse-fibred though no doubt he was. His genius was the genius of Augustan England before the romantic movement had helped to diminish its amazing gusto.

That gusto appeared in his passion for work. In spite of habits ostensibly easy-going and a self-indulgence that he never troubled to control or conceal, few men were more ambitious; none possessed greater application or showed a quicker grasp of any problem he was called to deal with. His energy and tenacity were Her-

---

The hardest censors, at the worst, believed
His temper was too easily deceived:
A consequential ill good-nature draws;
A bad effect, but from a noble cause!
    Lines by Lady Mary Wortley Montagu on Walpole's Portrait.
[1] Purchased by the Empress of Russia, it became the nucleus of the Hermitage collection; from which Rubens's portrait of his wife has passed into the private collection of M. Gulbenkian.

culean. "He had a strength of parts" (writes Lord Hervey) "equal to any advancement, a spirit to struggle with any difficulties, a steadiness of temper immovable by any disappointments. He had great skill in figures, the nature of the funds, and the revenue; his first application was for this branch of knowledge; but as he afterwards rose to the highest posts of power . . . he grew, of course, conversant with all the other parts of government, and very soon equally able in transacting them; the weight of the whole administration lay on him; every project was of his forming, conducting, and executing . . ." His personal judgments were swift and sure; "he had more warmth of affection for some particular people than one could have believed it possible for any one who had been so long raking in the dirt of mankind. . . . One should naturally have imagined that the contempt and distrust he must have had for the species in gross, would have given him at least an indifference and distrust towards every particular. Whether his negligence of his enemies . . . was policy or constitution, I shall not determine; but I do not believe anybody who knows these times will deny that no minister was ever more outraged, or less apparently resentful."

Even his bitterest foes were occasionally appreciative; and Pope, whose personal loyalties—if "loyalty" is not somewhat too strong a word to apply to any of Pope's literary or political attachments—were with Bolingbroke and other members of the Opposition, allowed that he could be genial and fascinating in private company. As a statesman perhaps his greatest weakness was an inability to work among equals on equal terms and a tendency to surround himself with vulgar subordinates whose chief merit was a complete subservience to the minister's will. Thus he was gradually drifting away from his brother-in-law, Townshend. Both were considerable Norfolk landowners; Lord Townshend, a haughty and unpractical man, was extremely jealous of the growing splendours of Houghton (which threatened to eclipse the mag-

nificence of Raynham), and their rivalry in questions of planting
and building soon spread to questions of statesmanship raised in
the council chamber. Townshend did not finally tender his resignation until the mid-part of 1729, and then only after a sharp tus-
sle over problems of foreign policy and a violent personal quarrel
in Mrs. Selwyn's apartments during which the two old friends
seized one another by the coat collar and were narrowly prevented
from drawing their swords, but the break-up of their coalition had
long been prophesied. Henceforward Sir Robert was alone in
command—alone to enjoy the consciousness of supreme authority,
alone to bear the attacks of the Opposition, which increased in
frequency and intensity as time went by. Walpole became the
scapegoat of the system he headed; but, though in many respects
that system was indefensible, and though the abuses it entailed
were grave and obvious, Walpole was not the originator of the
means he employed, and merely followed an established political
precedent.[1] He handled them, however, with unequalled cleverness, and with a touch of philosophic cynicism that enraged his
enemies.

To them he was the personification of political profligacy; and
it is indicative of the feelings Walpole aroused that when, during
the winter of 1728, Gay (finally disappointed in his hopes of royal
preferment, for he had made the capital mistake of courting Mrs.
Howard) produced his *Beggar's Opera* on the London stage, the
public at large should immediately have recognized the features of
Walpole in its swashbuckling highwayman hero, Captain Mac-

---

[1] He was to find an unexpected defender in Burke: "Walpole was an honourable man and a sound Whig. He was not, as the Jacobites and discontented Whigs
of his own time have represented him, a prodigal and corrupt minister. They
charged him . . . as having first reduced corruption to a system. Such was their
cant. But he was far from governing by corruption. He governed by party attachments. The charge of systematic corruption is less applicable to him, perhaps,
than to any minister who ever served the Crown for so great a length of time."—
Appeal from New to Old Whigs.

heath, and his differences with Lord Townshend in the squabble with Peachum. Gay's ballad opera enjoyed "a prodigious run"; and Walpole so far departed from his customary good-humoured indifference as to prohibit its feeble and foolish successor; upon which Gay's patroness, the Duchess of Queensberry, organized a fashionable subscription to have it printed, and carried the effrontery of a beautiful woman to such extravagant lengths that she was observed making the round of the drawing room and pressing even the King's attendants to "contribute to the printing of a thing which the King had forbid being acted." Having been discovered, she was at once forbidden the court, and riposted with a note, declaring "That the Duchess of Queensberry is surprised and well pleased that the King had given her so agreeable a command as to stay from Court, where she never came for diversion, but to bestow a great civility on the King and Queen. . . ." The court took her at her word, and *Polly* languished, while Gay ended his "blameless" life as the Duchess's pensioner.

But the Opposition were among Walpole's minor difficulties. His most brilliant opponents, Bolingbroke, Pulteney, Wyndham, were men who combined ability with instability, great gifts of the vituperative and critical order with a curious absence of any practical constructive *flair*. No party could afford to put its trust in Bolingbroke. Intellectually distinguished and personally charming, "he had fine talents, a natural eloquence, great quickness, a happy memory, and very extensive knowledge: but he was vain, much beyond the general run of mankind, timid, false, injudicious, and ungrateful; elate and insolent in power, dejected and servile in disgrace. . . . Those who were most partial to him could not but allow that he was ambitious without fortitude, and enterprising without resolution; that he was fawning without insinuation, and insincere without art; that he had . . . parts without probity, knowledge without conduct, and experience without judgment. This" (concludes the historian, a trifle breathlessly) "was certainly his character and situation"; and though Hervey would not "so far chime in with the bulk of Lord Bolingbroke's contemporaries as to pronounce he had more failings than any man ever had," he found it impossible when he considered Bolingbroke's record not to admit "that if he had not a worse heart than the rest of mankind, at least he must have had much worse luck." Sir William Wyndham (who had been brought up in Bolingbroke's school) had begun his career, like his master, as an ardent Jacobite, but now led that parliamentary faction known as the Hanover Tories who opposed Walpole while they professed allegiance to the reigning house. Pulteney, on the other hand, had been born a Whig and a Whig he remained—but in opposition; for he detested Walpole with an intensity that equalled Bolingbroke's, and Pulteney's hatred was as firm as his friendship was variable. He, too, had genial qualities and brilliant accomplishments but, qualifying them, a vehement, restless and uneasy temper.

Such opponents might annoy and distract, but they could not annihilate. As long as Walpole retained the support of the King —which meant, in fact, as long as he held the Queen—there was very little prospect of his falling from power; it was the royal family that presented a more serious problem. Could this odd team be successfully managed? Could the minister, himself so strongly English, co-operate with a master and mistress whose point of view was German when it was not royal, and whose personal prejudices were as ungovernable as their dynastic pride? Walpole's foreign policy was directed towards peace-keeping. It was a subject of the deepest satisfaction to him that, in a whole year of European bloodshed, of armed coalitions made and dissolved, cities besieged and taken and provinces ravaged, not a single English soldier had laid down his life. To the King and Queen, foreign policy meant family politics; while the King, who during his father's lifetime had professed to disregard his Hanoverian inheritance and give England and English interests the predominant place, since his father's death was swinging to the other extreme. He bore, indeed, a close resemblance to his hated parent; and Walpole, who had expected that on the accession of George Augustus his elder son would immediately be called to England, was surprised to notice that the King appeared most unwilling to give the necessary order, and seemed anxious that the Prince of Wales should remain abroad, an attitude in which the Queen herself supported and encouraged him. It was not until the Privy Council had formally remonstrated, and Sir Robert Walpole had added his pleadings to theirs, that George and Caroline prepared a reluctant welcome. Fully eighteen months had elapsed since the King's accession when Prince Frederick Louis stepped ashore upon English soil.

2

SEPARATED from his parents since the age of seven, brought up by a stern and reproving tutor, to most Englishmen the Prince of Wales was entirely unknown. His only contact with his family had been through his grandfather, who seems to have regarded him with some affection; while the little that he knew of his future inheritance was derived from occasional English visitors. On their memories the impression he left was favourable. Lady Mary Wortley Montagu, in 1716, had enjoyed a long interview and had reported that the nine-year-old princeling possessed "all the accomplishments and understanding, and something so very engaging and easy in his behaviour that he needs not the advantage of his rank to appear charming." The sprightliness grew more apparent as he approached maturity. There could be no doubt of the Prince's desire to please or of the natural friendliness that made him an easy talker, but with these virtues went certain complementary shortcomings. He was excitable, restless, lacking in dignity. With a greater share of imagination than of common sense, and good intentions but a curious lack of restraint or reserve, he was perpetually embarking on new projects, tumbling head over heels into new adventures, forming new connexions, many of them extremely discreditable. He saw the world fragmentarily, in bursts of enthusiasm, and himself always in some gallant and conspicuous role.

Thus, not long before, he had adopted the part of romantic lover. The plan of a double marriage between himself and the daughter of the King of Prussia, and the Prussian Crown Prince and his sister Amelia, had been held up by the opposition of the English court; and Frederick, having conceived the notion that he was desperately enamoured of the Princess Wilhelmina (whose portrait he may have admired but whom he had never seen) decided that the moment had come to force the issue. A confidential agent dispatched to Berlin, amid conditions of melodramatic secrecy, announced to the Queen of Prussia that the Prince intended to leave Hanover by stealth and, her parents willing, marry the Princess, in defiance of his royal father's orders. The Queen entered the plot as a zealous accomplice. She was delighted to further her nephew's scheme—so delighted that she confided in the English envoy, who felt obliged to send a courier post-haste to London, whence messengers as promptly flew back to Herrenhausen. The King had already agreed to his son's return, but he now insisted that it must take place without delay; and Frederick, who had been discovered at a court festivity, left for England as soon as the dancing was over. Willy-nilly he abandoned the unfortunate Princess (who, as it happened, had always been averse from the marriage) and precipitated her entire family into the depths of gloom. Her ferocious father gave way to an access of rage, and fell on and brutally thrashed both his son and daughter; the Queen of Prussia collapsed completely and retired to bed. Meanwhile Frederick Louis continued his journey homeward, reaching England during the first week of December 1728.

No drums were beaten, no cannon discharged, to mark his arrival. No glass coach waited at the quayside to drag him in triumph through a cheering city; no deputation of mayor or aldermen delayed his progress. All signs of public welcome had been carefully omitted. Having landed at Whitechapel, he finished his journey in a hackney coach, "alighted at the Friary, and walked down to the Queen's back-stairs, and was there conducted to her Majesty's apartment." Next Sunday he appeared briefly at the Chapel Royal. But though his parents certainly were at no pains to present him to advantage, his native liveliness stood him in good stead, and once again the impression he produced was pleasing. "Without being the least handsome"—like the King, Frederick Louis was extremely short—he was "very well made and genteel," and had "the most obliging address that can be conceived." His temperament betrayed itself in his mobile features. Eyes remarkably outstanding, and of a pale lively blue, projected from a pink Germanic countenance, which had the prominent lower jaw and bulging underlip of his father and grandfather. His nose was long and inquisitive, his forehead was lofty; but together they ran back in so flat a line that the effect of his profile was somewhat saurian, while his heavy eyelids increased the resemblance to a youthful lizard. About the whole face there was an unsettled and unfocused look; it was spirited, irresponsible, amusing and foolhardy—the face of a young man who might balk at discipline but would respond to the insidious suggestions of an experienced counsellor.

Counsellors and friends were not slow in arriving. But, for some months at least, Frederick Louis remained content with the modest and subsidiary position to which his father and mother obviously desired to relegate him, and his behaviour was a model of filial dutifulness. He crosses the stage only in a minor role—now giving a ball upon "the Island in St. James's Park," now surprising "the Queen and all his dear sisters with a very pritty entertainment at Richmond," where a company of players performed a piece entitled *Hob in the Gardens,* now supping at Cliveden among his family, now at Claremont pledging "a bumper of rack punch to the Queen's health" and strolling through the pleasure-grounds "till candle-light, being entertained with very fine French horns." For many references our authority is Peter Wentworth, the gouty and impecunious brother of Lord Strafford, whom Caroline had appointed her secretary and Groom of the Bedchamber to her younger son. A reformed drunkard who attributed his reformation to the condescending benevolence of the "Glorious Royal Family"—he enjoyed little jokes with the Queen about his reputed love for strong liquors "at free cost"—Peter Wentworth was the most uncritical of hangers-on, and there were other courtiers who looked more closely at the Prince's development. How long would his parents succeed in dominating him? When George Augustus, following his father's example, prepared to visit Hanover in May 1729, he left Caroline to occupy the position of Regent and delegated no share of authority to Frederick Louis. The Prince of Wales was much chagrined and disappointed. Above all things he needed a feeling of responsibility, for his good intentions were not of the sort that improve with keeping, and sooner or later his erratic energy would demand an outlet. That outlet the King and Queen had refused to supply. By the time George Augustus returned to England—that is to say, by September of the same year —the Prince's attitude had undergone a considerable change, and he began to allow himself some sarcastic pleasantries at his father's expense, adding many petulant criticisms of his father's ministers. It was in this state of indecision and increasing restlessness (further aggravated by a most embarrassing shortage of funds) that he encountered the mercurial genius of John Lord Hervey.

They had already met—but briefly and casually—at Herrenhausen. Hervey, who was something of a hypochondriac, had absented himself from England in a search for health and pleasure at the beginning of 1728, and only reappeared in the September of 1729. He was thirty-four, married, an accomplished courtier; but to understand the character of this singular being, and to realize the impact of his character on that of Frederick, it is necessary to go back at least a decade, to the period when, as plain Mr. John Hervey (for his brother, Carr Lord Hervey, the reputed father of Horace Walpole, did not die till 1723), he had made his first entrée in the drawing rooms of the Princess Caroline, and added charm and gaiety to the rebellious gatherings at Leicester House. He had been very young then, and very good-looking. His beauty, indeed, was so obvious as to be almost scandalous; and it was natural, given his constant desire to shine, that the handsomest young man of the Prince's household should have carried off the prettiest Maid of Honour, whom a dozen high-placed admirers had despaired of capturing. Mary Lepel was famed for her grace and vivacity; the marriage was as brilliant and romantic as it promised to be fortunate; and Chesterfield and Pulteney, in an anonymous ballad, had paid joint tribute to the superlative elegance of bride and bridegroom:

> Bright Venus yet never saw bedded
> So perfect a beau and a belle
> As when Hervey the handsome was wedded
> To the beautiful Molly Lepel.

> Had I Hanover, Bremen, and Verden,
> And likewise the Duchy of Zell!
> I'd part with them all for a farthing,
> To have my dear Molly Lepel. . . .

For some years, it is true, they were exceedingly happy. Youth, beauty and fortune had brought them together; and these powerful divinities still accompanied and favoured them in their progresses from Ickworth to London and leisurely back again. As in some Augustan conversation-piece we see Hervey in his chaise with his wife and child, driving along the avenues of Ickworth Park and, earlier, before the children had begun to be born, catch a glimpse of the pair, through the sharp and hypercritical eyes of Lady Mary Wortley Montagu, ringed round and secluded by their own contentment. The felicity of these "birds of paradise" (said Lady Mary) was so self-sufficient as to be somewhat exasperating. . . . Then, very gradually, the situation changed. Lord Hervey continued to beget children; his wife, in the intervals of bearing and rearing them, continued to play her part in the fashionable comedy, always well-bred, attractive and perfectly mannered; but, as time went on, their alienation grew more and more evident. Lady Hervey did not protest nor, according to all appearances, was she very much chagrined. If not a cold woman, she was certainly cool, with the rather chilly freshness of a fine spring day, for there was nothing bleak or forbidding about her temperament; but beneath the charm lurked an unusual stock of worldly prudence. No gossip ever credited her with an extraneous love-affair. Perhaps she was unresponsive to sexual love, but it is clear that she had an aptitude for friendship, great good sense and an intellect above the ordinary, not so brilliant as, but far steadier than, that of her husband. In Chesterfield's view she was the woman of the world *par excellence,* and he specially enjoined his son to frequent her drawing room, since she had "been bred all her life at Courts," of which she had "acquired all the easy good-breeding and the politeness without the frivolousness" and possessed "all the reading that a woman should have, and more than any woman need have, for she understands Latin perfectly well, though she wisely conceals it."

"No woman" (explained Lord Chesterfield) "ever had more than she has *'le ton de la parfaitement bonne compagnie, les manières engageantes, et le je ne sçais quoi qui plaît.'*" Hanbury-Williams's character-sketch will complete the portrait, adding just that touch of inner insignificance, that suspicion of intellectual and emotional nullity often hidden by a well-bred and well-balanced exterior, to which the flamboyant and the impulsively generous are equally alien. "Nature" (he writes) "took great care of her person, but quite forgot her mind, which had this effect, that she was of the same mind with every person she talked to. If she did not understand 'em she still assented with a smile. In which she dealt much, but which in all the years I knew her never grew to a laugh. . . . She affected to be lively, which was expressed by a smile and opening her eyes a little wider than ordinary, which ended generally in an exclamation of some things being charming. . . . Incapable of love and ignorant of friendship . . . she was a fine lady. . . . Her total real indifference to mankind has hindered her ever having a lover. For I am sure it was not love to her Lord prevented her: he not suffering her to be upon such an equality for many years last past, as produces that passion in its true light." The "indifference to mankind" that Hanbury-Williams noticed was certainly real enough to preclude the possibility of an open and disgraceful rupture; and there was no definite separation between husband and wife who, as long as they existed under the same roof, "lived together" (in the words of another historian) "upon very amicable terms . . . without any strong sympathies, and more like a French couple than an English one."

Lady Hervey's was essentially a cautious character—temperate, reserved, averse from experiment. "I look upon felicity in this world" (she was to admit to a correspondent during middle age) "not to be a natural state," remarking that she dreaded to see people she cared for "quite easy and happy," and always wished them "some little disappointment or rub, for fear of a greater." Very different was the spirit that possessed her husband. Though dearly bought, her mode of happiness was unexacting—it rested upon a tolerably secure foundation; while his greatest pleasures were usually the product of excitement and hazard, and could only exist in an atmosphere of emotional strain. He had a man's ingenuity but a woman's intensity. Now and then the feminine side turned uppermost—it was in this mood that he had flung himself during his early thirties into a passionate and tumultuous friendship with Stephen Fox, who followed him as his companion and attendant when he travelled abroad. The young man became the object of his intense devotion. Hervey's health at the time was extremely precarious; and images of love and death, deathless fidelity and eternal separation, flicker through the copious verses that streamed from his pen and lend a hectic colouring to the protestations that fill his letters. In violent passion there is a tinge of exhibitionism; and Hervey's letters to Fox are unusually revealing, as if he had dared himself to confess the truth and the world to believe it. Thus he delighted to exaggerate his feminine role; and, in a letter describing a banquet at Lord Harrington's, written in 1731, he dwells with a sort of gratified but uneasy relish on the emotion that had overcome him when his friend's name was proposed in a toast, how he had blushed and "felt just as I imagine your favourite and fondest mistress would have done upon the same occasion."

Habits of emotional subterfuge are always demoralizing. Even after Hervey's return to England, when he had plunged once again into the life of the court, Stephen Fox was still the object of his adoration, addressed in their correspondence as *"mon bien aimé," "mea vera et sola voluptas,"* the being whom he adored "better than all others in the world bundled together." Outwardly he was at pains to conform to the conventional pattern. In an age devoted to intrigue, when the pursuit of place, preferment and pecuniary advantage was an occupation that limited the views and controlled the existence of the most intellectual and highly gifted men, Hervey emerged as a master of court chicanery. He loved power, but the power he sought was not power of the brutal, direct and all-embracing kind achieved, for example, by Sir Robert Walpole. Hervey's methods and aims were more insidious. With serpentine and undulatory grace, he wound his way into the private counsels of others and, being an exceptionally adroit flatterer and a delightful companion, he did not find it difficult to twist his acquaintances the way he pleased. But, if he was fascinating, he was also treacherous. There was some element in Hervey's composition that made it impossible for him not to betray those whom he had subjugated. Perhaps his treachery was based on his love of diversity. To subdue was the first process; and, having subdued, he must necessarily betray, since betrayal was the only move that then remained. Like other unusually attractive personalities, he responded to the admiration and affection he could not help arousing, but despised his victims for the readiness with which they fell to his charm. Though he was not without feelings, his feelings (at least, in ordinary human contacts) were mercurial and rarely attached themselves to the same object for longer than a very short period: disenchantment and bitterness were bound to follow.

Typically devious was his treatment of his old friend Pulteney. When he returned to England, Hervey discovered that his wife and friend had been putting their heads together with the object of persuading him to desert the court and government party and devote his talents to the service of the Opposition. Pulteney's hatred of Walpole has already been mentioned, while Lady Hervey disliked the great man because he had once attempted to seduce her —"but unsuccessfully," as Hervey proceeds to explain, with an absence of indignation that his Victorian editor found peculiarly shocking—"love in these cases being like a ball, which the greater strength it comes back with, if it meets with resistance the further it rebounds back from the point at which was aimed." Various methods were adopted to sway his judgment. Lady Hervey, no doubt, recapitulated the story of the attempted seduction, though, knowing her husband as well as she did, she cannot have imagined it would have much effect; and her confederate poured out a flood of indignant oratory, inveighing against the "huffing military jackanapes of a king," his corpulent queen and his venal minister, suggesting that the whole country was thoroughly disaffected and hinting at the possibility of a *coup d'état*. It was true, added the conspirators, that Lord Hervey had his court pension of a thousand pounds a year which he could not be expected to forgo. Very well, then! his father, good old Lord Bristol, who was devoted to his brilliant and charming son, should supply a thousand a year from his own pocket, thus enabling Lord Hervey to give up his official stipend. Hervey listened—at first with an air of approval. Secretly he did not believe that his father would agree and hoped to escape from the proposal without the odium of definitely declining it; but the old gentleman was unexpectedly accommodating—anything to assist the fortunes of his "dear Jack"!—and Hervey found himself in the position of being "at last forced to say with an ill grace what he might at first have said with a good one" and to do "with the air of a mean shuffle and double dealing" what he might have done "with openness and reputation."

"From this time" (he concludes) "the friendship between Lord Hervey and Mr. Pulteney began to cool and soon after turned to the other extreme." Henceforward Hervey would devote his attention to the court and government, and for a person so intelligent and so experienced the subjugation of a young man as inexperienced and as impressionable as the Prince of Wales plainly presented very little difficulty. Frederick needed a mentor, and at last he had found one. Hervey was informative, worldly, entertaining. He knew a great deal about politics at home and abroad; he spared no pains to amuse and instruct his royal pupil; and very soon they were on terms of such intimate friendship that Hervey described himself as Frederick's Pylades, sent him long facetious letters in doggerel verse and received the Prince at his bedside when he had fallen ill. Stephen Fox, indeed, grew positively jealous. To this his admirer can only have objected that, though the devotion of princes may be very gratifying, it often imposes an intolerable strain on the courtier's energy, and that his own health and spirits were far from good. It was no sinecure, the position that he occupied. There were moments when it seemed that he must relapse into a state of chronic invalidism and that not all the doctors of Europe could set him right. Apparently he suffered from an affection of the gall-bladder; and having exhausted the science of ordinary practitioners (which resolved itself into the complex and excruciating formula: "a vomit to clear your stomach, a glister to give you a stool, laudanum to quiet the pain, and then a purge to cleanse your bowels," diversified by bitters to restore the appetite, spa water to raise the spirits, and ass's milk with powder of crab's eyes and oyster-shells to sweeten the blood), he had recourse to the superior knowledge of the celebrated Dr. Cheyne, who put his patient on to "a total and strict milk, seed and vegetable diet," in which Hervey persisted, with modifications, for many years. But even the regimen of fasting, bathing and purging was not wholly efficacious. Terrible attacks of vertigo would suddenly descend upon him. It had happened in the drawing room while he waited for the King to pass by; then he had saved the situation by clinging to a neighbour's arm and afterwards pretending he had been attacked by cramp. On an earlier occasion, while talking to the Prince, he had "dropped down at once, without the least warning," and had been carried by Sir Robert Walpole, Lord Scarborough and others into the Queen's bedchamber, "where they pulled off all my clothes, half drowned me with water, and crammed drops and gold powder into my mouth." Thence he was removed to his lodgings, "sometimes fainting and sometimes recovered." The King was exceedingly kind and solicitous; and the Prince (Hervey hastened to inform his friend) "sat with me all yesterday, and has promised to do so again today."

It is characteristic of Hervey's curiously flexible nature that, among the gloomiest premonitions of his approaching end, from which his passion for Stephen Fox gained a morbid intensity, he should have revealed himself in his most masculine and pugnacious aspect. At the beginning of 1731, only a few days after his collapse in the Queen's drawing room, his differences with Pulteney had flared up into a violent public quarrel. The Opposition, through its outrageous organ *The Craftsman,* was carrying on an intensive campaign against the court and government (with which Hervey had now finally identified his fortunes by accepting the office of Vice-Chamberlain) and the Government had retorted in a pamphlet entitled *Sedition and Defamation Displayed,* with a *Dedication to the Patrons of the Craftsman.* This *Dedication* contained a sharp attack on Pulteney and Bolingbroke; and Pulteney, who believed it to be Hervey's composition (which his former friend indignantly denied), entered the arena with *A Proper Reply to a Late Scurrilous Libel,* in which he popularized his theory of the anonymous authorship. The alleged pamphleteer was spared no wounding reflection. At first (wrote Pulteney) he was at a loss to imagine who could have composed the offensive work, though "the little quaint antitheses"—antithesis was an obvious feature of Hervey's prose style—"the laboured jingle of the periods, the great variety of rhetorical flourishes, affected metaphors, and puerile witticisms," prompted an attribution to some Eton boy or schoolgirl at a boarding establishment. Eventually, however, he had been informed that it was "the production of pretty Mr. Fainlove"; but his informant had added a plea that he would not treat the young gentleman with too much severity! *"Look at his youth and innocence! . . . What would the ladies say?* Nay, you know that he is a *Lady* himself; or at least such a nice composition of the two sexes that it is difficult to distinguish which is most predominant." Even more damaging and abusive references followed. They included an extremely broad insinuation that Hervey was guilty of offences then punishable by death, driven home with further gibes at his known effeminacy. Hervey's challenge reached Pulteney on January 25th. They met in the Green Park one snowy morning. Hervey faced his opponent with considerable sang-froid; according to some accounts he was wounded and disarmed, and according to another, "Mr. Pulteney once had so much the advantage that he would infallibly have run my Lord through the Body if his Foot had not slipped," upon which the anxious seconds took occasion to part them. Pulteney approached his adversary and attempted to embrace him. Hervey returned a stiff bow and they parted unreconciled.

There could be no doubt that Hervey had vindicated his physical courage. Lady Hervey's attitude towards this affair remains uncertain. Indeed, since her attempted intervention in her husband's career two years earlier—indirectly the cause of his duel with Pulteney—she had taken less and less part in his public life, which grew stormier and more busily occupied as time proceeded. He was now the inseparable companion of the Prince of Wales. It is tempting to imagine how, in somewhat different circumstances and given a slightly different turn to their respective characters, this association between Prince and courtier might have worked itself out. Hervey had a lively and polished intelligence. Frederick was all willingness to improve his mind, and possessed several qualities that his father and grandfather were completely lacking in. He was sociable, good-tempered, open-minded. Nothing pleased him so much as the opportunity of meeting his father's subjects upon equal and friendly terms. He had no reigning passion (noted Lord Egmont in 1732) if it were not "to pass the evening with six or seven others over a glass of wine and hear them talk of a variety of things. . . . He loves to play, and plays to win, that he may supply his pleasures and generosity, which last are great but so ill placed, that he often wants wherewith to do a well-placed kindness, by giving to unworthy objects. . . . He can talk gravely according to his company, but is sometimes more childish than becomes his age. He thinks he knows business but attends to none;

likes to be flattered. He is good-natured; and if he meets with a good Ministry, may satisfy his people; he is extremely dutiful to his parents, who do not return it in love, and seem to neglect him by letting him do as he will, but they keep him short of money." Too staunchly respectable in his own existence to be a very sympathetic critic of a rather dissipated and improvident young man, even Lord Egmont could not deny that the Prince had virtues; and an extreme readiness to learn was certainly one of them. Suppose that his new mentor had made the most of his opportunities—suppose that he had promoted a harmonious understanding between the Prince and Walpole, and that Walpole had persuaded the King to increase the Prince's income, thus removing the main grievance under which he laboured—it is possible, then, that the strain of liberal-mindedness and generosity which had been so evident in Frederick's character when he came to England might have developed to the exclusion of shabbier traits, and the strains of levity and infantile vanity have disappeared. But Hervey's was no benevolent, constructive genius. It was not calculated to secure his own peace or the peace of others.

On Frederick his influence was at least disturbing. There is no need either to sentimentalize the Prince's character or to subscribe to the opinion of it afterwards propagated by determined enemies; for it was irresolute rather than conspicuously noble or sordid. Hervey acted first as an excitant and then as an irritant. The various stages of their association are hard to follow, since Hervey's descendants, in the interests of decency or public policy, seem to have deleted from his *Memoirs* the sections he had devoted to this relationship, and an air of mystery envelops the whole episode. During the year 1730 and for the greater part of 1731, Frederick and Hervey were on terms of the very closest friendship; Frederick was present as godfather at the christening of Hervey's third son, the notorious Earl-Bishop of a later period, and they are said to have collaborated in writing a comedy which proved a failure and provoked a riot at Drury Lane.[1] It was towards the end of 1731 that a change occurred. Frederick, like his father and his grandfather, considered that gallantry was an obligation he owed to his rank, and he had already provided himself with several favourites, one of the latest being "an apothecary's daughter of Kingston." But now he ventured into a more serious entanglement. Miss Vane was his mother's Maid of Honour; she was also—or had been until very recently—Lord Hervey's mistress, shared by him with another nobleman about the court. For Hervey, at any rate, there was no question of jealousy. In fact he may have encouraged his friend's *liaison,* convinced that Miss Vane could be relied on to act as a useful secret agent and in her own interests would hesitate to betray his cause. Besides, the Prince was beginning to tire and annoy him. . . . Hervey's scruples usually vanished when his patience expired, but, in common with a great many cynical strategists, he made the mistake of over-simplifying the situation and under-estimating the complexity of human motives. Miss Vane was much less docile than her lover expected. Maybe she was piqued by Lord Hervey's desertion. Perhaps she did not appreciate the part he designed for her and took the bold line of confessing to Frederick her affair with Hervey, suggesting that Hervey was ready and willing to renew their passages. Whatever move she decided on, it was entirely successful. Hervey discovered, to his stupefaction, that he had fallen from favour.

Nothing is more exasperating than to be anticipated in one's own bad intentions. Hervey's surprise when he learned that he had been outwitted was so unaffected as to seem for the moment almost ingenuous; his indignation assumed the accents of offended virtue. During November he had been amusing the Prince with impromptu doggerel. In December, "That fool plagues my heart out" (he wrote angrily to Stephen Fox). "He is as false as he is silly," and

---

[1] See *Egmont.* October 11th, 1731, and January 16th, 1732.

in a subsequent letter he complains that he is continually receiving fresh evidence "of the falsehood as well as folly" of the Prince. . . . Not content with making bad blood between her old and new lovers, Miss Vane had had the effrontery to produce a candidate for Hervey's vacant place; and her candidate was the egregious George Bubb Dodington. A disappointed Walpole henchman and inveterate opportunist, Dodington, who, thanks to the good graces of Miss Vane, now entered the Prince's life as friend, political adviser and unpaid buffoon, was one of the strangest minor personages of the Augustan Age. In history he usually appears as an unscrupulous nobody. Dodington, nevertheless, had brilliant talents, but those talents could not redeem his reputation; and though he had liberal and cultured sympathies, he was to become notorious under the foolish figure of a mock-Mæcenas who collected dedications by dispensing port to his starveling poetasters. Among the many abusive epithets showered on his head, the word "coxcomb" occurs with startling regularity. It is clear that he had his ridiculous and vulgar side; and the element of coxcombry in his make-up, complicated by his extreme fickleness and selfishness, managed to overlay all his good and genuine qualities. He had the weaknesses of a very rich man and the vices of a *parvenu*. Having inherited the name and fortune of an opulent uncle, he maintained a state that was in proportion to his enormous wealth: sometimes established at his London residence in Pall Mall; sometimes receiving in his splendid villa La Trappe at Hammersmith, where the approach was embellished with "a large and handsome obelisk, surmounted by an urn of bronze, containing the heart of his wife," the chimney-piece was "hung with spars, representing icicles," the gallery was of marble and lapis lazuli, and he slept in a bed of purple and orange, "encanopied with peacocks' feathers"; sometimes driving down in a coach-and-six to his Dorsetshire mansion, which had been built by Vanbrugh in a similarly oppressive and splendid style. To Augustan critics this parade of plutocratic taste by a man whose father had been a tradesman and who had been born to the plebeian name of Bubb was particularly reprehensible and doubly preposterous. At the present distance, however, his foibles are at least as endearing as his virtues, and it is pleasant to read how Dodington, though he had a wardrobe "loaded with rich and flaring suits" ornamented with "a vast expense and profusion of brocade and embroidery," economized by never changing their cut, so that, with his huge "tye-periwig and deep-laced ruffles," he suggested "the picture of an ancient courtier in his gala habit, or Quin in his stage dress"; how the gold and silver carpeting around his bed was "a mosaic of the pocket-flaps and cuffs of all his embroidered clothes" and "betrayed its derivation . . . by the testimony of pockets, button-holes and loops"; or how he would rumble from London out to the suburbs in an equipage of ambassadorial size and magnificence, "drawn by six fat unwieldy black horses, short-docked, and of colossal dignity."

Frederick was less sensitive than his English contemporaries. It was not the least of Dodington's virtues that he was prepared to lend the Prince money which he had no immediate hope of seeing repaid, in return for promises of future preferment; and a triangular confederacy was established with Miss Vane as the apex. Hervey grew even angrier while he watched their proceedings. The Prince, Miss Vane and Dodington had been closeted together "all last night at that pretty idiot Lady Deloraine's lodgings," he told Stephen Fox indignantly on December 30th, 1731. Miss Vane was dismissed from her position at court early the following month, and Frederick thereupon made her an allowance at the rate of £1600 per annum and took a London house for her in Soho Square, which he equipped with a "fine service of plate and furniture." Here (says Egmont) she was visited by "a great number of people of fashion, men and ladies . . . to the just scandal of all sober and religious folks." That people of fashion occasionally visited her against their will is proved by the predicament of the Hanoverian

Colonel Schütz, Keeper of the Prince's Privy Purse, who had declined the honour as long as he decently could, only to receive a severe scolding from the Prince, "who said that she was a woman of quality whom he had done the honour to make his mistress, and his servants ought to respect her." Very well then, replied the Colonel. "If your Royal Highness commands me to wait upon her, I must go"; to which "the Prince replied such things are not to be commanded; meaning that servants ought not to wait till they are commanded." Miss Vane, at the time, was already pregnant. According to Egmont, she was no beauty, being a "fat, and ill-shaped dwarf," with "nothing good to recommend her . . . neither sense nor wit"; and it was feared that she was of a mischievous and ambitious turn, and might draw the Prince off "from that strict compliance with the King and Queen's desires and commands for which he was so distinguished." Hervey, too, observed her uneasily, but for other reasons. On first discovering the perfidious conduct of his former friends, he had vowed that they should never know he had detected them; but, as his mortification increased, he broke his word. The fury of his resentment grew irrepressible. Miss Vane was within two months of her confinement when she was handed a letter in which Hervey (having told the friend to whom he entrusted it that he wished merely to recommend a midwife) proceeded to overwhelm her with all the resources of his very considerable vocabulary, accompanying his invective with a storm of threats. Miss Vane was so affected that she fell in a swoon. The messenger, hearing that he had been deluded, swore that he would be the death of Lord Hervey; and "to prevent murder, Miss Vane was obliged to acquaint the Prince with what happened." Frederick used his influence to avert a duel, but his last spark of kindness towards Hervey was effectively suffocated. He "much resented the ill-treatment of his mistress, as did the King and Queen and Sir Robert Walpole. . . ."

"Mr. Fainlove" had definitely over-reached himself. Even Sir

Robert, not a severe critic of morals or manners, realized that his ally had gone too far; even the Queen, who had little indulgence for her son or his mistress, must needs resent this brutal affront to the Prince's dignity. The world at large sat back and smiled at Lord Hervey's discomfiture. The trouble was (considered Hanbury-Williams) that Hervey could never let well alone. He wished to be important in too many quarters: his ambition was too restless and too grasping; he had both too little loyalty and too little balance. Thus, quite apart from the treachery of Miss Vane, he had failed to hold Frederick because he had also set his mind on the subjugation of Frederick's mother, "attempting the management of the Queen and the Prince of Wales at the same time, though they were at that time, to every person's eye at Court except his, almost declared enemies." For several months Hervey was under the shadow of court disgrace; and during this period he made repeated and ignominious efforts to wheedle his way back to his old position, and attended the Prince's levee day after day. Miss Vane's child—christened Fitzfrederick, though gossips called it "the child of a triumvirate" and declared that Frederick, Hervey and his friend Lord Harrington could claim equal credit for its begetting—had been born in Soho Square during the month of July. Miss Vane was still a powerful and respected personage. She was powerful enough to humiliate Hervey. At one of the Prince's receptions they came face to face; and, while Hervey was conciliatory and deferential, she carried off the situation "with the haughtiness of an injured Princess, and would not allow him either a word or a look. . . ." Hervey digested the snub: he had other prospects. It was not in his nature to remain crestfallen for very long.

*F*INALLY disappointed in his hopes for Frederick, towards whom he now conceived a mortal hatred, Hervey focused his attention upon the Queen. For the Queen's star was growing steadily larger and brighter; the years of patience and self-suppression had brought their reward. Caroline, solidly supported by Sir Robert Walpole, could enjoy the preponderant power she had dreamed of wielding. The results of this alliance were extremely complete. A time had come when the minister, outwardly the frankest and readiest of English servants, and the Queen, apparently the gentlest and most submissive of German wives, had subjugated and encircled their royal master, and had done their work so thoroughly that the King himself had not an inkling of his new position. No pity need be wasted on the sovereign's plight. It was part of the plan—indeed, it was a condition of the whole agreement—that the King should continue to have the pleasure of thinking he ruled, while all the dangers and difficulties of exercising a truly royal function had been cleared from his path. Everything was done *through* him— nothing *by* him; yet he never lost the satisfaction of believing that he had initiated courses which, in fact, had been discussed and determined before the subject was allowed to come up at their councils, just as he retained—or appeared to retain—the royal, and husbandly, prerogative of having the last word.

Let him rage then, for the more blusterous the outburst, the quicker it would go by. Let him snap at the minister and so humiliate the Queen, in the presence of her friends and children, that the tears started into her eyes and she bent over her knitting with flushed cheeks and hurried, uncertain fingers; for when his fury had passed he would soon slip back into the habit of dependence, and, having gleaned the opinions of his two trusted counsellors, would boisterously proclaim them as his own. That they were not so only the King could have failed to recognize. The Opposition, at least, had been quick enough to appreciate the true state of affairs; and the task of Queen and minister was made yet more delicate by the frequent appearance of squibs at the King's expense, many of them published by that indefatigable organ, *The Craftsman.*

You may strut, dapper George, but 'twill all be in vain;

gibed a Tory versifier, in a jingle that was widely circulated even at court—

We know 'tis Queen Caroline, not you, that reign—
You govern no more than Don Philip of Spain . . .

and wound up with a pointed and painful reference to the fate of the King's mother:

Then if you would have us fall down and adore you,
Lock up your fat spouse, as your dad did before you.

While he was still smarting under this kind of attack George Augustus became unusually hard to manage, and all Sir Robert's bluff good-humour and Caroline's submissive charm were called into play. They had an interested spectator in the ambitious Vice-Chamberlain. He was their adjutant, too, once they had forgiven him for his behaviour towards the Prince. According to his own methods he helped to amuse the monarch, who remarked, nevertheless, that it was surprising a man of Lord Hervey's rank should lower himself by scribbling verses like "little Mr. Pope"; while his conversation and assiduous attendance in her leisure hours did much to soften the rigours of the Queen's existence. So feminine himself, Hervey could not withhold his admiration—never given very readily—from this triumph of a woman's insinuating cleverness over a man's brutal obstinacy and absurd conceit. His *Memoirs* grow almost lyrical as he describes the manœuvre. By long study (he observes) the Queen had learned "how to instil her own sentiments, whilst she affected to receive his Majesty's," and to appear "convinced whilst she was controverting, and obedient whilst she was ruling . . . She managed this deified image as the heathen priests used to do the oracles of old, when, kneeling and prostrate before the altars of a pageant god, they received with the greatest devotion and reverence those directions in public which they had before instilled and regulated in private. And as these idols consequently were only propitious to the favourites of the augurers, so nobody who had not tampered with our chief *priestess* ever received a favourable answer from our god; storms and thunder greeted every votary that entered the temple without her protection; calms and sunshine those who obtained it."

Such a system demanded endless discretion and delicacy. As often as Walpole appeared for a private interview, Caroline, much to the minister's interior amusement and the monarch's overt satisfaction, would rise, make a dutiful curtsy and prepare to withdraw, her husband sometimes permitting her to take her leave, sometimes condescending to bid her stay; at which Caroline, who had already discussed the matter with Walpole and decided on the course that should be adopted, would remain quietly engaged with her needlework throughout the audience. The King, who had a horror of petticoat government, was delighted to find his consort so well disposed, and ever and again would comment on her good behaviour. Charles I, he would remind acquaintances, had been governed by his wife, Charles II by his mistresses, James II by his priests, King William by his male and Queen Anne by her female favourites, his own father "by anybody that could get at him." "And who do they say governs now?" he would conclude triumphantly, sweeping a broad smile round the circle of embarrassed courtiers. The King's blindness was the measure of the Queen's diplomacy. He had never the misfortune of being undeceived; and yet, from his accession to the day of her death, Caroline exercised an authority more real, more solid and more continuous than that of any other Queen Consort or most Kings Regnant—one that extended to the smallest details of public affairs. She shared her power with Walpole and with Walpole alone. Walpole himself had the temperament of an autocrat; and, since the retirement of Townshend in 1729, the Duke of Newcastle, promoted to the Secretaryship of State, had become his chief supporter, a man of vast wealth and enormous territorial influence, but too muddle-headed ever to emerge as a dangerous rival.

The chronicler of this remarkable coalition between Queen and Prime Minister was their friend, Lord Hervey. Up till now his literary gifts had been confined to the writing of letters, the scribbling of comedies and *vers de société* and the composition of several energetic but rather over-elaborately phrased pamphlets defending the administration. But now he was to sit down to a more serious task. It was some time during 1733, according to internal evidence, that he embarked on the composition of his *Memoirs,* and for a number of years he continued to add to them regularly. They must have been written in brief snatches of privacy and leisure, by candle-light after the insufferable tedium of a royal card-party, or on odd days that he had managed to rescue from a life of routine. He tried his hardest to keep the tone of the work impartial, even going so far as to refer to himself usually in the third person, but his own temperament colours and qualifies the entire narrative. If style is an index of personality—if it be true that, notwithstanding every precaution, we must needs give ourselves away as soon as we take to pen and ink and paper—then Hervey's *Memoirs* form one of the strangest, sharpest and most incriminating self-portraits yet composed. They are brilliant—but with a brilliance so uncomfortable that after a time we look back to other and less interesting writers who have covered the same period, as a traveller through torrid regions looks back to the memory of some blank, drizzling, fog-enshrouded English afternoon. Oh, for the soothing obscurity of such humdrum pages! In Hervey's world, there is no dullness; equally, there is no relief from the sense of strain. It is not that Hervey wrote with exceptional effort. Indeed, he appears to have been gifted with very uncommon literary aptitude; but the facility that he possessed was facility of a peculiarly febrile kind, which exhausts and distresses, while it delights, the reader.

His method was idiosyncratic to the point of extravagance. Well might Pope gibe at this love of antithesis; and there is no doubt that, in the *Memoirs,* his habit of balancing sentence against sentence, and epithet against epithet, begins to assume the character of a nervous *tic,* till we feel that it had some hidden origin in the writer's mind. Hervey was a student and admirer of Tacitus, but nothing could be more unlike the sonorous and measured gravity with which the Roman historian delivers his most damning pronouncements than the enthusiastic distaste with which Hervey clings to a subject and will not let it go. Shaft after shaft attacks his victims; adjective on adjective, phrase on phrase, is piled up in a crescendo of personal antipathy; and the final effect is so intense as to be almost shrill.

It is the more surprising, then, that the *Memoirs* should have a heroine—that from the hurly-burly of accusation and recrimination, from the bewildering criss-cross pattern of hate and self-interest, should arise a single figure, large, alive, heroic and admirable. For genuine quality he still preserved a genuine reverence. The qualities of Caroline of Anspach were not moral qualities—had they been, Lord Hervey might have failed to recognize them—but they were of a piece with the physical fortitude that had always upheld her. The Queen was man-woman to his womanly man. Through force of circumstances, her proceedings were often devious; but in a certain robust integrity she never failed and, though she dissimulated, she remained obstinately and grandly herself. She bulks bigger and bigger as the story proceeds; and, as

CAROLINE AND HER SON,
WILLIAM DUKE OF CUMBERLAND

Engraving by Cooke after Kneller

FREDERICK AND HIS SISTERS

Engraving by Cooke after Nollekens

Hervey was drawn deeper into Caroline's intimacy and his knowledge of the family she ruled over grew more intensive, so did his regard for her talents increase. He became the *ami de la maison* of the royal family. Besides the Prince of Wales, whose alienation from his parents was now common knowledge, the King and Queen had five children still living, the three elder princesses being now practically grown up. The Duke of Cumberland was his parents' favourite, a stocky, sullen, obstinate adolescent, very unlike his volatile and capricious brother. He had the makings in him of an absolute monarch and a martinet. Anne, the Princess Royal, was of similar stuff and envied her father and mother their position and privileges; for she was distinguished by her meddlesomeness and her love of power. The Princess Amelia was of a masculine turn, both ill-natured and spiteful. Only Princess Caroline set an example of sweetness and mildness; she endured ill-health and suffered from an unhappy love-affair.

In fact, she was hopelessly attached to Hervey. While the Princess Royal dreamed of a splendid marriage, and Amelia busied herself with horses and dogs or engaged in coarse flirtations with the Duke of Grafton, Caroline devoted her energies to assisting her mother, but poured her whole spirit into a passion she could never gratify. Beyond a certain stage the relationship could not hope to progress. A curious essay might be woven around the careers of these royal virgins, doomed each of them to some degree of frustration, and round the effect of rank and birth on their private characters. They were repressed yet exalted, ignored yet flattered. Records speak of the sums of money that went in their maintenance (in the purchase of "three flower'd coats, one of them with silver," "two coats embroider'd, one trim'd or rich stuff, and one velvet or rich silk," damask nightgowns, silk under-petticoats, "shoes: a pair every week," "gloves: sixteen dozen in the year; 18*s*. per dozen," ribbons and lawns, patches and artificial flowers, powder and combs and quilted caps) or were distributed to dressers, tiring-women and gentlemen ushers, to pages, chambermaids and the man who tuned their harpsichord. None of the sisters was particularly good-looking; and we imagine them, with their large-featured, pouting, rather sulky Hanoverian faces, their hair in small flat curls on the tops of their heads or unrolled in one long ringlet that swept the shoulder, the upper part of their bodies squeezed into tight tubular bodices terminating in a pointed stomacher, their lower limbs enveloped in substantial petticoats, yellow and silver, dark green velvet or heavy brocade—but the whole organism taut and tremendous with frustrated energy.

On Anne and Amelia the effect of their position was coarsening. In Caroline it helped to develop a vein of romantic sensibility that afterwards degenerated into melancholia. Hervey knew of her passion for him and no doubt exploited it. Among the *jeux d'esprit* he wrote to amuse the Queen there is a dramatic episode in which (like Swift) he gives an imaginary account of the impression produced at court by the announcement of his own sudden demise. Princess Caroline alone is deeply affected. She controls her grief, but the movement of her hands betrays her feelings and her mother turns upon her with puzzled annoyance—"My God, Caroline, you will twist off the thumbs of your glove." Princess Amelia, on the other hand, pretends no sorrow, and is extremely scornful of her sister's somewhat faltering attempt to defend the dead man's memory: "Mama, Caroline is *duchtich* [1]; for my part I cannot *paroître,*" a remark which the Queen immediately crushes: "Ah! ah! You can *paroître* and be *duchtich* very well sometimes; but this is no *paroître;* and I think you are a very great brute. . . . My dear Purcel, this is the nastiest fruit I ever tasted. . . ."

Apart from the light it throws on the emotions of the unfortunate Princess, *The Death of Lord Hervey or A Morning at Court* is memorable for its portrait of the Queen herself and for its de-

---

[1] A slang word current in the royal family, based on *tüchtig* (strong, capable), which had apparently come to mean "clever," "designing."

tailed delineation of her talk and habits. It depicts Caroline during her husband's absence at Herrenhausen; free for a short time from the wearisome necessity of anticipating his whims and obeying his humours, she is particularly lavish of an easy-going and affable charm. The scene is laid in the Queen's gallery, at nine o'clock; Caroline is attended by two of her daughters, Mrs. Purcel, her tiring-woman, and Lord Lifford, a French Protestant exile raised to the English peerage who, with his sister, Lady Charlotte de Roucy, acted as domestic drudge and general whipping-boy of the royal household. It is Lord Lifford who brings news of Lord Hervey's death. *"Ah! grand dieu!"* gasps the Princess Caroline. *"Comment, est-il véritablement mort?"* exclaims the Queen, striking her hand —with what, no doubt, must have been a characteristic gesture— against her knee. "Purcel, my angel, shall I not have a little breakfast?" "What would your Majesty please to have?" "A little chocolate, my soul, if you give me leave; and a little sour cream and some fruit." The question of breakfast settled, she returns to Lord Lifford's story, scolds Princess Emily for laughing aloud, complains of the quality of the fruit on the table—"Is there none of the Duke of Newcastle's? or that old fool Johnstone's?"—then retires to write one of the enormous letters with which she entertained members of her family in the courts of Europe.

Next the scene shifts to the Queen's dressing room. The Queen is at her toilet, cleaning her teeth; Mrs. Purcel is busily tiring her head; and around, like attentive worker-insects, circle her Ladies of the Bedchamber, Pembroke and Burlington, and her Woman of the Bedchamber, Lady Sundon. From the adjoining room the Royal Chaplain and his assistant can be heard engaged in a perfunctory recital of morning prayers. This service regularly accompanied the Queen's private levee and was usually held in an outer room which contained a picture representing a large naked Venus. Dr. Madox did not object to its proximity, though he had once commented on it "archly" to Mrs. Selwyn as "a very proper altarpiece"; but, out of respect for his feelings and his parsonic dignity, the door between the two rooms is not entirely closed; and fragments of the liturgy come floating through. *"From pride, vain glory, and hypocrisy, from envy, hatred and malice, and all uncharitableness . . . Good Lord deliver us!"* intone the two unseen ministrants. Deeply devoted to theology in the abstract, Caroline was somewhat impatient of religious observances and now appeals to Lady Sundon to "shut a little that door: those creatures pray so loud, one cannot hear oneself speak." Lady Sundon, whose sympathies were notoriously Low Church, proceeds to close it as far as she decently can, but Caroline moderates her excessive zeal: "So, so, not quite so much; leave it enough open for those parsons to think we may hear, and enough shut that we may not hear quite so much." With quiet restored, the talk flows back to Lord Hervey. Lady Burlington [1] admits that he could be very entertaining, yet adds that he reminded her of "a party to Vauxhall, where the glare and the bustle entertain one for a little while, but one was always tired of one as well as of t'other in half an hour." Lady Sundon rallies stiffly to her friend's defence, declaring that she is sure he loved the Queen, to be immediately contradicted by Princess Amelia:

"That is, you are sure he said so, my good Lady Sundon, and so will all Mama's pages and gentlemen ushers."

"But he has said it in a way that I think I could see whether he felt what he said or not. . . . And I assure your Royal Highness I think the Queen will have a very great loss of him, for, besides the use he was of in Parliament, which I do not pretend to be a judge of, he was certainly a constant amusement to the Queen in private, and gave up his whole time to amuse her; and I must say I do not

---

[1] For Lady Burlington, wife of the great building magnifico, Hervey had a particular dislike, which found expression in his doggerel verses *To the Queen:*

Let . . . Dame Palladio, insolent and bold,
Like her own chairman, whistle, stamp, and scold. . . .

think it is everybody (if they would give their whole time to it) is capable of amusing the Queen." *Queen:* "Oh! upon my word he amused me exceedingly. I pray give me the basin to wash." (*Lady Pembroke kneels and gives the basin.*)

Presently, Sir Robert Walpole is introduced; but, considering the informality with which he arrives and the alacrity with which the Queen does him the especial favour of offering him a chair, it might be more accurate to say that he "drops in." Caroline is evidently delighted to see the minister:

"Come, come, my good Sir Robert, sit down. Well, how go matters?"

"Everything very well, Madam, pure and well. I have just had intelligence out of the City—all is very quiet."

"But we must hang some of these villains," remarks the Queen, referring to recent disturbances that had been put down by the military, and proceeds to inveigh against the necessity of reading the Riot Act—"Ah! *mon Dieu!* they are all so *ennuyant* with their silly forms and their silly Acts"—and to give her views of "your fine English liberty! The *canaille* may come and pull one by the nose, and unless one can prove which finger touched one's nose, one has but to put a plaster on one's nose, and wait to punish them until they pull it again . . ." an outburst to which Sir Robert, with placid dignity, remarks that "there are inconveniences and imperfections attending all systems of government, and these are ours," then changes the subject by inquiring for news from Hanover.

Caroline replies that she has just received from the King a letter of forty-five pages, but she has no time to discuss it now, since the Drawing Room waits, and the last scene opens to reveal her in full royal splendour as she bears down upon a curtsying and bowing assemblage. The drama ends a little lamely with Lord Hervey's reappearance. Caroline's comments on this production we do not know, but it is typical of her good nature that she was not offended and took no umbrage at some of the grosser pleasantries that were put in her mouth. Lord Hervey was certainly very diverting. Herself, she needed all the diversions that came her way; and, besides the companionship of this dazzling *cicisbeo,* who talked with her, played cards with her, brought her gossip and, at hunting parties, always rode at the door of her chaise, she found them in pursuits as diverse as theology and gardening.

Her gardening and building activities (which remodelled the whole of Kensington Gardens and swept imposing prospects through Richmond and Kew) must be mentioned elsewhere. Her theological opportunities she took especial delight in—not so much because she was a woman of deep convictions or had a very real understanding of religious faith, as because theology gave her intelligence the stretch it needed and provided an excuse for the type of discussion she loved. Over breakfast she might often be discovered delving into a volume of new sermons or topical religious controversy. As Princess of Wales she had followed the example of her guardian, the Queen of Prussia, by arranging the celebrated metaphysical set-to between her old friend Leibniz and Dr. Samuel Clarke, the famous incumbent of St. James's, Westminster, on the relation of Time and Space to God; and, as Queen, she remained speculative and latitudinarian, a firm supporter of the more advanced and unorthodox bishops. Like them, she inclined to Erastian and Arian principles. Benjamin Hoadly, Bishop in turn of Bangor, Hereford, Salisbury and Winchester, was a prelate whose learning she particularly favoured; and Hoadly, whose Erastianism had been demonstrated in an early pamphlet defending the supremacy of the state in church affairs, was also suspected of heretical views on the nature of the Trinity, which he preferred to regard from the Unitarian standpoint. During an earlier period both Clarke and Hoadly might have been burnt as heretics; at the beginning of the century in which they flourished a religious issue was still powerful enough to bring out the mob; the Augustan Age had assigned theology to its proper sphere. The thunders of the Bangorian controversy were deep but distant: they aroused no disturbing echo in popular feeling.

Thus, the intricate structure of Christian belief was considerably simplified. Clarke, who had boggled at the Trinity, also hesitated at the idea of revelation; and, in a series of lectures on the *Being and Attributes of God* and the *Evidence of Natural and Revealed Religion,* attempted to show that the existence of a Deity might be proved by *a priori* arguments. Pope opposed his pretensions at length in the *Dunciad:*

> Let others creep by timid steps and slow,
> On plain experience lay foundations low. . . .
> All-seeing in thy mists, we want no guide;
> Mother of arrogance, and source of pride!
> We nobly take the high Priori road,
> And reason downwards, till we doubt of God!

And it is, in fact, recorded of Dr. Clarke that after delivering his second series of lectures he fell victim to a severe attack of religious doubt, or, at least, that his nimble and ingenious mind "first wavered on the grand principles of our faith, as members of the Church of England."

Those who shared his scepticism certainly included the Queen. Disdainful of, or disappointed in, human affection, more ambitious than she ever admitted or was allowed to show, Caroline adopted church affairs as an absorbing hobby, in which both the King himself and Walpole were content to humour her. Religious exiles from abroad she received and pensioned. At home she extended her patronage to the dissenting sects. In the Anglican Church, Berkeley was promoted to an Irish bishopric, while Butler, author of *The Analogy between Natural and Revealed Religion,* a divine widely celebrated in his day, she made Clerk of the Closet and often invited to visit her, for philosophical and metaphysical discussion, on her leisure evenings from seven to nine o'clock. No church appointment was made without her approval; and if the well-bred passivity of the Church of England, maintained for the best part of a hundred years, had something to do with the constitution of Augustan culture, and if that culture be considered harmonious and dignified, then Caroline as dean- and bishop-maker deserves much of the credit. Her nominees were always Whigs; they were usually learned. They preferred discussion to devotion, and reason to zealotry.

In her own character vitality took the place of enthusiasm, and intelligence of the more delicately shaded virtues. It is often dangerous to see a period through an individual, particularly when the individual is of royal birth and his or her character has been correspondingly changed or distorted; but Caroline's affinity to the age she lived in is a very obvious one. Like Walpole, she is part of the Augustan setting, shrewd, lively, courageous, unsentimental, yet blessed with a certain native generosity, sometimes ruthless yet tolerant to the point of cynicism. Her prejudices were violent, her language was strong; but even in her aberrations she remained a realist—and it is that strain of realism which gave its quality to the Augustan mind where shadows were few and prospects were open, and romantic melancholy and religious mystery were equally strangers. But, for all her cheerfulness, Caroline of Anspach was not a happy woman; and her robust good-humour concealed incessant physical suffering.

Chapter Four

1

*I*T IS one of the chief beauties of the early Augustan Age that, since comparatively few figures demand our attention and since the tenor of the period was generally placid, those few figures should stand out in the greatest relief. Each of them fits compactly into the niche he built for himself. No opponent could dispute the powers of Walpole; no critic ever doubted the brilliance of Boling-broke; Lord Chesterfield was the grand exemplar of worldly wis-dom; Pope's position as the foremost poet of the age he lived in seemed as secure in 1730 as it seems today. His development had been regular; his gifts were harmonious. But, just as the apparent calm of the period depended upon the maintenance of an unpopu-lar dynasty, and just as Walpole, its representative and guardian, was the cleverest and strongest but also the worst-hated minister of his time, so Pope's career conceals an element of contradiction. His life story might be plotted in two separate graphs. First, there is the curve of his literary development—a smooth upward line unbroken by any of the brutal disappointments, maddening false starts or major reverses that fall to the ordinary writer's share. For-tune had been invariably, extraordinarily benevolent. Born in con-ditions that had neither the disadvantages of downright poverty nor the distractions of overwhelming affluence, he was free from financial embarrassment as long as he lived. He showed youthful promise, which was immediately recognized; and, though not al-

ways generous towards his friends, he recorded his indebtedness in
flowing couplets:

> *Granville* the polite,
> And knowing *Walsh,* would tell me I could write;
> Well-natur'd *Garth* inflam'd with early praise,
> And *Congreve* lov'd, and *Swift* endur'd my lays:
> The courtly *Talbot, Somers, Sheffield* read,
> Ev'n mitred *Rochester* would nod the head,
> And *St. John's* self (great *Dryden's* friends before)
> With open arms receiv'd one Poet more.

Thus encouraged, he had moved on swiftly from triumph to triumph. The *Pastorals* were slight; but they were correct and charming. *An Essay on Criticism* had followed them two years later and,
to show that he was as versatile as he was gravely accomplished,
was itself followed in the year 1712 by the exquisite apparition of
The Rape of the Lock. His translation of the Iliad had secured his
fame. True, the Odyssey and the edition of Shakespeare had been
less successful; but they had entailed at the very most a temporary
set-back, while the Odyssey had earned him a handsome reward.
Then, in 1728, with his declaration of war on the Dunces, he had
revealed himself the supreme exponent of literary satire.

So easy and so continuous had been his progress. . . . But beneath the first graph we must trace a second; beneath that master-
ful smoothly ascending curve runs a line jagged and erratic as the
chart of an earthquake, scored in the blackest of ink with the wild-
est of needles, the graph of his emotional and nervous life. From
his father he had inherited the frame of a hunchback and, with it,
that odd mixture of vitality, susceptibility and extreme pugnacity
which sometimes inhabits a hopelessly crippled organism. In a
face sharpened by intelligence, malice and suffering were set large
and uncommonly beautiful eyes; the nose was long and high-
bridged and delicate; but "his mouth" (according to Sir Joshua

Reynolds, who remembered as a boy once having seen him) "had those peculiar marks which are always found in the mouths of crooked persons," and the muscles crossing his cheeks projected like cords. Violent headaches accompanied chronic insomnia; and Roubiliac, the statuary, who made a bust of him from life, observed that "his countenance was that of a person who had been much afflicted with headache; and that he should have known the fact from the contracted appearance of the skin above the eyebrows. . . ." Add to this an air of unquenchable liveliness. He might speak of his existence as a "long disease"; but there could be no question of the tenacity with which he clung to it or of his delighted preoccupation with the affairs of the world. He loved the world; it often hurt him; he struck back furiously. He loved his fame; at the smallest threat to it, he was up in arms, and in this mood sometimes attacked when he thought he defended. Intensely suspicious and absurdly sensitive, he saw all opponents as of the same size if they aroused his enmity.

Then no manœuvre was too black or too devious. The history of Pope's campaign to discredit the Dunces (which included the administration of an emetic to a piratical bookseller, the composition of scurrilous and indecent lampoons, the employment of anonymous letters and disguised emissaries) is a melodrama that often lapses into farce or a comedy with decidedly tragic undertones. No affront was too slight for Pope to remember; no adversary so vulgar as to be beneath him; and among the small fry of bankrupt publishers and struggling critics, he raged with the ferocity of a sectarian prosecutor and the high moral indignation of a religious reformer. As a controversialist, Pope is at his best when he is broadly scurrilous—for example, when he dashes off his spirited and Rabelaisian account of *"a Horrid and Barbarous Revenge by Poison on the Body of Mr. Edmund Curll"* (the episode of the emetic administered in a glass of sack)—but at his feeblest when he strikes an attitude of superior virtue. Pope himself never paused to query his motives. As the editor of his early prose works has pointed out,[1] it is an extremely interesting and illuminating fact that his third onslaught on Edmund Curll, the most abusive and improper of all his lampoons, should have been composed at about the same time as his splendid dedication to the Iliad, one of the nobler prose achievements of the eighteenth century. In Pope's character such a dichotomy had always existed. At his most petulant, he continued to see himself as the peace-loving private citizen dragged from his dignified retirement by mercenary scribblers:

> Whom have I hurt? has poet yet, or peer,
> Lost the arch'd eye-brow, or Parnassian sneer?

—at his most untrustworthy, as the truest and staunchest of friends. His own mind never alighted on the contradiction. He remained incorrigibly aggressive and fiercely proud.

Pope had a deep respect for magnanimity. Conscious in himself of generous and noble impulses, unconscious perhaps that they did not often appear in his private dealings, he made it his business to present an estimable character to the world at large. Few poets have designed more flattering self-portraits; and, not content with the limitations of poetic portraiture, Pope carried the same method into his correspondence, carefully calculating the effect it would produce on his friends and posterity. He must seem lofty, good-humoured, calm, disinterested. Incidentally, he let slip no opportunity of editing and re-touching the letters he had already written and posted, and for this purpose sometimes reclaimed them from the original addresses. He detested the slipshod and the second-rate; he abominated the petty and the meretricious. Was it not natural, then, that he should polish up his private character as diligently as he polished and revised his couplets and that, loving

---

[1] Norman Ault, *The Prose Works of Alexander Pope, 1711–29.*

POPE AND HIS HOUSE AT TWICKENHAM

Engravings by Faber after Vanloo (above), and by Cooke (below)

LADY MARY WORTLEY
MONTAGU

Original by Zincke

MRS. HOWARD,
LADY SUFFOLK

Engraving by Cooper

MARY LEPEL HERVEY

From a Miniature

the virtues he omitted to practise with platonic enthusiasm, he should pay them the tribute of persistently believing they had always been his? At least, the aspiration was there, the passion for goodness—a passion that, like many others in Pope's life, was thwarted by the accident of physical infirmity. Personal happiness had eluded him as well as virtue. Uncommonly susceptible to the charm of women, with a sensuous predilection for their friendship and company and an absorbing interest in every detail of the lives they led, he was doomed to a series of abortive love-affairs. Martha Blount remained a devoted companion to the very end; but Theresa Blount deserted and betrayed him; while one of the strongest attachments he ever conceived had the bitterest aftermath. Overshadowing a multitude of minor reverses loomed the dreadful story of Lady Mary Wortley Montagu.

On Pope's side, it had been a profound and serious passion. On Lady Mary's—well, Pope was a famous writer; she herself was a fashionable and accomplished woman; and his protestations (she may have considered) did both of them credit. Lady Mary had a high opinion of her charms and abilities. From her father, the extravagant Duke of Kingston, she derived her pride, her gusto and her eccentricity. It had been (as she remembered) the happiest moment of her life when, at the age of seven, she had been sent for by her father to the Kit-Cat Club, lifted onto a table and solemnly toasted, elected a reigning beauty of the day, then passed "from the lap of one poet, or patriot, or statesman, to the arms of another" and "heard her wit and beauty loudly extolled on every side"— mere "pleasure" was much too mild a word to describe her sensations! She had grown up in the dashing paternal style. Her marriage, against her father's wishes, to the good-looking and talented Edward Wortley Montagu, had been romantic and at first extremely happy; and it was some two or three years afterwards that she had encountered Pope. This was probably during the course of 1715. A year later, she departed with her husband on his celebrated embassy to the Sublime Porte; and Pope's devotion pursued her as she travelled eastwards.

During 1718 Lady Mary returned to England; Pope helped his friends to find a house at Twickenham; and for at least two years the visionary pursuit continued. That it remained visionary was Pope's tragedy and the friendship's undoing. Lady Mary, a woman exceptional in all things, was exceptional in her bold and forthright epicureanism, to which she brought a certain strain of inherited rakishness. "Considering what short-lived weak animals men are," she had written to the Abbé Conti on her travels, "is there any study so beneficial as the study of present pleasure?" Her "present pleasures" were one day to become notorious, and in 1720 they did not include the love of Pope, who possessed none of the qualifications of a successful amorist. He was to be flattered, corresponded with, but kept at arm's length. The delight he felt in thinking of her return (he had declared in October 1717) "transports me beyond the bounds of common sense and decency"; but her return had procured him little of the joy he hoped for, and a sense of deep frustration clouded his spirit. Forlorn, he watched the growth of his house and gardens, the enlargement of avenues and the planting of coppices, the erection of urns and obelisks and rustic temples, "twisted and twirled and rhymed and harmonized" into a miniature landscape.

Had Pope's mind been attuned to disappointment or capable of substituting the charms of regret for the pleasures of love, the conclusion of the story might have been less disastrous. But he was naturally proud and naturally irritable; his aspirations were the aspirations of an impetuous lover; and it was in this role, according to Lady Mary, that he flung aside reserve and suddenly declared himself. Alas, the effect was comic when it should have been moving! He was received not with rapture, not with hesitation, not even with grave looks and talk of friendship, but with a burst of laughter so immoderate it could not be contained, with a wild explosion of fashionable scorn and feminine spitefulness. Pope's response was as electric as the affront was unmerited. The revenge he took was elaborate; he prolonged it indefinitely.

Lady Mary was subjected to a succession of pinpricks. But since each pin consisted of a couplet forged by Pope, dipped in a distillation of several years' hatred and aimed at some vital spot in the victim's character, his campaign proved far more damaging than a frontal attack. The public was reminded of a somewhat shady transaction in which Lady Mary was supposed to have been engaged at the time of the South Sea Bubble; it was regaled with references to a rumour that she had once suffered, or was still suffering, from a disgraceful and disfiguring disease; it was diverted with a passing mention of her personal sluttishness. At the same time, Pope was careful to keep a retreat open; and, charged with having slandered an individual, he would reply that his intentions were purely general—his *Lady Marys* and *Sapphos* were generalized figures—as for the application, it had been supplied by the complainant herself! Employing a similar method, he also escaped from the imputation of having slandered the "princely" Duke of Chandos, master of Canons, and that alarming personage, the old Dowager Duchess of Marlborough, both of whom at different periods had befriended him. For, though Pope was courageous, he was usually circumspect; and the disconcerting streak of obliquity that ran through his temperament—his liking for strategic and secretive methods, his preference for "genteel equivocation" and his tendency, as Lady Bolingbroke once remarked, to "play the politician about cabbages and turnips"—had its origin in the physical conditions he had to contend against, in the withdrawnness and defensive craft that are bred of suffering. But then, vices may return as virtues through the alchemy of genius, which rears strength from infirmity and success from failure.

Thus, it is the sense of quivering frustration that Pope in his own life must so often have experienced—the possessor of a powerful brain lodged in an almost powerless body, of strong passions continually thwarted and made ridiculous by the infirmities inseparable from his constitution—that gives his verse its peculiar delicacy and nervous fineness. To look beneath the surface of his greatest poems is to become aware of an intensity of feeling developed to a point where it would be difficult to say whether it were pleasure or pain that predominated. As a recent critic has remarked, while discussing the characteristics of Pope's imagery, his "most sensuous descriptive poetry is seldom independent of physical irritation." [1] His imagination, like one of his own sylphs, seems to be composed of some substance exquisitely attuned to every delight but unprotected against a multitude of minor distresses. Only Pope could have devised that fascinating inferno reserved for the disobedient celestial beings:

> Whatever spirit, careless of his charge,
> His post neglects, or leaves the fair at large,
> Shall feel sharp vengeance soon o'ertake his sins,
> Be stopp'd in vials, or transfix'd with pins;
> Or plung'd in lakes of bitter washes lie,
> Or wedg'd whole ages in a bodkin's eye;
> Gums and Pomatums shall his flight restrain,
> While clogg'd he beats his silken wings in vain;
> Or Alum styptics with contracting pow'r
> Shrink his thin essence like a rivel'd flow'r:
> Or, as Ixion fix'd, the wretch shall feel
> The giddy motion of the whirling Mill,
> In fumes of burning Chocolate shall glow,
> And tremble at the sea that froths below!

or evoked in images, at once so ludicrous and so brilliantly imaginative, the phantom shapes that surround the Goddess Spleen.

---

[1] *On the Poetry of Pope,* Geoffrey Tillotson.

But to appreciate the full range of Pope's achievement, we should observe his performance at opposite ends of the keyboard. If *The Rape of the Lock*—which must be numbered among the most perfectly sustained poems in the English language—is an example of delicacy combined with strength (for the material of the work is as light as thistledown, yet the execution never becomes weak or flimsy) the *Epistle to Arbuthnot* displays his genius at the other extreme. Here imaginative grace is allied to satirical hardihood. In its concentrated vigour of denunciation Pope's attack on Sporus may be compared, in eighteenth-century prose literature, to Junius's famous attack on the Duke of Grafton. Whether the attack itself was just or fair is beside the point; since, when satire arrives at a certain degree of excellence, we abandon ethical in favour of æsthetic standards, and it is as unimportant to us whether the victim was worthy of hatred as whether the object of some great amatory poem was deserving of love. What counts is the organization of violent feeling, its expression through the management of rhythm and the choice of imagery, and its distribution in the rise and fall of the satirist's eloquence. Here Pope's mastery of his medium reaches its highest pitch. Addressed to an imaginary or a forgotten character —and by how many is Junius's arch-villain today remembered?— the poem would still be brilliant, effective, exciting; but Pope's audience knew the character he had in mind (though they knew little of the circumstances of the actual conflict) and understood the private sting of each poetic sally.

It is appropriate that for this—his fiercest diatribe—Pope should have selected one of the period's most furious haters, a man who enjoyed a quarrel as he did himself. During the aftermath of his differences with Lady Mary Wortley Montagu, Pope had also fallen out with her friend Lord Hervey—for what reason and on what occasion we may never know. At all events he fondled a lingering grievance; and, since Hervey was a poetaster as well as a peer, young, fashionable, flippant, beloved of women, in the writer's attitude there was a disturbing mixture of contempt and envy. Pulteney's pamphlet had already popularized the legend of Hervey's effeminate manners and ambiguous morals; and two years later, in 1733, when he published his *First Imitation of Horace,* Pope pilloried him, under a derogatory nickname, as the foolish scribbling nobleman who wrote with ease:

> The lines are weak, another's pleased to say:
> Lord Fanny spins a thousand such a day.

Hervey and Lady Mary retorted in rhyme. But, though the intention was virulent, the effect was feeble. Pope's deformity was likened to the brand of Cain; he was reproached with his insensibility to Youth and Beauty:

> Not even Youth and Beauty can control
> The universal rancour of thy soul . . .

when his uncommon susceptibility was more at fault; he was threatened with vague but dreadful punishments. In the original production, Lady Mary had had the greater hand, but her collaborator continued the war on his own account; and *A Letter from a Nobleman at Hampton Court to a Doctor of Divinity* lent colour to Pope's opinion of Lord Fanny's verses. From that moment the strife became unequal; the persecuted poet turned relentless persecutor, destined to harry his victim to the grave and beyond it, then elevate him to the pantheon of undying Dunces. Caught and for ever imprisoned in the amber genius, the may-fly nobleman achieved an immortality beyond his hopes and fears.

In fact, the *Letter to a Noble Lord* did not reach the printing-press—some said that Pope had been bought off by Walpole—but there is no doubt that it was circulated and widely read. "Pope" (Hervey had written to Stephen Fox, soon after the appearance of his *Letter to a Doctor of Divinity*) "is in a most violent fury and *j'en suis ravi"*; but for the purposes of literature he controlled his rage—though, now and then, it quivers out in a line or an epithet —and composed a masterpiece of ironic retaliation. The satirists had made clumsy play with his lameness and ugliness.

It is true, my Lord, I am short, not well shaped, generally ill-dressed, if not sometimes dirty. Your Lordship and Ladyship are still in bloom; your figures such, as rival the Apollo of Belvidere, and the Venus of Medicis; and your faces so finished that neither sickness nor passion can deprive them of *colour*. I will allow your own in particular to be the finest that ever *man* was blest with. Preserve it, my Lord, and reflect that to be a critic would cost it too many frowns, and to be a statesman too many wrinkles!

Elsewhere he dealt with the question of the satire's authorship:

Your Lordship indeed said you had it from a lady, and the lady said it was your Lordship's; some thought the beautiful bye-blow had two fathers, or (if one of them will hardly be allowed a man) two mothers; indeed I think both sexes had a share in it, but which was uppermost, I know not. I pretend not to determine the exact method of this witty fornication; and if I call it yours, my Lord, it is only because, whoever *got* it, you brought it forth.

A pause followed: then came the *Epistle to Arbuthnot*. One mention of Lord Fanny in three hundred lines. Pope is at his most majestic, delightful, discursive, heaping scorn on the scribblers who disturb his rest, paying a noble tribute to his old patron Bolingbroke, drawing a brilliant sketch of Addison and his coffee-house coterie—till suddenly, from a clear sky, the bolt descends. It is as though the poet's voice had actually risen. Arbuthnot intervenes; but the real purpose of his pacific query is to introduce a reference to Hervey's consumption of ass's milk and the unnatural, unearthly pallor of his delicate skin, which he had already begun to conceal beneath coats of rouge:

> Let *Sporus* tremble—*A*. What? that thing of silk,
> *Sporus,* that mere white curd of ass's milk?
> Satire or sense, alas! can *Sporus* feel?
> Who breaks a butterfly upon a wheel?

This check merely gives fresh impetus to Pope's invective; and, springing from couplet to polished couplet, he pounces in turn on the defects of Hervey's oratory—a mouthing manikin controlled by Sir Robert Walpole—on his sinister exploitation of the Queen's friendship—on his love of antithesis, his fund of small talk and *jeux d'esprit*—on his dreadful handsomeness, his alleged perversity and his mincing gait:

> Yet let me flap this bug with gilded wings,
> This painted child of dirt, that stinks and stings;
> Whose buzz the witty and the fair annoys,
> Yet wit ne'er tastes, and beauty ne'er enjoys:
> So well-bred spaniels civilly delight
> In mumbling of the game they dare not bite.
> Eternal smiles his emptiness betray,
> As shallow streams run dimpling all the way.
> Whether in florid impotence he speaks,
> And, as the prompter breathes, the puppet squeaks;
> Or at the ear of *Eve,* familiar toad,
> Half froth, half venom, spits himself abroad,
> In puns, or politics, or tales, or lies,
> Or spite, or smut, or rhymes, or blasphemies.
> His wit all see-saw between *that* and *this,*
> Now high, now low, now master up, now miss,
> And he himself one vile antithesis.
> Amphibious thing! that acting either part,
> The trifling head, or the corrupted heart!
> Fop at the toilet, flatt'rer at the board,
> Now trips a lady, and now struts a lord.

Eve's tempter thus the Rabbins have exprest,
A cherub's face, a reptile all the rest,
Beauty that shocks you, parts that none will trust,
Wit that can creep, and pride that licks the dust.

Retort would have been impossible; nor did Hervey attempt it. From the point of view of the world that has inherited his portrait, Hervey himself is of less consequence than the emotions he roused and the forms those emotions took in poetic imagery. Pope's *sæva indignatio* may have been mean or magnificent; there can be no question but that the shape it assumed was splendid. Here, crystallized in art, are the qualities of which, in terms of life and conduct, he had never presented more than an awkward travesty. Compare Pope's motives in attacking the Duchess of Marlborough, Addison or Hervey with the grace, speed and energy of the attack itself, and the paradox of his existence becomes doubly clear. The noble and the ignoble—the mean and the dignified—are at length reconciled by the mysterious processes of æsthetic creation.

2

IF POPE stands for the creative genius of the Augustan Age— loftily overlooking the Youngs and the Parnells, the Tickells and the Thomsons—Chesterfield epitomizes its genius in another sphere. Like Hervey, he had seemed marked out for uncommon achievements at a time when, as Lord Stanhope and Mr. John Hervey, they had been companions and rivals at Leicester House; but it was Chesterfield who had reaped the lesser rewards. To some extent, his private character might be held responsible: he inspired respect, but he did not inspire attachment; and his wit (which was unusually sharp and biting, and often employed with a reckless disregard of time and place) had earned him more

enemies than it had gained him admirers. Then his alleged friendship with Mrs. Howard had annoyed the Queen. Caroline (according to a piece of court gossip retailed by Horace Walpole)
"had an obscure window at St. James's that looked into a dark
passage, lighted only by a single lamp at night which looked upon
Mrs. Howard's apartment." One Twelfth Night, Chesterfield,
who had won a large sum at cards which he was afraid to carry
home upon his person, visited Mrs. Howard very late, to leave it
in her charge; whence (says Horace Walpole) "the Queen in-
ferred great intimacy"—which had little or no foundation in
fact—and made it her business to thwart him at every juncture.
The anecdote is perhaps completely fictitious, but it is clear that
Chesterfield did not obtain advancement in proportion to his
merits (which were considerable) or in accordance with his ideas
of his own value.

Disappointed he may have been, but he was not embittered. The
British Embassy at the Hague (which he occupied from 1728 to
1732) was a relatively modest appointment, but Chesterfield discharged his functions with grace and diligence. This was the busy
and formative period of the Ambassador's life. In 1732, by a humble *dame de compagnie,* Madame du Bouchet, he became the
father of the son whose education was to be the delight and despair of his middle age; and a year later, soon after his return to
England, he contracted a marriage of convenience in the grandest
style. Impossible to look higher or choose more prudently! Petro-
nilla Melusina von Schulenburg—to give her her English title,
Lady Walsingham—was not young, not beautiful and not amusing; but she was related on the left hand to the royal family, being the daughter of the Duchess of Kendal and George I, and
possessed a substantial fortune, which her husband subsequently
enlarged to the extent of another twenty thousand pounds by
threatening to reveal George Augustus's unwise suppression of his
father's last will and testament. Husband and wife maintained

entirely separate households, but it is recorded of Chesterfield that he treated his wife always in the most courteous and suavely considerate manner, while he made not the smallest sacrifice of his personal liberty. Such was the perfect balance he held between duty and inclination. From the point of view of the politician and the careerist it might be said that he was only moderately successful and that clumsier and stupider men had often outstripped him; but, from another point of view, his triumph was dazzling. Lord Chesterfield was his own masterpiece, complete and flawless, a finished product beyond the petty scope of success or failure.

Self-discipline had made him extraordinarily self-sufficient. The incomparable letters that, in 1739, he began to address to the shy and awkward being who bore his name but had inherited so little of his grace and wit, are much more than a series of helpful suggestions intended for the use of any one particular young man; they are the painstaking crystallization of a life's philosophy. That philosophy is typical of the age that produced it. A quarter of a century later, in a world already tainted by the progress of religious enthusiasm and romantic unreason, Chesterfield would figure as the devil's advocate, the—

> Polished and high-finished foe to truth,
> Greybeard corrupter of our listening youth,[1]

and Johnson (who had a personal grudge against his memory) would declare that his letters instilled "the morals of a whore and the manners of a dancing master." The early Augustan Age, to its credit, had no such qualms. Safely latitudinarian and soundly classical, it judged of men and their problems by human standards, without immoderate optimism or wild foreboding. It possessed, moreover, a homogeneity, moral and intellectual, that has been achieved by very few other periods; and just as Pope, in his

---

[1] Cowper's *Progress of Error*.

pursuit of literary correctness, appealed to the whole body of educated and cultivated human beings, so Chesterfield invoked the consensus of "polite society." The only passport to its approval was the art of pleasing; but the application this art demanded was painfully strenuous.

For birth without elegance he had no regard. Indeed, in Chesterfield, there was something of the visionary and of the ascetic, haunted throughout his youth by dreams of continuous self-improvement, dominated in his maturity by the desire to instruct. A very old and very infirm man, he would still spend long hours with his godson at his knee, holding the little boy's head between his hands, and obliging him to look up into his eyes, or gently treading on the child's toes if his attention wandered. As a young man he had been an indefatigable student, "and I can assure you" (he told his son in 1751) "that what little figure I have made in the world, has been much more owing to that passionate desire I had of pleasing universally, than to any intrinsic merit or sound knowledge I might ever have been master of. . . . Without this passion for the object, I should never have been so attentive to the means; and I own I cannot conceive how it is possible for any man of good nature and good sense to be without this passion. Does not good nature incline us to please all those we converse with, of whatever rank and station they may be? And does not common sense and common observation show of what infinite use it is to please? Oh! but one may please by the good qualities of the heart, and the knowledge of the head, without that fashionable air, address, and manner, which is mere tinsel. I deny it. A man may be esteemed and respected. But I defy him to please without them. Moreover, at your age, I could not have contented myself with barely pleasing; I wanted to shine and distinguish myself in the world as a man of fashion and gallantry, as well as business. And that ambition or vanity . . . was a right one; it hurt nobody, and made me exert whatever talents I had. It is the spring of a thousand right and good things."

Essentially aristocratic in all his prejudices, Chesterfield, nevertheless, envisages his perfect Augustan courtier as, in certain respects, a "self-made man," self-moulded from the raw material of human nature. He has obligations to fulfil, and they are numerous—not to his superiors (though he owes them worldly respect) —not to his inferiors (though he is kind and tolerant to persons beneath him)—not to God (though he may profess a gentlemanly Deism)—but to the men and women with whom he exists on terms of equality. Here are his friends, and here his tribunal. It is for his friends' benefit that he should cultivate the Graces, till those goddesses (a rather formidable and, indeed, almost witch-like trio as Chesterfield describes them) have a share in every transaction of his daily existence. Chesterfield's hero does not seek to remodel society (a preoccupation of which the Augustan Age was entirely innocent) nor does he seek to distort his nature by suppressing the natural human appetites: his duty is to arrive at that perfect compromise between duty and interest, between "awkward, disagreeable merit" on the one hand and vulgar debauchery upon the other, which will entitle him to the consideration of his fellow-men.

Chesterfield had an almost mystical faith in the virtues of high life; at the touch of the true *homme du monde* (he liked to believe) ordinary vices lost their degrading and weakening properties, since the man of the world always pursued them with moderation. It would ease his mind (he remarked to Philip Stanhope) if he were convinced that "your pleasures, whatever they may be, will be confined within the circle of good company and people of fashion. . . . I confess, the pleasures of high life are not always strictly philosophical, and I believe a stoic would blame my indulgence; but I am yet no stoic, though turned of five-and-fifty.

. . . The pleasures of the table among people of the first fashion may indeed sometimes, by accident, run into excesses; but they will never sink into a continual course of gluttony and drunkenness. The gallantry of high life, though not strictly justifiable, carries, at least, no external marks of infamy about it. Neither the heart nor the constitution is corrupted by it . . . manners, possibly, improved. Play, in good company, is only play, and not gaming, not deep, and consequently not dangerous, nor dishonourable. It is only the inter-acts of other amusements."

Yet a certain weariness is inherent in the search for perfection. "We must take most things as they are" (concludes Chesterfield at the end of a long and particularly improving letter); "we cannot make them what we would, nor often what they should be"; and a vein of stubborn eccentricity runs through human nature that even the wisest and blandest of mentors cannot wholly surmount. Philip Stanhope, the "dear friend" and "dear child" of his father's interminable yet fascinating correspondence, was to grow up, not as the *"galant homme,"* the *"homme de la cour,* a man of business and pleasure; *estimé des hommes, recherché des femmes, aimé de tout le monde,"* but as an unpolished, if good-natured and industrious, booby. Chesterfield did not flinch when he discovered his failure, nor did he descend to recriminations when he learned of Philip's unworthy and secret marriage—his letters to Mrs. Eugenia Stanhope are models of courtesy and delicate kindliness. So thoroughly had his own philosophy taken possession of him. His last recorded words, uttered with the supreme effort of a dying man: "Give Dayrolles a chair," are in tune with everything that we know of his life and conduct, for his remarkable consistency was not the least of Chesterfield's virtues. He remained faithful to the plan he had originally set himself. We may object that this plan was an extremely limited one—that it excluded many of the nobler human impulses and left out of account many of the deeper human experiences—but, granted its limitations, it is extremely complete, and as logical in its design as a Palladian villa, with Chesterfield playing the part of a modern Vitruvius, emulating Kent and Burlington in the sphere of morals. A classical structure may look odd in an English landscape; cold winds may whistle down those shining corridors; but it is much to be preferred to the Gothic extravagances of Walpole and Beckford.

Chesterfield's structure is a dwelling house; it is not a folly. And though he existed partly in the world of the imagination—in an atmosphere of impossible perfection and ideal consistency—he was also a practical man and had a solid foothold in the contemporary universe. It is interesting to compare his letters with those of his friends. The society in which Chesterfield had been brought up, whose standards he made it his business to clarify and enlarge upon, were shared by the circle that centred in Mrs. Howard and included Pope and Swift in its literary circumference. Selections from the letters they exchanged have already been published; and though the two volumes of the *Suffolk Correspondence*—Mrs. Howard had become Countess of Suffolk on the death of her unruly husband's brother in 1731—do not make always very brilliant reading, they are a valuable addition to our knowledge of the social background. Extremely distinctive are the conventions and tastes they embody. Something of the bohemianism of Leicester House and Hampton Court, cultivated at a time when the Prince and Princess and their attendants had existed precariously under the ban of royal displeasure, is reflected by the slang and nicknames and "coterie-speech" that Lady Suffolk, Lady Hervey and Mary Bellenden—Mrs. Campbell since her romantic and unpopular marriage—continued to employ in their middle years. The affectation is one of simplicity, ease and liveliness—the height of good taste is to combine the inimitable arts of pleasing (*"le ton de la parfaitement bonne compagnie . . . et le je ne sçais quoi qui plaît"*) with a touch of philosophic indifference to the affairs of the world. Mrs. Howard was a model of worldly conduct; and the "sensible soft melancholy" Pope had praised—based upon a recognition that "we must take most things as they are" and can seldom twist circumstances the way we would have them—provided the mellow background that set off her qualities to the greatest advantage. From the lofty golden drawing room of Marble Hill, built out of the profits of her former servitude, she could look back across a life of forbearance and compromise, traversed with hardly a false step and never a solecism. Like Chesterfield, she had endured reverses, but they had failed to sour her. It was her strength not to ask more of the world than the world could give.

Thus she was pensive yet cheerful, philosophic yet worldly. And it is to be remarked that the peculiar combination of qualities most admired in the society Mrs. Howard knew is also reflected in the physiognomy and dress of the period, as they are illustrated by the series of contemporary portraits. Long-waisted and long-necked, with their regular oval features, large eyes and lofty egg-shaped foreheads, these willowy personages are hardly recognizable as the parents and grandparents of men and women who would one day pose for Reynolds, Romney and the later Gainsborough, or as the descendants of a generation that had sat to Lely. Simplicity and formality combine in their attitude; just as, in women's fashions, voluminous hooped skirts, dipping and undulating over the ground, go with bodices so plain as to be almost milk-maidish, unrelieved by lace or kerchief or jewelled gewgaws. Thus Mrs. Howard is depicted against a rustic landscape, half-reclining, her hair unbraided, her bosom bare, one finger lifted thoughtfully towards her cheek, and Miss Lepel lightly handling a chaplet of flowers, gathered, no doubt, in the sophisticated wilderness of Kew or Kensington. Even Hervey, languid and easy as he faces the portrait-painter, has a look of candour, almost of innocence, that belies his temperament.

To this society William Kent was builder and decorator, the

most indefatigable of artists and the most ingenious of journey-men, whose style "predominated authoritatively" during his life-time. Pope's "bold associate" and Burlington's protégé, Kent had a fluency and versatility that enabled him to combine the develop-ment of "modern" gardening, where the romantic and the irregu-lar were the height of taste, with the revival of classical ornament in English architecture. It would be rash to assert that nothing he touched he did not beautify—for as the manufacturer of gigantic frescoes he was often weak and as a portrait-painter definitely untalented—but considering the vast number of commissions he handled, from the Horse Guards to Holkham and Devonshire House, from the design of river-craft to the embellishment of royal weddings, the level of execution that he maintained was ex-tremely high. "He was not only consulted for furniture" (writes Horace Walpole) "as frames of pictures, glasses, tables, chairs, etc., but for plate, for a barge, for a cradle. And so impetuous was fashion that two great ladies prevailed on him to make designs for their birthday gowns. The one he dressed in a petticoat decorated with columns of the five orders; the other like a bronze, in a copper-coloured satin with ornaments of gold." Kent's furniture was characteristic of his imagination, and also characteristic of the general tendency of the period he lived in. While a romantic gar-den might lap the steps of a Palladian portico or a carefully culti-vated wilderness surround a Grecian garden-temple, behind that portico he allowed his fantasy again to stretch its wings. For rooms of sumptuous classic splendour, constructed on correct Vitruvian principles, he planned chairs, mirrors and side-tables of a rococo oddity, rich and heavy and complicated as the heart could desire. The sphinx was a *motif* he particularly favoured; and, encour-aged by Kent, it littered in house and garden, established itself at the end of grassy avenues, or perched itself amid the foliage of gilded consoles. Were we to seek an emblem of the age of Caro-line, with its brutality, its freakish delicacy, its romantic classicism, we might find it in Kent's version of the Theban monster, cruel and placid, magnificently ornamented yet clumsy and vigorous. Around the slender throat there is a heavy collar; beneath its swelling youthful breasts are spread the massive claws.

Chapter Five

1

*I*T WAS not until 1733 that Sir Robert Walpole, who had masterfully bestridden the government for several years, holding the reins of policy in his easy yet decisive clutch, was taken by surprise and almost unseated. The cause was both unexpected and unreasonable. In many respects Walpole's methods were hard to defend, but his management of the country's finances was always adroit, and that ingenuity very nearly proved his undoing. For some while, the landed interest had complained that they were expected to carry more than their fair share of the national taxation; and Sir Robert (anxious to please a section of the community that included a great many inveterate Tories) devised a scheme by which it would be possible to reduce the land-tax from four shillings to one shilling in the pound, without increasing the weight of taxation elsewhere.

This was to be done by substituting inland duties for the duties on tobacco and wine then payable at the time of importation—in other words, by transforming the Customs (which were notoriously inefficient and expensive) into Excises. Sir Robert himself had no doubt of the project's success. Indeed he appears to have looked forward to a considerable increase of his popularity. But the Opposition saw their chance and immediately snatched at it; by talk, by the publication of articles and by the distribution of pamphlets all over the country, the scope of the scheme was so distorted and magnified that it came to be regarded as a *general*

Excise, which would entail the ruin of trade and the extinction of personal liberty. Comparatively slow to indignation, the British public is apt to prove proportionately unreasonable once its indignation has been aroused. A blaze of fury swept through the entire realm. All the necessities of life (it was believed) were to be subjected to the most oppressive and merciless taxation; the liberties decreed by Magna Carta were at an end; the power of the Crown was to be made absolute; a horde of tyrannous Excise officers would soon be hammering at every Englishman's front door.

So widespread was the effect of this propaganda that, long before the scheme had assumed definite shape, it had already become a popular bogy, and from every part of England and from the city itself memorials had been sent to members of Parliament, begging or insisting that they should oppose "all new Excises and all extensions of Excise laws" however and under whatever shape they might be presented. But Walpole, relying perhaps too much on the efficacy of sober common sense, or too confident of his ability to present his case, declined to give way without a trial. Parliament met during the middle of January, but the scheme was not immediately brought forward; and it was left to the Opposition to open the battle. This they did when a group of Walpole's opponents in the House of Lords, the Duke of Argyll, Lord Chesterfield and a number of their friends, decided to try conclusions with the Queen herself, and Lord Stair, a veteran of Marlborough's campaigns and formerly successful Ambassador to the Court of France, was deputed to ask Caroline to grant him an interview. Their meeting was long and exceedingly stormy. Caroline listened, patient but unconvinced, while Lord Stair railed against the Minister, declared that he was universally despised and detested, assured her that the Excise scheme was contrary to the fundamental principles of British freedom; but when he presumed to speak of his conscience, she cut him short:

"*Ah, my Lord*" (she exclaimed in her positive fashion), "*ne me parlez point de conscience; vous me faites évanouir."* Lord Stair was "extremely shocked and nettled"; and Caroline, carrying the war into her opponent's camp, proceeded to give him her opinion of Carteret and Bolingbroke, from whom (she said) she supposed that he got his politics and "whom you may tell, if you think fit, *that I have long known to be two as worthless men of parts as any in this country, and whom I have not only been often told are two of the greatest liars and knaves in any country, but whom my own observation and experience have found so."* The ex-Ambassador realized that his cause was hopeless, but he did not withdraw till he had worked himself up into a violent passion and come as near to insulting his interlocutress as a subject dared. Ejaculating, *"Madame, vous êtes trompée, et le Roi est trahi,"* he hastened unceremoniously out of the presence chamber.

Among the Opposition, there was much praise of the frank and forthright manner in which Lord Stair had elected to speak to the Queen for her own good; and, in the House of Lords, Carteret discovered a means of making an oblique comparison between Walpole and Mazarin on the one hand, and Caroline and Anne of Austria upon the other. Hervey and the Queen laughed over this comparison; and Hervey, who had mastered the art of seeming attractively bold without ever becoming obviously impertinent, ventured to interpolate a couplet of Racine as more applicable to her Majesty's situation:

> *Derrière une voile, invisible et présente,*
> *Je fus de ce grand corps l'âme toute puissante.*

The Queen was not at all displeased with the compliment, adding "as you often tell me of my pride, I will now confess to you an instance of it, and to carry on the parallel you have drawn between me and Agrippina, will own to you that I very often feel myself, in conference *avec ces impertinents—*

> *Fille, femme, et mère de vos maîtres."*

At last, the day arrived when Sir Robert, finding it impossible to postpone the trial any longer, had determined to bring the Excise scheme before Parliament. The time was mid-March, but opinion was still as excited as during January, and the country still reverberated with the popular battle-cry of *No slavery—no Excise—no wooden shoes!* On the day itself London was full of alarming rumours. It was expected that a vast mob would besiege the House, and besides the provision of justices, constables and civil magistrates, who were instructed to attend for the purposes of keeping the peace, secret orders were given to Foot and Horse Guards to hold themselves in readiness. The mob, however, though considerable in size, was neither quite so large nor so disorderly as had been anticipated. Members, with some shoving, were able to make their way through the crowd; and when they emerged, the government on a first reading having obtained a majority of sixty-one votes, they got to their carriages without much difficulty. But, now and then, when a supporter of Walpole was sighted, there would be a hiss from the ranks of angry citizens, and a loud, hostile whisper of *"That's one of them!"*

Hervey's duties for the evening were not yet done. He drove to St. James's Palace, where the King drew him into the Queen's Bedchamber and kept him answering questions till three o'clock in the morning. This was his function during all the debates on the measure that followed. No sooner had he discharged his obligations in the House of Commons and extricated himself from a crowd that grew every day more riotous in Palace Yard, than he must report on the position of affairs to the King and Queen, satisfying George Augustus not only as to how So-and-so had voted but what his general behaviour had been and how he had looked. Such was the trust the King now placed in Sir Robert Walpole that he had begun to regard the passing of the Excise Bill as a matter that affected his personal honour; and day by day the violence of his feelings increased and his bitterness towards any malcontent who dared oppose it. Not for the first time had he come into collision with his subjects' obstinacy, and he quivered with resentment at the intolerable restrictions his rank imposed.

Yet the prospects of the Bill's passing steadily diminished. Every night Lord Hervey, received in private audience, had to report a smaller minority, further defections from the ranks of Walpole's supporters, scenes of greater disorder around the House. When Hervey (curious to see to just what extent the King's real opinion of his Minister had changed since the beginning of the reign) repeated some of the attacks that had been made upon him and described Sir Robert's retaliation, the King, flushing furiously and swearing volubly, often with tears in his eyes as he spoke, would declare that Walpole was a brave fellow, that he had more spirit than any man he ever knew. Caroline, who was primarily responsible for her husband's *volte-face,* seconded him in applauding their intrepid adjutant, and Hervey, in duty bound, completed the chorus.

Nor did the King exaggerate Sir Robert's courage. For three weeks, exposed to the attacks of adversaries as gifted and unscrupulous as Pulteney and Carteret, as respected and influential as Sir William Wyndham, he continued not only to hold his own but to ripost with all the bravado of an experienced fencer. Outside, the situation was even more disturbing. There were moments when the flimsy ancient parliament buildings, slightly and insecurely guarded, resembled a vessel adrift on a stormy sea. Roars of indignation shook the windows of the Chamber. It was often doubtful whether the Minister and his friends could escape from the House without physical injury; and when news came that the army was disaffected (for word had gone round that the price of tobacco was likely to rise) Walpole at last admitted that he must withdraw the scheme.

On April 9th he visited the King and Queen at St. James's Palace, acquainted them with his decision and at the same time offered his resignation. This (as he had probably anticipated) they refused to accept. Never had they felt so close in spirit to their valiant Minister; any memories of past grievances or early suspicion had completely disappeared during the excitement of the last few weeks; and both were highly indignant at the suggestion that they could think of deserting him. But, in the face of a possible upheaval, the Excise must go. It was agreed, nevertheless, that Walpole should hold on for some days longer—at least till the city was safely delivered of a monster petition against the Excise Bill which it intended to present the following day. Accompanied by a train of coaches, which stretched at one moment from Westminster to Temple Bar, and chaperoned by the Lord Mayor in full civic splendour, the petition arrived on April 10th; and that evening Walpole's majority fell to nineteen. Caroline's tears and her husband's profanity were uncontrollable; Hervey was worn out retelling his story and describing the treacherous conduct of separate members, while the King discovered an abusive epithet for each of them. The Opposition prepared to celebrate its return to power.

Of this evening George Augustus's nephew, Frederick the Great of Prussia, reports (in an anecdote that, although probably fictitious, throws much light both on the situation and on the persons involved) how, after the debate, Walpole was obliged to run the gauntlet of the Westminster mob disguised beneath the folds of an old red cloak, shouting "No tyranny! no Excise!"; how he at last struggled through the crowd to St. James's, and there found the King and Queen in a state of perturbation bordering on distraction, the King armed to the teeth, wearing the cockaded hat he had worn at Malplaquet and trying the edge of the sword he had carried at Oudenarde, demanding that he should be put at the head of his royal guards and allowed to march out and make an example of the mutineers.

Frederick's portrait of his uncle is certainly a likeness. On the other hand it was as little in Walpole's character to run risks, when to take them was entirely unprofitable, as it was to shirk danger when the situation demanded hardihood. Hervey made an energetic and efficient emissary; and, in fact, that night, far from venturing among the mob disguised as one of his own opponents—his face and figure were not easily travestied—Walpole assembled his most trusted subordinates at his house in Arlington Street and, after supper, when the servants had gone, rose to address them. *"This dance"* (he remarked), "it will no further go," speaking "with a sort of unpleased smile," the nearest he came to betraying his feelings. "And tomorrow I intend to sound a retreat. . . ." But though a withdrawal was inevitable, it need not be headlong; they must make it quite clear that they were still convinced of the project's value.

False shame had never been one of the Minister's weaknesses; and, next day, instead of the humbled and broken figure whom the Opposition had looked forward to hounding out of office, they encountered an adversary apparently little the worse for wear, who first treated them to a "long and artful speech," in which he handled his own defence with the greatest dexterity, then blandly proposed that further discussion of the Excise Bill should be postponed until the early summer months. No talk of defeat! None of resignation! Nor, when through their spokesman, Sir William Wyndham, they declared that this "wicked attack upon the liberties of British subjects . . . ought to be stigmatized with every mark of ignominy"—that it was not sufficient for the Bill to be dropped, it must be rejected—could they arouse much enthusiasm in the House of Commons; by some mysterious means Walpole had regained his ascendancy and come unaltered through the fiercest tempest of his whole career. The florid declamations of Sir William Wyndham sounded flat and empty: Walpole's fellow-members were perfectly content to let the matter slide.

But the disposition of the mob was less pacific. During the entire debate its voice had rolled and rumbled through the Chamber and, when the House had risen, Walpole's friends suggested that he would do well to make his escape by a back way. Walpole refused, with a quotation from Suetonius; and a phalanx of supporters was therefore marshalled, including Hervey and the Minister's eldest son, which set out on the difficult journey home. Forty constables struggled to keep order; oaken staffs cracked about the heads of friends and enemies alike; blows were given and received; and such was the confusion and the weight of the crowd that anyone who had fallen would have been trampled to death. Walpole escaped and returned to his house; but that evening he was burnt in effigy by the citizens of London. Beside him on the bonfire blazed a female figure, grotesquely fat, to represent his royal confederate.

Their association amid flame and smoke had a symbolic value. Far from weakening his position with the King and Queen, Walpole's troubles over the Excise Bill had strengthened his hold on them and increased their conviction that he was the mainstay of the House of Hanover. His late adversaries were not allowed to go unpunished; and Chesterfield, who since his return from the Hague had occupied the position of Lord Steward to the Household, was peremptorily deprived of his White Wand and dismissed the court. But the Bill had had an adversary whom Walpole could not touch. It was an open secret that the Prince of Wales had expressed himself very strongly against the measure and had taken some part in the confabulations of Walpole's enemies, with many of whom he was on terms of the closest friendship. That incorrigible young man was breaking loose. At home, he still existed in a condition of tutelage, dining every day with his brother and sisters, defraying his pleasures as best he could out of the small income allowed him by the King; but away from the home he had begun to cut a more considerable figure and choose his own friends, quite regardless of his parents' prejudices. In the family, he was merely "Fretz" or "the Griff"—to be scowled at or quarrelled with; in London, he was Prince Frederick Louis and his father's heir.

Up to a certain point the antagonism that existed between the Prince and the other members of his family is not difficult to understand; beyond that point its development becomes mysterious. The parents were neglectful; the son was undutiful. In Hanover Frederick had annoyed his tutors and run into a variety of escapades, but he had done nothing to deserve the reception he met with in London. Even so he had proved singularly reluctant to thrust himself forward, and it was not till several years after the inauspicious moment when a plain hackney coach had discharged him on the outskirts of St. James's, and he had climbed the Queen's back-stairs to greet his mother, that their relations grew so strained as to be politically threatening. Meanwhile, he had been stinted, ignored and snubbed. His allowance (as his favourites carefully explained to him) was exactly a quarter of what his father had once received, the balance returning straight to the King's pocket; and for this arrangement he was chiefly indebted to Sir Robert Walpole. It is not surprising that he should have acquired an intense distrust of his father's Minister, and learned to look upon the Opposition as his advisers and allies.

By them he was flattered, by them appealed to. Bolingbroke poured out for the young man's benefit all the treasures of his philosophy, all the resources of his experience and erudition, refined and etherealized during years of abstention from public life. Frederick's attitude to the old statesman was attentive and charming. Only a person of the most saintly courage or the most accomplished worldly wisdom could have borne his parents' neglect without some show of resentment; and Frederick was neither a saintly character nor a very sensible one. Intrigue attracted him for its own sake; a chance of adventure had always appealed to his hare-brained temperament; but whereas, at an earlier period, he might have ridden out with his father's armies on a crusade or, becoming involved in some wild dynastic conspiracy, have lost his eyes or his life in a royal dungeon, he was condemned by circumstances to a petty round of underground politics which inflamed his excitability and weakened his balance—the last a quality in which, as it happened, he had never been strong. At his best he had displayed a hot-headed and engaging frankness; the reverse side of that enthusiasm would soon appear.

During the interval his protean personality had flowed through many moulds but taken shape in none. To his mother, mature even as a young girl, and his father, still obstinately childish in advanced middle age, the Prince's character was naturally incomprehensible. There was no holding down—no making sense of—their ridiculous offspring. Now he was the man of pleasure running after women in suburbs and back streets—Caroline laughed and shrugged when she learned how poor "Fretz" had lost his watch and seals during a nocturnal adventure in St. James's Park. Now he was for playing the politician and one heard of him closeted with that villain Dodington or those arch-villains Bolingbroke, Pulteney and Carteret. Now he was pestering his father to select him a consort—his real motive, one imagined, was to get his allowance raised—or attempting to acquire a wife on his own initiative. This desire to marry had already had serious consequences. First there had been his intrigue with the Court of Prussia; more recently, some time before 1731, he had engaged in clandestine negotiations with the Dowager Duchess of Marlborough—old Sarah, "ever proud and ever malignant"—who had offered him her favourite granddaughter, Lady Diana Spencer, and a portion of a hundred thousand pounds. The day had been fixed for a private ceremony and the place agreed on—the Duchess's hunting lodge at Windsor—when Walpole's secret service had got wind of their plans and Walpole had quietly seen to it that the project miscarried. Frederick's second attempt at a romantic breakaway had ended in ridicule; the Prince himself was flung back into financial servitude.

In this embarrassing state his disposition did not improve. Where previously he had been thoughtless, he now became sly; and, where he had once appeared meddlesome and indiscreet, he now evinced an unusual aptitude for making mischief. He did not love his sisters and was at pains to exasperate them. Frederick's most endearing taste was a passion for music; in the earlier days of his reunion with his family, there had been little concerts with the Princess Royal at the harpsichord and Frederick sawing energetically at the bass viol. But presently music itself provided matter for discord. Because Princess Anne was the patroness of Handel and the King and Queen regularly attended his operas, the Prince of Wales posed as a champion of Buononcini. The dispute over the merits of German and Italian operas soon assumed a political complexion. To be a Handelist was to be known as an adherent of the court party; but the King and Queen at that moment were far from popular and Handel's audiences at the Haymarket proved extremely thin, though George and Caroline continued to honour him night after night and preside with dignity in an almost deserted auditorium. At the opera house in Lincoln's Inn Fields, on the other hand, the Prince of Wales and half the nobility had established their stronghold, whence Italian singers trilled defiance at German dullness and the notes of a famous *castrato* set the lustres trembling. The King and Queen were vexed and indignant; their daughter outraged; but as the generalissimo of "a faction of fiddlers" the Prince had won.[1]

Any elation, however, that he may have experienced was swallowed up in feelings of extreme annoyance when he discovered that the Princess Royal had stolen a march on him. The dynastic marriage she had always aspired to had at length materialized.

---

[1] Handel was consoled with a royal grant of £1000 a year.

Certainly it was less magnificent than she might have hoped, since the Prince of Orange was neither rich nor well established and was reputed to have the figure of a hunchback; but in the Princess's character was a vein of iron and she calmly set aside every attempt to postpone the sacrifice—she had determined to make a marriage, and married she would be. While she waited Anne amused herself at the keys of her harpsichord, unsmiling but unruffled, among her favourite opera-singers.

In fact the period of the Princess Royal's engagement (during which Anne behaved always with complete insensibility or the most consummate sang-froid) was prolonged over a period of several months; for no sooner had the Prince arrived in England and satisfied gossips that, although he suffered from an unsightly curvature of the spine, his face was intelligent, good-humoured and distinguished, than he fell seriously ill and came near to dying. The royal family did not visit him during his illness, for the King considered that his dignity would not permit him to wait upon a Prince of inferior rank and, without the King's example, no one else could take the initiative. By March 1734, he had sufficiently recovered to attend his wedding. In a suit heavily embroidered with gold and silver thread, wearing a long perruque that flowed down to conceal his crookedness, he gave his hand to an equally resplendent bride, stiffly fenced about with petticoats of silver tissue, against a background of fringes, tassels and gilded sconces, which William Kent had designed at the Queen's command. A supper party was followed by the public presentation to the whole court of the married couple sitting up in bed. Caroline had wept during the ceremony; but, when the Prince of Orange entered the apartment wearing his nightcap and a dressing-gown of brocaded stuff, looking "behind as if he had no head, and before as if he had no neck and no legs," she had been afraid (she told Lord Hervey next morning) that her self-control was deserting her and she would swoon away. *"Dites-moi, My Lord Hervey"* (she demanded), *"avez-vous bien remarqué et considéré ce monstre en ce moment? Et n'aviez-vous pas bien pitié de la pauvre Anne? Bon Dieu! c'est trop sotte en moi, mais j'en pleure encore!"*

To this Hervey, whose experience had been just the reverse and whose wife's beauty had long ago ceased to move him, replied judiciously that "in half a year all persons are alike; the figure of the body one's married to, like the prospect of the place one lives at, grows so familiar to one's eyes, that one looks at it mechanically, without regarding either the beauties or deformities that strike a stranger." Nor was the Princess particularly deserving of her mother's sympathy and, if her husband repelled her, she did not show it—so intense was her absorption in her future prospects and so single-minded her devotion to the idea of sovereignty. From her father she had inherited pride, from her mother fortitude. She did not expect to be happy; it was enough to be regal.

2

IF ANNE had achieved her independence, then why not Frederick? And soon after the Princess's departure for Holland, the Prince of Wales, on the advice of his favourite George Bubb Dodington, approached the King and laid before him a modest petition. Firstly, he asked that he might be allowed to go abroad and join the army of the Emperor, then engaged with the French forces in the Rhineland. Secondly, he begged his father to increase his allowance, explaining that his creditors had begun to press him. Thirdly, he reverted to the subject of marriage and requested that he might be properly provided for as soon as possible. To none of these suggestions did the King agree; and, though he hinted that if his son were to improve in his conduct towards his mother he might perhaps assist him to pay his debts, he showed no immediate signs of becoming more generous. Grievances based on a lack of money increase by compound interest. As the Prince's position deteriorated, his temper grew worse; he soon fretted at the restraining influence of his former favourite. With the suddenness that was characteristic of all his movements, and the touch of spitefulness that had begun to appear in his character, he turned against Bubb Dodington and broke off their intimacy.

Poor Dodington's life as Frederick's adviser had not been a happy one. A somewhat parsimonious millionaire, he had had the annoying experience of lending his patron money and then learning that the Prince, in his flippant undignified style, had boasted to his circle that, though Dodington was supposed to be a clever man, he, the Prince, had just "nicked" him of several thousand pounds! A corpulent and ceremonious personage, he was sometimes the victim of extremely obstreperous horse-play; there had been an occasion when the Prince and his friends had rolled him in a blanket and had bumped the unfortunate Grand Vizier down a flight of stairs. But the manner of his dismissal was excessively galling. Frederick had taken Carlton House (presumably for purposes of entertainment, since his regular residence was at St. James's) next to Dodington's mansion in Pall Mall. He had given his favourite the key of a small door in the party wall that separated their gardens. This door was now ostentatiously bricked up; trees were planted to serve as an additional screen; the creditor-favourite was ignored in public by the debtor-patron. Dodington had little talent for arousing loyalty, and the story of his humiliation was extremely popular.

While gossips commented acidly on the fall of Dodington, another favourite, in a very different *milieu,* also experienced the revolutions of royal caprice. But here the fall from favour had been long anticipated and the favourite retired, not only without the slightest display of reluctance, but even with a certain suggestion of relief and alacrity. Lady Suffolk was heartily sick of the posts she occupied. It was true that, since her husband's elevation

to the peerage, she had rid herself of some of her more onerous
duties by exchanging her appointment as Woman of the Bedchamber for that of Mistress of the Robes; but the Queen's attitude had grown no gentler with familiarity and the King's attentions no more agreeable with the passage of years. The wife
was still jealous, the husband tyrannous. Yet it was always Caroline who kept the King and his mistress together; and George
Augustus had frequently been heard to grumble that he could not
conceive why the Queen prevented his dispensing with the services of this old, dull, deaf, peevish woman for whom he had ceased
to feel any trace of liking! . . .

What the relationship so evidently lacked in romance it had
once made up in regularity and decorum; but, during the summer of 1734, there were hints of strife, and Lord Hervey's mother,
who occupied a bedroom at Richmond adjoining Lady Suffolk's,
spoke of colloquies she overheard in the morning hours—Lady
Suffolk talking earnestly and at length in low hushed tones, the
King interrupting her with the repeated exclamation: "That is
none of your business, madam; you have nothing to do with
that." Constantly snubbed and, as time went on, more and more
neglected, Lady Suffolk behaved with her usual *savoir-vivre*. The
world had taught her much and could give her little. All that she
now aspired to was the quiet of Marble Hill, her friends, her
books, her correspondence—the visits of Pope and Arbuthnot and
the letters of Swift. The house she had built was in the highest
traditions of Augustan correctitude. Outwardly plain, its white
façade looking down a gentle tree-bordered slope towards the
silvery stretches of the river, indoors it displayed a sober magnificence; a wide painted staircase swept up from the spacious
entrance-hall to reception rooms and the mistress's bedchamber on
the first floor, lofty apartments frescoed in gold and brown, with
vast windows, marble chimney-pieces and carved overmantels.
Even today their splendour has scarcely been tarnished; they are

rooms that combine an air of ceremony with an impression of intimacy—planned for leisurely conversation and long-drawn visits, for comfort and candle-light, knotting and the arts of the embroidery frame, for a life neither vegetable nor particularly vivid but irradiated by the mild glow of sense and sentiment.

Of all the afflictions Lady Suffolk had experienced, the worst was boredom. Left to her own devices, Caroline might have established a court as entertaining as it was intellectually distinguished; but since the King hated books, distrusted writers and was naturally suspicious of clever men, and the Queen never contradicted or opposed her husband, its atmosphere as the years went on grew more and more dismal. Every evening the same monotonous scenes were repeated. A sly visitant from the realms of fashion, gaiety and dissipation, Hervey wound his way through the royal underworld, dropping a glance here and a whisper there, producing his best stories to amuse the Queen, his latest political news for the King's benefit, throwing his lightest and subtlest snares round the Princess Caroline. But even Hervey could not dissipate the prevailing ennui; and in a letter to Lady Sundon (written during 1733) he describes the unrelieved tedium of existence at Hampton Court, where "no mill-horse ever went in a more constant track, or a more unchanging circle." Walking, audiences and levees filled the morning. At night the King played at commerce and backgammon, and the Queen at quadrille, poor Lady Charlotte de Roucy at the quadrille table running "her usual nightly gauntlet—the Queen pulling her hood, Mr. Schütz sputtering in her face, and the Princess Royal rapping her knuckles all the time. . . . The Duke of Grafton takes his nightly opiate of lottery, and sleeps as usual between the Princesses Amelia and Caroline; Lord Grantham strolls from one room to another (as Dryden says) *like some discontented ghost that oft appears, and is forbid to speak,* and stirs himself about, as people stir a fire, not with any design, but in hopes to make it burn brisker, which his lordship constantly does, to no purpose, and yet tries as constantly as if he had ever once succeeded. At last the King comes up, the pool finishes, and everybody has their dismission. . . ."

Lady Suffolk's life for more than two decades had been of this texture—with the added drawback that her privacy was not her own. Now, deaf and tired and growing elderly, she determined to escape from a servitude that could bring her no further material advantage but of which the humiliations were increasing day by day. At the end of October 1734, she begged the Queen to grant her leave of absence. Six weeks later, when she returned from Bath, the King made it clear that she had been discarded; there were no further visits punctually at nine o'clock; happening to meet her at the ceremony of the Queen's dressing, he merely accorded her a few brief and indifferent words. But the Queen must still be persuaded to dispense with her rival; and this Caroline was exceedingly loath to do, for, though she disliked Lady Suffolk, she found her useful and, though jealous, she was constantly reassured by the decline of her beauty. A stiff battle was fought at their farewell interview.[1] To Lady Suffolk's attempts to tender her resignation the Queen merely replied with baffling blandness. Lady Suffolk, she insisted, was being romantic. What reason had she to imagine that the King was displeased? Perhaps she had been reading too many novels? She suggested that she should postpone her decision till she had thought it over, implying that she would certainly reconsider it. But Lady Suffolk, with the utmost deference, declined to give way. She retired first to her brother's house, then to the country; and the King himself did nothing to prevent her going.

Caroline's temper had been ruffled by the affairs of her house-

---

[1] Two accounts of this conversation have been preserved: one given to Lord Hervey by the Queen some time after the event: the other in a curious memorandum (possibly made by Lady Suffolk herself) now in the Manuscript Room of the British Museum.

hold—except from her husband she was not accustomed to contradiction—and violently excited by the catastrophe of Sir Robert's Excise Bill; but at the same time she was taking a passionate interest in foreign politics. Here, on the whole, her influence was a definitely disturbing one. Reasonable enough in domestic questions, if somewhat prone to fly out during her conferences with the Minister into tirades against "your fine English liberty," in problems of foreign policy she was harder to manage. For once she was with the King and against Walpole. As Elector of Hanover, George Augustus owed allegiance to the Holy Roman Emperor; and since 1733 the Emperor's position, attacked by a coalition consisting of France, Spain, and Sardinia, had been growing steadily more and more precarious. Was Hanover to come first, or should England prevail? The King and Queen wished to sink England in Hanover; their loyalty and their dynastic pride were both involved; while the King, whose devotion to all things military was perhaps the strongest feeling of his entire existence, received with delight the Emperor's tactful suggestion that he should take command of the Imperial army on the Rhine.

Walpole was subjected to a double fire. Not only did several members of his government, including his chief supporter, the blundering and pompous Duke of Newcastle, favour armed intervention and a break with France, but the royal couple now constituted a separate war party. Caroline was no longer his secret confederate. Openly and vehemently, she championed the Emperor; for "wherever the interest of Germany and the honour of the Empire were concerned, her thoughts and reasonings" (noted Hervey) "were often as German and Imperial as if England had been out of the question; and there were few inconveniences and dangers to which she would not have exposed this country rather than give occasion to its being said that the Empire suffered affronts unretorted . . . whilst she, a German by birth, sat upon this throne an idle spectatress, able to assist and not willing to interfere." The King's emotions, though equally strong, were less disinterested. Such an opportunity might never occur again. It infuriated him to think of his fellow-princes shining against the glorious background of camp and battlefield while he himself rusted at home among politicians. Even his hateful brother-in-law, the King of Prussia, had flown to arms. . . . And whenever Walpole entered his Cabinet with twenty different matters of business to discuss and decide upon, George Augustus would treat him to a long harangue always centred in the theme of his military grievances. After an hour or so the Minister would take his leave, his questions unanswered and his business unsettled.

Yet, little by little, he achieved his object. Realizing that he could not hope for the Queen's support and that his own colleagues in the government would be of small assistance, Walpole shouldered the entire burden of negotiations. An emergency always showed him at his strongest and cleverest. "Step by step," he remarked, "I can carry the King and Queen perhaps the road I wish, but if I ever show them at a distance to what end that road leads, they stop short." Every dispatch, incoming or outgoing, was read by him personally. Through an extensive correspondence, carried on with his brother and emissary, the elder Horace Walpole, and other agents at the various courts of Europe, he secured an exact knowledge of what was occurring behind the scenes—knowledge that he employed piecemeal as suited his purpose. It was clear that the outcome of hostilities must depend upon the intervention or non-intervention of the two great maritime powers, England and Holland; and by exerting differing degrees of pressure in different quarters, taking care that the prospect of Dutch and English intervention should not raise Austrian hopes, or the certainty of non-intervention heighten the intransigence of the French attitude, finally by raising difficulties between Madrid and Paris, he was able at last to persuade the belligerents to consent to terms.[1] Fifty thousand men, he told the Queen, had been killed in Europe—not one Englishman had died on a foreign battlefield. Here was the justification of twelve months' incessant manœuvring. Caroline's comments or congratulations are not recorded.

At any rate she bore Walpole no personal grudge. Nor did she take it amiss that Hervey, in the capacity of Walpole's aide-de-camp, should have addressed her an extremely lengthy memorandum which he slipped into her hand as she rose from cards, criticizing the Emperor and supporting peace. Never had he stood so high in his mistress's favour. She had persuaded the King to increase his salary by a thousand pounds; and each morning, as soon as her husband had left her, she sent for Hervey and kept him talking to her over the breakfast-table. She gave him a hunter which, on royal hunting parties, when the rest of the court was scattered across the landscape, he never failed to ride at the door of her chaise. About their friendship there was, indeed, something almost tender. Caroline called him her "child," her "pupil," her "charge," told him that he dared to be so impertinent only because he knew very well that she could not live without him, and once observed that it was just as well she was so old, or she would undoubtedly be "talked of for this creature."

Hervey "really loved and admired" the Queen. It was not that his point of view was in the least uncritical; but, as fresh springs bubble up from the depths of the sea, so disinterested, generous, even kindly impulses mingled with the general bitterness of his composition and helped to temper the extreme cynicism of his private policy. He loved her courage, her humour, her common sense. He respected, though he often deplored and ridiculed, the strength of mind with which she bent her will to the King's caprices, submitted her intelligence to his stupidity, but from sub-

---

[1] Articles of peace were finally signed, after several diplomatic hitches, in October 1735.

mission managed to extract her greatest triumphs. Caroline was fourteen years older than Hervey; her growing corpulence made her physically unprepossessing. Yet between a man and a woman the issue is rarely a simple one; and some element which, if it could not be called attraction, bordered on the feelings of an *amitié amoureuse*—that blessed half-way state between love and friendship—added warmth to the association of these extraordinary beings, both proud, both unscrupulous and both determined. They were alike, yet very different in character and upbringing. In one another, they found a temporary refuge from vexation and ennui.

By the Prince of Wales their connexion was fiercely resented. With some reason he regarded Hervey as his worst enemy, and he was deeply chagrined to see the man who had insulted and vilified him now installed as his mother's most intimate friend. He declined as Hervey rose in the Queen's favour. Had anything been needed to convince Frederick that he was the victim of a diabolical domestic conspiracy, Hervey's growing influence would have removed his doubts. As far as Hervey was concerned his suspicions were justified. There is no question but that he did his best to harass Frederick and encouraged the Queen in her dislike of her elder son, while he sympathized with the frequent complaints of the Prince's sisters. Obliged to listen to stories of the young man's misconduct—and with scrapes, squabbles and debts upon the one hand and suspect political acquaintances upon the other, the supply of damaging anecdotes was always copious—he could usually cap them by producing stories of his own collection. Frederick knew that the Vice-Chamberlain was a dangerous antagonist. What he did not know was that, since the summer of 1734, Hervey had picked up the threads of an old *liaison* and that for several months Miss Vane had been visiting him secretly, or receiving his visits at her house in Grosvenor Street. Hervey's motives may have been more complicated than is at first apparent; at any rate, they were scarcely those of the ordinary amorist.

There are diplomatic love affairs as there are dynastic marriages. And from our knowledge of Hervey's personal temperament, and from various slight hints that he drops in his *Memoirs,* it seems improbable that he was the victim of a thoughtless passion. It delighted him to hoodwink and cuckold Frederick; he was gratified to reassert his former supremacy over a woman who had once ventured to cast him off; and Miss Vane was still a valuable secret agent. Yet the intrigue had also its romantic side. Miss Vane, leaving her chair and footmen at St. James's, would slip through the Park and join Hervey at "an out of the way scrub coffee-house, little frequented, behind Buckingham House." Later he used to visit her in Grosvenor Street. Her household, except for one old man and a maid-servant, had gone to a villa the Prince had taken for her at Wimbledon, and when Hervey arrived, on foot and cloaked to the eyes, Miss Vane would open the door herself. Lady Hervey, at the time, was abroad with friends; and as the difficulty of procuring tea, fruit and supper made the deserted house in Grosvenor Street a somewhat inhospitable place of assignation, they presently transferred their meetings to St. James's Palace, where they spent the night in the Vice-Chamberlain's private apartments. It was a hazardous, very nearly a disastrous, move. For one night Miss Vane fell violently ill, writhed in agonies of "cholic" on her lover's bed and appeared to be hovering every moment between life and death. Hervey confronted a prospect of certain ruin. Call his servant or seek assistance obviously he dare not. On the other hand, supposing Miss Vane should die and the dead body of the Prince's mistress be found in his bedroom, not even the Queen's protection could avert disaster. Then he would perish in the trap he had laid for Frederick. . . . Distraught and terrified, he flung himself on the helpless young woman and dosed her liberally with cordials and gold powder—in spite of which her symptoms grew worse and she swooned away. After a time, however, she regained consciousness; and

Hervey, who had almost abandoned hope, by dint of more gold powder and more cordials, and with the help of hot napkins applied to her stomach, was able to get her up and into her clothes. Finally, since it would have been imprudent to call a carriage, he managed to support her to the street outside, and in Pall Mall was lucky enough to find a sedan-chair.

Yet their meetings were not entirely discontinued, and Hervey's reward came during 1735, when Frederick decided at length to pay off his mistress. In this decision he was influenced partly by the vague promises he had received from his father and mother that a marriage would be arranged for him very soon, partly by the development of a new friendship. Lady Archibald Hamilton (on whom the Prince's prominent pale-blue eye had rested more and more attentively for several months) was the mother of ten children and neither young nor fascinating, but clever, sympathetic and an adroit diplomatist. Her husband was as good-natured as he was unsuspicious. Frederick became a frequent visitor at the Hamiltons' house, walked and talked with Lady Archibald hours on end, while at Drawing Rooms he whispered to her so assiduously that "his nose and her ear were inseparable." To please his *confidante,* and also clear the way for his approaching marriage, Frederick instructed Lord Baltimore, one of his Lords of the Bedchamber, to approach Miss Vane with the suggestion that she should go abroad for two or three years. Her allowance, he promised, should be continued; and the education of her son, little Fitzfrederick, would be provided for in England. Unfortunately, he was so tactless as to include a threat. The allowance (Lord Baltimore was told to insinuate) would only be paid if Miss Vane consented to the Prince's conditions; otherwise it would immediately come to an end. Miss Vane was "extremely shocked" and summoned Lord Hervey; and Hervey, "not a little pleased," took up pen and paper.

The letter he drafted was a minor masterpiece of dissimulation.

Written in a style that owed something to current romances, it dwelt in pathetic terms on the brutal harshness of the Prince's behaviour to a woman who had deserved only good of him, and proceeded to enumerate the sacrifices she had already made:

"Your Royal Highness need not be put in mind who I am, nor from whence you took me. . . . That I have long lost your heart I have long seen and long mourned: to gain it, or rather to reward the gift you made me of it, I sacrificed my time, my youth, my character, the world, my family, and everything that a woman can sacrifice to the man she loves. . . . I have resigned everything for your sake but my life; and, had you loved me still, I would have risked even that too to please you; but as it is, I cannot think in my state of health of going out of England, far from all friends and all physicians I can trust. . . . My child is the only consolation I have left. I cannot leave him nor shall anything but death ever make me quit the country he is in." Concluding with a salvo of good wishes for Frederick's "health, prosperity, and happiness," and signing himself (on his mistress's behalf) "with unalterable affection," Hervey handed this production to Miss Vane and insisted that she should copy it out before she left the room. The effect on the Prince of Wales was all that he had hoped for. Frederick flew into a violent rage as soon as he received it; but, although he realized that both the style and the sentiments did rather more than justice to Miss Vane's capacity, he had no means of detecting the writer or exposing the fraud. Miss Vane's partisans were highly indignant, and the shocking brutality of his message to her was eagerly canvassed, till he was obliged to blame Lord Baltimore and deny its authorship. The Vane faction then retorted with a second letter (also written by Hervey at Miss Vane's request) in which she accepted his repudiation of his agent's authority and once again raised the standard of injured innocence. But meanwhile the scandal had become public property and found its way into lampoons and pamphlets and news-papers.

Vanilla on the Straw and *Vanessa, or the Amours of the Court of Modern Gallantry,* gave that part of the world not already in-structed in court gossip a lively and scurrilous account of their heroine's seduction, betrayal and later sufferings. They were not calculated to improve the Prince's credit; and on his personal pop-ularity Frederick (like his mother and father, during their term as Prince and Princess of Wales) was beginning to place the greatest value. There was no help for it, and he capitulated more or less grudgingly: Miss Vane received a settlement and the house she lived in, with full permission to dispose of herself as she pleased. But she did not long survive to enjoy her triumph or Lord Hervey's favours, dying at Bath of some mysterious internal ail-ment. About the same time, her child expired in a "convulsion fit"; and (his family noted with some surprise) the Prince seemed sorry.

3

During the summer months of 1735 the King, for no better reason than that he had previously done so, and what he had once done he did again, set out to Hanover on his triennial holi-day. There he celebrated his release from England by falling in love. The immense letters that came posting back to Caroline were soon enlivened by references to his new passion, and by long descriptions of the beauty and virtues of Madame de Walmoden. She was young; she was "of the first fashion"; she was extremely accommodating. It would, indeed, have been remarkable had she refused the King, since she was related to Madame Schulenburg and the Countess Platen, and came of a family that had a long and gallant record. All this, and much more, the King confided, mingling his confidences with protestations of his love for Caroline and with a detailed and painstaking chronicle of his daily life. His letters, which never filled less than forty, now often exceeded sixty pages, certain paragraphs being annotated with a request that the Queen would show them to Sir Robert: *Montrez ceci et consultez là-dessus le gros homme.* The Queen, as it happened, showed his letters both to the Minister and to the Vice-Chamberlain; and Hervey, among other characteristic oddities, was particularly entertained by a suggestion that the Queen should give proof of her wifely loyalty by arranging that, when the Prince of Modena visited England, he should be accompanied to London by the Princess; for the King was acquainted with her reputation and was anxious to have the pleasure of making his court to a daughter of the late Duc d'Orléans, the celebrated Regent, "a pleasure" (he added) "that I am sure, my dear Caroline, you will be delighted to procure me when I tell you how ardently I desire it."

In her reply (according to Sir Robert Walpole) the Queen did not hesitate to humour these velleities and to sympathize with the account he gave of his present adventures. She wrote to tell him of Lady Suffolk's unexpected and far from brilliant marriage to an old admirer, Mr. George Berkeley. The King responded that he was "extremely surprised at the disposition . . . my former mistress has made of her person in marriage to that gouty old fellow, George Berkeley; and I am delighted that it should be so. I would not wish to confer such presents upon my friends; and, when my enemies rob me, pray God they may always do it thus!" Balls, suppers and masquerades filled the monarch's time; but among these amusements (of which he decreed that a special series of pictures should be painted to amuse the Queen when he returned to England) he was also able to arrive at an important decision. On encountering the Princess Augusta of Saxe-Gotha, who had purposely been thrown in his way at Herrenhausen, he selected her as an appropriate bride for his elder son.

At last, and most reluctantly, he made ready to travel. There was a farewell banquet at which the King toasted Madame de Walmoden, and his mistress, "in a mixture of tears and smiles," pledged the 29th of May, when the King had given a solemn promise they should be reunited. Then his equipage was assembled and the yachts prepared. George Augustus, like his father, was a headlong traveller. On Wednesday, the 22nd of October, he had begun his journey; the following Sunday, just before dinner, he arrived at Kensington, where his hand was kissed by the Queen at the great gate. He embraced her and led her upstairs with the accustomed ceremony. But so fast had he travelled across Europe, and so few halts had he allowed his suite to make on the road, that (as it soon appeared) he was both feverish and out of humour. George Augustus was usually at his mildest when he returned to Caroline and would dismiss the court, that they might be alone together, as soon as possible. This afternoon he seemed in no hurry for a private interview.

His irritability increased during the next few days. Furious at his separation from Madame de Walmoden, and further exasperated by a severe attack of piles—the result of the constant jolting he had endured in his carriage—he lavished his ill-temper on the world at large. England and his English subjects became definitely hateful to him. Pursuing a theme that had once been the mainstay of his father's conversation, at a period when he himself had championed exactly the opposite point of view, he inveighed against English cooks and English confectioners, English jockeys, English coachmen and English players—Englishmen who had never learned to enter a room and who could talk of nothing but their insufferable politics; Englishwomen, not one of whom knew how to dress though they were incessantly occupied in discussing their clothes. By way of contrast, he spoke at length of Hanover, where the blessings of absolute monarchical government were combined with splendour, wealth, magnificence, gallantry, learning, where his subjects were loyal to him and his advisers devoted and he rewarded them in proportion as they did their duty.

Even Caroline appeared to have lost the art of managing him; and for her he reserved his cruellest snubs. No detail was too small to catch his attention and little that he noticed he did not criticize. So she and Lord Hervey had presumed to re-shuffle his pictures? In fact they had removed several very indifferent canvases by unknown artists and substituted works by Van Dyck and others. But with this arrangement his Majesty was not at all content. Hervey, in a spirit of extreme daring, inquired whether he would not allow the two Van Dycks, at least, to remain where they were, to which the King retorted that he had a great respect for Lord Hervey's taste in matters that Lord Hervey understood, but in questions of picture-hanging he begged leave to follow his own. He supposed (he remarked bitterly) that Hervey had assisted the Queen with his "fine advice" while she was pulling his house to pieces and spoiling his furniture. Thank God, she had left the walls standing! "As for the Van Dycks, I do not care whether they are changed or no; but for the picture with the dirty frame over the door, and the three nasty little children,[1] I will have them taken away and the old ones restored; I will have it done too tomorrow morning before I go to London. . . ."

"Would your Majesty," next inquired Lord Hervey, growing more and more bold, "have the gigantic fat Venus restored too?"

"Yes, my Lord," replied the King, with a touch of sarcasm that Hervey would not appear fully to have understood. "I am not so

---

[1] It has been suggested by Hervey's modern editor, Mr. Romney Sedgwick, that the King probably referred to the well-known Van Dyck portrait of Charles I's children.

nice as your Lordship, I like my fat Venus much better than anything you have given me instead of her."

Hervey reflected (though he did not permit his thought expression) that, had the King liked his "fat Venus" as well as he used to do, life at court would have been an easier and simpler business. Unfortunately the picture asked for had been carted away; other pictures had been sent to Hampton Court, and their frames either cut down or else enlarged. But the King, in common with most domestic tyrants, had a memory that was not to be depended upon, and next day he gave his ill-nature a different direction. Meeting the Queen at breakfast in the gallery of Kensington Palace with her children and the Vice-Chamberlain, he snubbed his wife, who was drinking chocolate, "for being always stuffing," the Princess Emily because she had failed to hear him, the Princess Caroline because she had grown fat, his second son for the awkward way in which he stood, and "Lord Hervey for not knowing what relation the Prince of Sultzbach was to the Elector Palatine . . . then carried the Queen to walk and be re-snubbed in the garden."

The court in general and members of the government were also subjected to sallies of the King's ill-temper. Though not noticeably infected with humanitarianism, he professed to be shocked by the English devotion to blood sports; and when the Duke of Grafton requested his permission to go into the country for the hunting he declared that it was a pretty occupation for a man of the Duke's quality and age to spend his time "tormenting a poor fox, that was generally a much better beast than any of those that pursued him." Besides, what could the Duke himself know of the hunting field? "For, with your great corps of twenty-stone weight, no horse, I am sure, can carry you within hearing, much less within sight, of your hounds."

It was with a certain rueful pride—even with a kind of inverted satisfaction—that the courtiers compared notes as to their personal sufferings and the various affronts that they had received during the course of the day. The position of the Queen was much more serious. Sir Robert and the Vice-Chamberlain were both alarmed: if the Queen were to forfeit her hold on the King's affection, the alliance they had built up would lose its cornerstone and the King, under other management, grow quite intractable. Sir Robert, therefore, recommended submission and patience, flavouring his good advice with a number of broad pleasantries which shocked Hervey and ruffled and hurt the Queen, though, "great comedian" as ever, she laughed them off. Sir Robert was particularly suspicious of Lady Deloraine, the younger Princesses' governess and George Bubb Dodington's former ally, for whom the King seemed to have developed a predilection and with whom he used to talk "a little indecently" on his leisure evenings, which were generally whiled away in his daughters' apartment. Walpole considered her a dangerous fool, possessed of a weak head, a pretty face and a deceitful nature. He advised the Queen to send for Lady Tankerville, who was "a very safe fool," good-natured, good-looking as she was simple-minded, and would amuse the husband without damage to the wife's interests.

Caroline was not pleased, but she did not disagree. At no time easy or safe or calm, her life had never been more distracted than during these autumn and winter months of 1735, when every hour almost produced some new injury to her self-esteem and the whole court was the witness of her humiliation. Walpole, with his coarse realism, did not spare her feelings, and Hervey was often surprised that a man in many respects so delicately perspicacious should in other things have been so obtuse and so heavy-handed. After all, the Queen was a woman in love; and if her love was no longer exclusive or personal and now hard to separate from her love of the position she occupied, she was still exquisitely sensitive to neglect or ill-treatment. Yet she continued to smile in depths of misery—at Sir Robert, when he ventured to repeat his lesson, preach philosophy and remind her of her middle age, and at the King himself when, with cheeks flushed and eyes protuberant, he would bully and contradict her or stamp from the room.

Even more tedious and more melancholy became evenings at court. While the King, pacing restlessly to and fro with the stiff military, impatient stride that had once been his father's, kept up a continued flow of complaint and criticism, the Queen would smile and nod in the right places and Lord Hervey seek to humour him by a tactful diversion. These attempts often served to redouble his spleen. At one such interview George Augustus, having given his opinion of the Vice-Chamberlain's friend, Bishop Hoadly —"A pretty fellow for a friend! Pray what is it that charms you in him? His pretty limping gait, or his nasty stinking breath?— phaugh!—or his silly laugh, when he grins in your face for nothing . . ."—afterwards took his text from the Queen's interest in building and planting, unburdened himself on the subject of "Merlin's Cave," a little folly Kent had designed for Richmond Park, and proceeded to exclaim against her love of pictures. Why must she be perpetually gadding and sight-seeing? "You do not see me running into every puppy's house, to see his new chairs and stools. Nor is it for *you*" (he added, turning upon his wife) "to be running your nose everywhere, and trotting about the town to every fellow that will give you some bread and butter, like an old girl that loves to go abroad, no matter where. . . ." Caroline blushed and tears filled her eyes but she did not speak. Hervey thereupon observed that, since the Queen was fond of pictures, it was natural she should wish to visit private collections; but the torrent of the King's fury could not be stemmed, and it presently overflowed into the German language, again without eliciting a reply from Caroline. But she coloured miserably and her hands shook so that she tangled her knotting thread and, in endeavouring to snuff the candles, she snuffed them out.

Only his elder son escaped the full blast of the King's resentment, for his choler was a partial sign of regard or affection, and his dislike of Frederick was now so deep as to be almost voiceless. Thus, although he would sometimes speak in general terms of unworthy, designing sons and excellent, long-suffering, deserving parents, he did not condescend to notice the Prince when he entered the room, and gave the impression of looking through him as through a spectre. But Frederick was a phantom that would not be ignored. An irrepressible household imp or malicious *Poltergeist,* he was continually popping up in the most unexpected situations and contrived to make himself felt though he remained unseen. Besides, the King had now definitely fixed his marriage and was anxious to get the ceremony over and done with, that he might return to Hanover and Madame de Walmoden, to the pleasures of absolute monarchy and youth and love. He therefore hurried on the preliminaries of Frederick's union, which he settled should take place during the early spring.

One other consideration delayed his flight. The British Parliament—symbol of all that he found most inexplicable and most exasperating in the English constitution—was devoting its energies to a lengthy wrangle over church affairs, with particular reference to the oppressive legislation still in force against Quakers and Nonconformists. Walpole realized that on grounds of social justice alone the Test and Corporation Acts could not be defended; but he knew that the more orthodox members of the clergy—as distinct from those "less believing" bishops patronized by the Queen and Lady Sundon—were bitterly opposed to the idea of repeal and it was not his method to create unnecessary awkwardness. In consequence the support he gave was lukewarm, and the hopes of the Nonconformists were defeated after a long and acrimonious struggle, stubbornly contested by both sides. Caroline had been all for religious freedom; her husband, on the other hand, who lacked his wife's passion for divinity and was exceedingly contemptuous of English bishops, with their cushioned stalls, abundant incomes and sleek self-interest, wished that the devil might rid him of the whole affair and flew into "fretful transports" if he heard it mentioned. That Parliament, as a result of it, should rise later than usual and thus cause some postponement of his visit to Herrenhausen, seemed an intolerable, and typically English, assault on his dignity.

At any rate there should be no postponement of the Prince's marriage. Towards the middle of February, a deputation of five members of the Cabinet Council brought Frederick a formal message from his father, announcing that, if the Prince of Wales gave his assent, the King would demand the Princess of Saxe-Gotha for him in marriage. Frederick, as if to show that, granted considerate treatment, he could be relied on to behave with due propriety, responded that he was delighted to accept his father's choice. An embassy was then dispatched to claim the Princess, and on the 25th of April 1736, the seventeen-year-old girl landed at Greenwich, where Frederick immediately visited her and spent several hours in conversation, returning next day to join her at dinner. Quite clearly the Prince of Wales was enjoying himself. Courteous and attentive to his betrothed (whom none of the other members of his family had yet greeted since "the laws of precedency had not settled the rank of the Princess before she became Princess of Wales") he allowed her to appear in the gallery of the Palace to a vast crowd gathered beneath the windows and heard her welcomed with "the most lively acclamations." There were also a public supper-party and an expedition up the Thames in the Prince's own finely ornamented barge (designed for him by William Kent in 1732), a long slender craft as rich as gilding and tritons could make it, which supported amidships a small painted cabin like a sedan chair. Perhaps (as he had previously done to the grave Lord Egmont [1]) Frederick boasted to Augusta of the

---

[1] *Egmont.* August 10th, 1732.

vessel's design and how much more speedily his barge could be rowed than his father's, adding that he considered it a Prince's function to provide liberally for the entertainment of a loyal populace.

Already he saw himself in the attractive guise of the people's champion. Bolingbroke had entertained him with philosophic disquisitions on the nature of kingship and the opportunities awaiting some truly disinterested, exclusively patriotic and non-partisan sovereign; Chesterfield and young Lyttelton had enlarged on the theme. More simple-minded than the majority of those who advised him, Frederick loved the warmth and glitter of popularity and, if he did not fully understand his mentors' precepts, at least appreciated the chance they seemed to offer him of playing a distinguished personal role. He enjoyed cheers, deputations, civic addresses. It was particularly annoying, then, that his father and mother should have decided to marry him off with few trappings and an air of almost surreptitious haste and emergency, as though the job were disagreeable but must be done. His return to England had been obscure; his marriage was subfusc. On a Sunday the Princess had landed at Greenwich; the following Tuesday, she was conveyed to Lambeth by coach, ferried across the Thames to Whitehall steps and thence transported in the King's chair to St. James's Palace. The King, attended by the Queen and the entire court, had been waiting, not very patiently, in the Great Drawing Room for the better part of an hour, but the Princess was no sooner presented by Frederick than she conciliated him by executing a series of Oriental obeisances and flinging herself full-length at their Majesties' feet. Was she as crafty (wondered the courtiers) as this action suggested? Somewhat awkward in figure and not at all pretty, the Princess had the charm of youth and freshness, and an expression that implied health and serene good-humour.[1]

---

[1] "The Prince led her in. She is about his height, much pitted with the small-pox, and had a great colour from the heat of the day and the hurry and surprise

According to outward appearances she was quiet and childish; but she came with credit through a long and difficult day, and seemed neither brilliant nor stupid, neither *gauche* nor thrusting —a good-natured, well-mannered puppet in brocade and diamonds, uttering the commonplaces and performing the gestures that custom demanded. The only difficulties that occurred were raised by Frederick, with his brother and sisters, over details of precedence at their separate dinner-table.

The others, he insisted—seized by that demon of perversity which now sometimes rendered him as aggressive over small questions as he had once been patient and easy-going under major provocations—must sit on stools while he and his future wife occupied high arm-chairs. They alone, he commanded, should be served on the knee. But the Princesses, who were versed in their brother's stratagems, declined to leave the ante-chamber till the stools had been removed and instructed their attendants to treat them exactly as Augusta and Frederick were treated by theirs: with the result that they scored a technical victory, though obliged to refuse coffee for fear of a mishap. Such an introduction to family existence was not very promising. But there remained the greater trial of the marriage itself. At nine o'clock the brief religious ceremony was gone through and, after a supper-party, the scene shifted to the nuptial chamber.

Here the bride was undressed by her sisters-in-law and put to bed. Frederick, who in the meantime had been disrobed by his brother, and by George Augustus solemnly invested with his night-shirt, now entered wearing a dressing-gown of silver tissue and a tall imposing nightcap "of the finest lace." Ill-disposed observers found him slightly ridiculous; and Caroline, who had had much ado to prevent herself bursting into tears when she saw her eldest daughter consigned to the uncouth embraces of the Prince

---

she was in. But she has a peculiar affability of behaviour and a very great sweetness of countenance."—*Egmont*. April 27th, 1735.

of Orange, on this occasion was obliged to restrain her laughter. Had Lord Hervey noticed the height of her son's nightcap? It had reminded the Vice-Chamberlain of a grenadier's bonnet; both laughed over the Prince's expression at supper as he had gulped jellies while turning to wink at one of his servants. . . .

If his marriage had flattered the Prince's vanity, his animosity was gratified by its immediate sequel. For, among the congratulatory orations delivered in Parliament, the younger members of the Opposition—contemptuously styled by Walpole "the Boys" —who had begun to look on Frederick as a convenient figurehead, took the opportunity of aiming their shafts at the King and the Minister. Mr. Grenville, Mr. Lyttelton and Cornet Pitt rose one after another in the House of Commons and, having applauded the Prince and complimented the Princess, suggested, "not in very covert terms," that George Augustus deserved comparatively little credit, since the marriage had been forced through against his will, that he had merely given way to the demands of his son and the voice of the nation. Cornet Pitt, an ambitious but obscure young man, whose personality still concealed that of the great Lord Chatham, was afterwards dismissed his regiment on account of his speech. Though it pleased Frederick to stand forth as the people's hero, the princely advocate of freedom and honest government, his relationship with his family did not improve.

His income, it is true, from £29,000 a year was raised to £50,-000, but even that was only half what his father had received and barely sufficient for the needs of an expensive household. Worse still, on the eve of going abroad, the King sent him a message through the Duke of Grafton that, wherever the Queen had her place of residence, there apartments would be provided for himself and the Princess. This (contended Frederick), though it might have been interpreted by the court as an act of civility, was a deliberate attempt to tie him to the Queen's apron-strings; and there is every reason to suppose that he was right. The King had no intention of allowing his son to set up a separate establishment which would, in due time, become an opposition court—he had learned his lesson through his own experience with Frederick's grandfather. He remembered Hampton Court, the flight from St. James's, the splendours of Leicester House; and it was to Caroline that he again delegated all the powers of regency.

George Augustus left England during the middle of May. Immediately there developed between Caroline and her son and daughter-in-law a variety of trivial but trying differences. For example, it exasperated the Queen that the Princess should always come late to chapel and push in front of her along an unusually narrow pew. She therefore instructed the Princess's Chamberlain to bring her in, if she arrived late, by another door, but was promptly and publicly disobeyed at the Prince's orders. Hervey, however, warned the Queen that he suspected Frederick of wishing to foment a quarrel during his father's absence, and Caroline made it her business to avoid disputes. Augusta's share in these *contretemps* was a purely negative one. It was evident that her husband entirely dominated her. During her leisure hours she seemed to lapse back into a condition of childhood and spent much time dressing and undressing a big jointed doll, on the window-seat, in full view of the sentries outside. . . .

Caroline did not find her congenial company. But to give the Queen her due (noted the Vice-Chamberlain), "she was always remarkably and industriously civil to her and has often said to me she thought there was no sort of harm in her, that she never meant to offend, was very modest and very respectful. . . ." But family dinner-parties were not amusing. Lord Hervey, when he visited the Queen after the Prince and Princess had joined her at dinner, usually discovered his friend bored and nervous and out of spirits, declaring that "the *fades railleries* of her son," combined with "the silent stupidity of her *ennuyante* daughter-in-law," were so fatiguing that really she was ready to cry. . . .

Meanwhile troubled letters arrived from the King. His happiness in Hanover had not lasted long, and, like most pleasures eagerly looked forward to, his reunion with Madame de Walmoden was overclouded. During the spring months she had presented him with a bastard son. The King was delighted with this proof of his prowess, but soon after his arrival, when he was staying at Herrenhausen, one of the gardeners there happened to see a ladder standing at night against Madame de Walmoden's casement. A hue and cry having been raised, a man was caught hiding behind an espalier and dragged off to the captain of the guard. The intruder proved to be an officer in the Imperial Service, a M. Schulenburg, and a member of the Duchess of Kendal's family. He was released, but the scandal could not be suffocated, and George Augustus wrote to Caroline in deep distress. It was characteristic of him that he should immediately run to his wife for comfort. He included the usual request that she would consult Sir Robert Walpole, *"qui a plus d'expérience, ma chère Caroline, que vous dans ces affaires, et moins de préjugé que moi dans celle-ci."*

The repercussions of what came to be entitled "the ladder story" filled the King's correspondence for several weeks. Caroline laughed and sighed over the rambling chronicle. But at home she had more serious affairs to attend to, for during the summer of 1736 a "licentious, riotous, seditious and almost ungovernable spirit" showed itself in rioting and disorder all over the Kingdom. The West Country rose against the export of corn; in London itself the weavers of Spitalfields, enraged by the employment of cheap Irish labour, created violent disturbances, which were put down by the military, but not before lives had been lost and property damaged. A small bomb exploded in Westminster Hall, throwing judges and lawyers into the utmost panic and putting them to flight with the loss of wigs and gowns and dignity. Special precautions were needed at the passing of the Gin Act. Since the introduction of gin, which had made it possible to achieve insensibility for a threepenny piece, London and other English cities swarmed with drunkards whose presence was a source of constant scandal to the wine-drinking classes. But the proletariat liked the new liquor and meant to keep it. A crowd surrounded the Queen's coach as she returned from Kensington with shouts of "No gin, no King"; threatening letters were received by Sir Robert Walpole, warning him that he and gin would go down together; and for a considerable period before and after the bill's passing strong military detachments patrolled London and Westminster, while a double guard was posted at Kensington Palace.

But the most flagrant disorders of all occurred in Scotland. From Edinburgh, that still half-savage city, with its Old Town of crooked granite-paved streets and smoky house-tops crowded together beneath the Castle Rock, came news of a serious riot which had taken place at the execution of a well-known smuggler. When the mob began to stone the soldiers and the hangman, Captain Porteous, commander of the Town Guard, had given his men orders to open fire, and several people had been killed and many wounded. Captain Porteous was thereupon arrested, tried and condemned to death. But Caroline, having been handed a petition for mercy, signed by vast numbers of the nobility and gentry of Scotland, elected to exercise the royal prerogative. As soon as it was known that Porteous had been reprieved, the Edinburgh mob exploded in insurrection. They captured the gates, seized the arms of the City Guard, stormed the prison and, after releasing his fellow-prisoners, dragged Porteous from the chimney in which he had hidden and hauled him with a rope round his neck to the Grass Market. There he was lynched with all the solemnity of a proper hanging, amid a crowd which roared defiance at Queen and Government, but, as soon as they were satisfied of their victim's death, quietly melted away.

To Caroline and, presently, to George Augustus (for whose

benefit they were described in letters hardly less voluminous or less detailed than his own) these tumults seemed but another illustration of the incurable laxity and liberalism of an English government. With the "pert cruel air" of a royal martinet, he had often exclaimed against the ridiculous weakness of British methods and declared that rebels and traitors should be made an example of. It infuriated him that so many villains remained unhanged. And though Caroline by temperament was far more merciful and took an indulgent interest in the sufferings of Dissenters and in the abuses of prison life, she had a distrust, almost as deep and instinctive, of the mass of Englishmen. For she was a royal personage first, and intelligent afterwards. That is to say, although her education had shaped her mind, and reading and experience had enriched its texture, its rocky skeleton was still one of inherited prejudice: she never doubted the moral validity of the power she exercised. It was the privilege, pleasurable and painful, of a superior being, born to suffer and command, to be exalted and solitary.

Thus, in spite of all, she preserved her equanimity through these summer months. Her spirits and temper seemed exceptionally good; and it was only when the summer declined into autumn, and week after week no reports arrived of the King's return, that she grew moody and impatient and a little resentful. Her birthday came and went, but he delayed in Hanover. During the earlier part of his stay the letters they exchanged had been of the usual length and, on his side, contained the usual protestations, mixed with his customary descriptions of Madame de Walmoden. Now the quality and length of the Queen's missives began to give way. From thirty or forty pages they dwindled to seven or eight, and their general tone became measurably less obsequious. Again Hervey and Walpole were much alarmed. They realized that Caroline could not afford to seem distant, and Sir Robert undertook to speak to her privately and beg her to address her husband in a different strain. She must sacrifice her pride to advance her interest, and request the King to bring back his favourite when he returned to England.

It was not the first jolt her pride had received, nor perhaps the harshest. Caroline wept, then thanked Sir Robert for his good advice, laying on her thanks "so thick" and adding "such professions of friendship and gratitude" that he understood (explained Walpole) that he had "gone too far; for I am never so much afraid of her rebukes as of her commendations." Yet the unpalatable hint was absorbed and bravely digested; two or three days afterwards, in the garden at Richmond, she told him that she realized he had not expected her to take his advice, but that she had done so and was even then composing a letter. Its tone should be submissive, kind and affectionate: she would beg the King to do her the favour of importing his mistress. And, later, if Hervey returned to the subject, she spoke of jealousy as a foolish and immature passion, only worthy of the very young and the very stupid; or would hum a phrase from one of Handel's operas—

Se mai più saro gelosa mi punisca il sacro nume

—to indicate her complete affranchisement from these trivial feelings.

George Augustus, when he received her letter, was touched and delighted. Madame de Walmoden, not surprisingly, proved a little sceptical; but the King incontinently framed his answer in a style as naïve and open-hearted as it was persuasive and passionate. It was his dearest wish to live up to her good opinion of him. "But you know my passions, my dear Caroline! You understand my weaknesses; in my heart there is nothing hidden from you. . . . Would to God I could imitate you as I know how to admire you, and that from your example I could learn all the virtues that you have taught me to see, feel and love!" The King appended a further sketch of Madame de Walmoden's appearance—which (he

said) was engaging if not regularly beautiful—and of her mind—
"Not a brilliant wit, but lively and amusing . . . as regards heart,
she is certainly the best creature in the world"—and described the
emotion with which she had responded to the Queen's offer. Caroline handed this effusion to Sir Robert Walpole, who repeated it
from memory to the Vice-Chamberlain. Both agreed that, if the
King had been content to write, instead of talking to, and strutting
before, the women he courted, his natural eloquence would have
made him almost irresistible.

But the situation created by the King's absence did not affect
merely Caroline's *amour propre* or Lord Hervey's and Sir Robert
Walpole's political plans. It also precipitated a public scandal.
During the autumn Englishmen in every rank of life began to
murmur at the huge expense of maintaining as sovereign one who
preferred to spend the revenues he received abroad. Tradesmen
were uneasy because it cost them business.[1] "Ordinary and godly
people" sympathized with the poor Queen, who had borne so
many fine children and was treated so shabbily. Secret Jacobites
ventured out into the open. Englishmen are seldom indulgent to
a lawless love-affair, particularly when it crosses their own self-
interest; and there was much talk of the monarch's advanced age
and the absurdity of his attempting to cut such a youthful figure.
Various practical jokes showed the state of popular feeling. One
day an old blind decrepit horse came ambling through the streets,
with a pillion on its back and a broken saddle, and an inscription
fastened to its forehead. *"Let nobody stop me. I am the King's
Hanover Equipage going to fetch His Majesty and his whore to
England."* Another paper was pasted up on the gate of St. James's
Palace: *"Lost or strayed out of this house, a man who has left a*

---

[1] "The citizens of London cry out their trade is ruined . . . and last week one
of them in the presence of a friend of mine damned him, saying, if he will have a
whore, why don't he take an English one and stay at home; there are enough of
them to be had cheaper."—*Egmont.* October 28th, 1736.

wife and six children on the parish; whoever will give any tidings of him . . . shall receive four shillings and sixpence reward. N.B.—This reward will not be increased, nobody judging him to deserve a crown." A third notice appeared at the Royal Exchange: *"It is reported that his Hanoverian Majesty designs to visit his British dominions for three months in the spring."* And there were many more, of the same import and equal bitterness. Again the "Hanover rats" were damned and ridiculed, and toasts were drunk to His Majesty King James III.

Chapter Six

1

*I*N HER perturbation the Queen naturally fell out with Frederick. His conduct had not been ingratiating during the course of the summer; on the other hand, it had not been particularly scandalous, and no grave quarrel or open rupture had yet taken place. But now, when Caroline announced that she intended to stay at Kensington till the King's return, though it was almost cut off from London by boggy roads and at some points by "a great impassable gulf of mud," the Prince desired permission to go up to St. James's. This move his mother declined to countenance, and letters of a frozen politeness went backwards and forwards, bristling with expressions of assumed sympathy and feigned respect. Eventually Frederick gave in and stayed at Kensington, where he fixed for the rest of the autumn his *"séjour principal"* and lodged a part of his permanent household to please the Queen. But he and Augusta led a rambling existence between Kew and London and seldom slept at home more than two or three days a week.

They resembled gipsies (said Caroline) rather than royal personages. For though her attitude towards her elder son had once been qualified and she had even gone so far as to defend him against Lord Hervey—remarking that, though often very tiresome, he could also be very entertaining and, though mean and crafty, there was no doubt he had generous impulses—it was now undergoing a transformation of the utmost significance. Where before she had disapproved, she began to hate; and, as she hated, so her intellect lost touch with her feelings, till they had drifted beyond the control of reason or common sense. Such an intensity of unnatural aversion is hard to explain, nor has any contemporary diarist or later historian been able to provide a solution that is wholly satisfying. Was Caroline able to fathom her own emotions? Though an intelligent and highly cultivated woman, she was at heart too feminine to be entirely reasonable and too royal to employ ordinary human standards. Thus she felt instinctively that her son menaced her husband's position. By ranging himself with the opponents of Sir Robert Walpole he became an embodied threat to the King's authority and a traitor to what she conceived of as the family cause. Always passionately loyal to George Augustus (who represented both her private affections and her cult of power), she could not forgive, on the part of her offspring, this apparent disloyalty, which touched vital centres of love and self-interest. The self-subordination she had practised since childhood had made her prejudices as inflexible as her will was strong.

Other factors increased the difficulties of the situation. Lord Hardwicke, in his *Memoirs,* when describing Frederick's quarrel with his father and mother, declares that Sir Robert had informed him of "certain passages between the King and himself, and between the Queen and the Prince, of too high and secret a nature even to be trusted to this narrative," but which induced him to believe that "this unhappy difference . . . turned upon some points of a more interesting and important nature than have hitherto appeared." It has been suggested that these passages, high and secret and incommunicable, were probably connected with George Augustus's suppression of his father's testament, an ancient and scandalous episode in the family history. It had been believed at the time that a number of private persons, including the Duchess of Kendal and Prince Frederick Louis, had suffered thereby considerable pecuniary losses, but later research gives the transaction a more serious character. George Louis (for whose political sagacity Frederick always entertained the greatest respect) had long contemplated the disjunction of England and Hanover, and in his will attempted to entail Hanover on Prince Frederick's second surviving son, while England would, as a matter of course, go to the eldest. The whole question had been debated in secret on the old King's death, and since it was decided by the King's Hanoverian ministers that the bequest had no sort of legal validity, George II had decided to suppress the document. Frederick, however, threatened to reopen the question. He proposed to abandon his hereditary rights to the Electorate of Hanover (which would pass to his brother, the Duke of Cumberland) in return for an increase of his personal allowance. As it happened, the proposal was never brought forward, but the mention of it may well have upset his parents, who regarded their German Electorate with an exclusive love which they were very far from feeling for their island kingdom. Moreover, they were extremely jealous of their own authority and not disposed to accept any interference by the meddlesome Frederick.[1]

These questions did not come uppermost till the following year, and meanwhile the antagonism between the Prince and his mother was founded rather on personal differences than on problems of policy. With a more intelligent young man the Queen might have sympathized; a stupider and more downright son she might have understood; but the Prince of Wales's curiously fluid temperament, his constant variations of purpose and changes of mood, neither flattered her understanding nor aroused her sympathies. She saw his failings, and even his virtues she found antipathetic. In her eyes Frederick's free and easy habits, his love of taking his walks with a single attendant and meeting distinguished men over a glass of wine, suggested a Machiavellian plot to supplant his father. His natural friendliness she interpreted as craft

---

[1] There is an interesting exposition of this problem in Mr. Romney Sedgwick's foreword to his edition of Hervey's *Memoirs*.

or weakness. A certain touch of absurdity in Frederick's character (which, to a more indulgent critic, might have seemed slightly engaging) jarred on her essentially positive and literal mind. Whatever he undertook, he somehow overdid; and though Caroline would not have objected to his love of concerts, or resented his devotion to the violoncello, it seemed unnecessary to make music of summer nights at an open casement above one of the back courts of Kensington Palace, where he caroled a medley of French and Italian songs, for the delectation or amazement of the royal servants. There he sat haloed by rosy candlelight while his audience arranged itself opposite in ascending tiers, "the colonnade below" (Hervey noted) "being filled with all the footmen, scullions, postilions, applewomen, shoe-boys, and lower order of domestics, whilst the first-floor windows were thronged with chambermaids and *valets de chambre,* and the garret, like the upper gallery, stuffed with laundry maids and their gallants."

Thus far the Queen's more reasonable and explicit grievances. But there comes a moment when we find ourselves on another plane. Every family has its secret oddities, its *tics,* its manias; and in royal families their development is forced and unnatural, so that with each succeeding generation they may grow more fantastic. Already traditional in the House of Hanover was an intense mistrust, verging on hatred, between parent and offspring, which certainly ante-dated their arrival in England but derived an added stimulus from their elevation to the English throne. George I had disliked the Electress Sophia and felt something more than dislike for George Augustus. Instinctively George Augustus had avoided his elder son; and, if Frederick's conduct helped to justify his father's aversion, that conduct had been largely aggravated by the King's neglect. Nor with Frederick was the vicious circle finally completed. The old hatred blazed out again between his son and grandsons, and the old mistrust between his great-granddaughter and the Prince of Wales: Victoria once informed a sober statesman that she felt a profound repugnance to remaining in the same room as her son and heir.[1]

The origins of this tradition must remain mysterious, hidden in the darkness that surrounds the secret history of some small German court, where the trappings of the *Grand Siècle* concealed the manners of the Middle Ages. From its later development, on the other hand, we cannot entirely disassociate that strain of mental instability—sometimes amounting to insanity—afterwards known as "the hereditary disease." This disease, at any rate in an incipient stage, was not confined to its chief victim, George III, for George IV's behaviour and private table-talk often created a suspicion that he was partly deranged; and his niece, even during the lifetime of the Prince Consort, herself considered that she existed under the shadow of madness and used the hint of it as a useful weapon in moments of difficulty. Frederick's own mental balance was by no means solid, and frequently puzzled and bewildered his closest associates, so rapid and so irresponsible were his changes of humour, so much activity did he combine with so little direction. Given greater natural endowments, his course might have been meteor-like, but he flickered inconstantly and burnt unevenly—an *ignis fatuus*.

As yet the harm and the good he had done were trivial. George Louis had once posted back from Hanover to curtail the exuberance of George Augustus; but though detailed reports were undoubtedly sent him of Frederick's tiresomeness, the King was still in no hurry to return home. His birthday (like the Queen's) passed unnoticed; and it was not till the 8th of December 1736, after a magnificent ball and supper-party, that George Augustus finally bestirred himself and took the road. His favourite judged

---

[1] As a further example of this tendency, one may cite Queen Victoria's extremely uncomfortable relations with her eldest daughter, the Crown Princess of Prussia, and that daughter's even more uncomfortable relations with her son, Kaiser Wilhelm II.

it prudent to remain at Herrenhausen; even so, Caroline looked
forward to his homecoming with very mixed feelings, for though
she wished his return she regretted her liberty and did not expect
that she would be repaid with much husbandly tenderness. After
last year, her hopes were very moderate. . . . On the 22nd of
December the King reached Helvoetsluis. On the following Tuesday, when it was believed he was already at sea, a violent storm
swept up against the coasts of England and for several days there
was no news of the royal flotilla. Only the Queen remained calm
in the general hubbub, reading a new volume of Rollin's *Histoire
Ancienne,* the kind of work she found particularly to her taste,
and playing cards every evening with her attendants and daughters. But Frederick's excitement in the emergency would not be
controlled. His attitude was neither decorous nor diplomatic. On
Friday, when it was conjectured that the King might well have
been in serious danger of his life for three whole days, he gave a
great dinner at his private house in Pall Mall to the Lord Mayor
of London and all the Aldermen, and received from them the
Freedom of the City. His speech (Hervey informed the Queen
that evening, anxious to soften nothing of its ill-effect) was, so he
had been told, "the most ingratiating piece of popularity" ever
composed and he imagined that the toasts drunk were similarly
fulsome. Nor did the Queen fail to respond as he intended she
should, stirred to the depth of her autocratic being by this account
of democratic and disloyal antics. "My God" (she cried) "popularity always makes me sick, but Fretz's popularity makes me vomit.
I hear that yesterday—on his side of the House"—that is to say,
among the Opposition benches—"they talked of the King's being
cast away with the same sang-froid as you would talk of a coach
being overturned. . . ."

There followed a period of alternating hope and anxiety. First
a messenger arrived with news that the King had not yet quitted
Helvoetsluis; then, the storm having died down so that all au-

thorities agreed he would attempt to cross, it blew up once again
with hurricane violence. This time there seemed no doubt that he
must suffer shipwreck. Minute guns were heard booming off the
storm-bound coast. Bad report after bad report arrived at the
Admiralty. Sir Robert Walpole and Lord Hervey began to think
of the future. What little news arrived was by no means comforting. The second scare had begun on Monday the 20th, and on
Friday a disabled and dismasted sloop brought information that
the captain of the vessel had seen the King's yacht tack about for
Helvoetsluis but, after that single glimpse, it had disappeared.
Next day several men-of-war, also a part of the royal convoy,
struggled with difficulty into four separate English ports and were
able to confirm the previous message. At a prearranged signal the
fleet had disbanded, yachts making for the coast, larger craft driving out to the open sea; and, as in the canvas of some seventeenth-
century marine painter, a modern imagination fills the scene with
sky and billows, a vast prospect of tumbling discoloured surges,
scattered across it the plunging vessels of the royal fleet, their sails
swollen and pennants fluttering against an indigo background.

Christmas Day passed without further news; and Caroline, forgetting her Rollin and abandoning her sang-froid, gave way to
miseries of apprehension. Walpole and Hervey could bring her
little comfort. Ruin, proscription, disgrace, exile—they would face
them all on the accession of King Frederick I, while a dignified
obscurity was probably the best that the Queen could hope for.
Frederick, on his side, was surrounded with counsellors, but
whereas during the original scare his behaviour had been unbe-
coming, he now revealed a different aspect of his personality. It
was the first moment of real crisis he had yet experienced. The
King's popularity had never been at a lower ebb. Either he was
drowned or, his fleet dispersed, was laid up at Helvoetsluis and
likely to remain there, immobilized, for several weeks. No circumstances could have been more favourable to a *coup d'état*.

Should Frederick come forward and announce that in this un-precedented emergency he felt it his duty to take over the royal power? Many of his supporters seem to have expected some such step; Lord Stair, one of Walpole's bitterest opponents at the time of the Excise Bill, wrote that the only hopes men that wished well to their country could entertain was the Prince's "thinking right and acting accordingly." But Frederick hesitated at so great a de-cision. He commanded sympathy and popularity in his present state. Why sacrifice all for an unknown hazard, compromise his entire position by a stroke of daring? There was much to be said in favour of a dutiful attitude, even though it might sit upon him a trifle uneasily; and when members of the Opposition arrived "to assure him of their service," Frederick returned them a very prudent and becoming reply.

Within a short while he had reason to congratulate himself. For on Sunday, two days after Christmas, while the Queen sat at chapel "with a heavier heart" (she presently admitted) "than she had ever before felt in her breast," a letter was put into her hands from the King, informing her that, having set sail from Helvoet-sluis at eight in the morning, he had had much ado to get back to port at mid-afternoon the following day. His own obstinacy—though he denied having shown the smallest signs of impatience and Caroline was loyal enough to repeat his story—had very nearly involved his ships in disaster. For after a short stay at Hel-voetsluis he had grown restive and irritable, and declared that if Sir Charles Wager, the commander of the flotilla, would not set sail, he intended to take the ordinary packet-boat. He had also remarked that he was anxious to witness a storm at sea, but after many hours of continuous buffeting, with the yacht threatening to go down every moment and the sailors making ready to break up the royal cabin which had been constructed on the quarter-deck and throw overboard its rich furniture to lighten the vessel, he had admitted that his curiosity was more than satisfied and that he never wished to be in another tempest as long as he lived.[1] His first letter was comparatively brief and business-like; but, having received Caroline's reply, he wrote again, and on this occasion covered some thirty pages. His tenderness was as ebullient as his relief was profound. "In spite of all the danger" (he wrote) "that I underwent during the storm and all that I suffered—ill as I was to a degree that I had not thought it possible for the human body to endure—I would go through the same experiences again and again, for the satisfaction of receiving those marks of your tenderness that my situation has procured me. The affection you show me, the friendship, the fidelity, the inexhaustible kindness you display wherever I am concerned . . . are obligations that I shall never be able to repay, never deserve, but which I am equally incapable of forgetting." This letter (which also contained expressions of extreme amorous impatience) Caroline showed, as her practice was, to Walpole and Hervey, adding that she did not wish them to suppose, because she had shown it, that she was "an old fool, and vain of my person and charms at this time of day. I am reasonably pleased with it, but I am not unreasonably proud of it." They understood, nevertheless, that she was deeply gratified, for the King's regard meant more to her than mere self-interest and, when he hurt her, he cut deeper than surface vanity —so closely allied are selfish and unselfish passion, and so hard is it to unwind our own feelings from the person we love.

A spirit of peace and amity seemed to have gone abroad. Frederick, possibly somewhat disappointed but at the same time, no doubt, a little relieved, behaved exceptionally well now the crisis was over. An opportunity of rendering conspicuous service soon presented itself in the shape of a fire that threatened to burn down

---

[1] "Mr. Bronkar . . . told me that in the great danger the King was the last storm, one of the cabin boys saw him at his prayers, whereupon calling to another of the boys, he said the King is coaxing God Almighty, but by G—— he will be drowned for all that."—*Egmont.* January 17th, 1737.

the Temple, and Frederick, rushing to the scene of danger, took
charge of operations all through the night. It was said that the
crowd, drunk with enthusiasm, had shouted, "Crown him!
Crown him!" and though this story was not believed by his family there was no doubt that he had covered himself with distinction; while he claimed that in helping the firemen to carry buckets
he had sustained a couple of severe bruises beneath his periwig.
A further proof of his good intentions appeared when, happening
to meet Sir Robert in his mother's ante-chamber, he took him
aside and detained him in friendly conversation for two and a half
hours. He had always considered Walpole, said the Prince, "one
of the ablest men in England" and felt "the greatest regard" for
his talents and character; at which Sir Robert displayed suitable
signs of surprise and gratitude. But he took the opportunity of
reading Frederick a quiet lecture and warning him of the perils
attendant on domestic discord.

2

So BATTERED and exhausted as to be almost subdued, George
Augustus finally reached London on the 25th of January 1737.
Caroline, attended by her children and her entire household, was
waiting to greet him beneath the colonnade of St. James's Palace.
Climbing down from his coach he embraced them all, and even
Frederick's cheek was honoured with a paternal kiss. His behaviour was in the extreme sunny and affectionate. Towards both
the Queen and Sir Robert Walpole he turned the warmest rays of
his approbation. No eulogy was too enthusiastic for his devoted
consort—wise, faithful, intelligent and understanding—or for her
great and good adjutant whom he would always honour.

In his private apartments the King's behaviour was reassuring;
and, next day, when Hervey encountered Walpole, just as the

Minister was descending the Queen's back-stairs, the information they exchanged was of the most cheerful sort. Since a sentry stood close by, they spoke in Latin. *"Optime, optime"* (said Sir Robert) *"omnia rident,"* and, Hervey having replied with four lines of Horace: *"Dixit ad uxorem,"* Walpole added: *" 'quamquam sidere pulchrior illa est, tecum vivere amen, tecum obeam libens.' "* Fright and enforced abstinence had done their work, and Caroline triumphed in the possession of her recaptured husband—only Walpole held aloof and shook his head, for he was sufficiently cynical not to believe in sudden changes: the King (he thought) would be as difficult as ever once he had regained his spirits. Caroline had a great respect for Sir Robert's sagacity, but that sagacity did not endear him in her present mood.

Outside the court there were many sallies at the King's expense. Virulent, witty and improper epigrams were composed by Lord Chesterfield and Mr. Pulteney, which dealt with the rapturous re-union of George and Caroline and compared the sovereign to the "learned Hottentot" who returns to his kraal. The Queen's obesity and unattractiveness were liberally celebrated. George Augustus's course in foreign policy (which he himself had hardly counte-nanced and was the last to approve) also received the attention of an anonymous versifier:

> For nine long years George bullies, sneaks and treats,
> Pays useless armies and pacific fleets.
> When war's proclaimed, he shifts from court to court,
> Loth to engage, yet promising support.
> At length the peace is signed, Sir Robert says it,
> And George, we're told, has read it in the Gazette.

Nothing was forgiven him and nothing spared; but the King, broken down by his winter journey, retired to bed with a feverish cold and an attack of hæmorrhoids.

For some weeks he continued to keep his room. Caroline and her daughters maintained that his illness was trifling, but elsewhere it was said that his condition was serious, and these rumours naturally found their way to his elder son. Frederick's hopes and aspirations at once revived. It would be interesting to know whether, in the secret counsels of King, Queen and Minister, any mention were made of a squib let off by Frederick, apparently during the year 1736, to prepare the way for a more serious attack on the court and government. Frederick had a certain feeling for the art of literature; and it was through literature that he had decided to express his grievances and vent his dislike of his younger brother and the King and Queen. With the touch of almost comic oddity that never deserted him—the hint of frivolity that was inclined to crop up at the gravest moments—the form he chose was a fairy-tale in the manner of Perrault.

So *l'Histoire du Prince Titi* was turned loose on the world—a fantastic narrative written by the Prince in French, and translated by James Ralph, a party journalist. The hero of this not very amusing allegory is a gallant young man, cursed with two exceedingly unpleasant parents, *le Roi Guinget* (otherwise King Guinea), "haughty, fierce, partial in his affections . . . insatiably avaricious," and *la Reine Tripasse* (which may be rendered as Queen Tripes), who managed the monarch and hated his heir. There are various references to the meanness of his father and mother—to the King's crimson velvet parade suit, "lined with white rabbit, except at the edges to which were sewed strips of ermine cut from an old manteau," and his hat, grown somewhat shabby, battered— "less with wearing than with being kicked about the room when there was no other object for revenge. . . ." By his parents Titi and his devoted consort Bibi are subjected to all manner of persecutions. But Titi is as patriotic as he is long-suffering. He defeats an army of invaders, humbles their champion and, acclaimed by the populace, is eventually restored to his rank and privileges. Youth, beauty and virtue are at length triumphant; age, avarice, oppression hang their heads in shame.

Though the literary merits of this production were microscopic, at least it showed the change in the Prince's temper that had occurred since his association with the youthful "Patriots." The process of self-dramatization was now complete—private interest and public duty had become synonymous, and he laid his plans, in collaboration with Grenville and Lyttelton, fired by the agreeable belief that he was serving his country. Alone, like Prince Titi, he would face the foe and alone (he boasted) accomplish more than the Opposition, through its whole career since the beginning of the present reign; for what he aimed at was the final defeat of his father's minister. With that end, he proposed to submit his case to Parliament. Pulteney and Carteret had at first been against the scheme, but Pulteney agreed to sponsor it in the House of Commons and Carteret promised his support in the House of Lords. There was much clandestine soliciting of private members; then, after two months of preparation, the mine was sprung.

Sir Robert was taken unawares, the Queen incredulous. The King, suddenly informed that his son intended to make public and parliamentary property of something that he still regarded as a private dispute, behaved with better sense and greater self-control than his friends had anticipated. But Caroline grew angry beyond all measure. Hervey had observed the Queen in many vicissitudes—furious, discouraged, hurt and miserable; never had he seen her in such deep distress. Her dislike of her elder son amounted to detestation; then detestation itself became a kind of frenzy, and she was soon incapable of so much as mentioning him with restraint or reserve. A mere glimpse of him was enough to release her resentment; and, one day, when she stood at her dressing-room window and the familiar, dapper, strutting figure crossed the court beneath, "Look, there he goes" (she exclaimed, flushing with fury), "that wretch!—that villain!—I wish the ground would open this moment and sink the monster to the lowest hole in hell." Hervey himself was a little surprised at the Queen's behaviour. Caroline paused, remarking in a more moderate tone, "You stare at me; but I can assure you if my wishes and prayers had any effect, and that the maledictions of a mother signified anything, his days would not be very happy nor very many."

Yet in spite of these motherly and sisterly imprecations—for the gentle Princess Caroline echoed her parents—and some attempts, made on his father's behalf, to arrange a compromise, Frederick stuck obstinately to his original plan. Lord Scarborough scolded, but he would not be moved. A deputation of the Cabinet, including five dukes, three earls and other important members of the government, produced a message to the effect that the King would settle a jointure on the Princess and secure his £50,000 a year to the Prince for life; but Frederick declined to give way to their official pleading. He was sorry, he said, but they had come too late. The affair had now passed into the hands of others.

On February 22nd, therefore, Pulteney introduced a motion "that the House should address His Majesty to settle on the Princess of Wales a jointure such as the Queen had when Princess," and also make a settlement on Frederick "such as His Majesty had when he was Prince." Pulteney (according to Lord Egmont's informant in the House of Commons) "spoke extraordinarily strong and learnedly, showing the Prince had a right to a settlement of £100,000 a year, from reason, equity, law, precedent and policy." Hervey himself agreed that, in his speech "which lasted above an hour and half, there was a great deal of matter and a great deal of knowledge, as well as art and wit," though the impression it made was studied and somewhat laborious. Walpole's reply was equally long and equally careful. On the one hand he spoke of the King's expenses—far heavier than those incurred by his predecessor—and of the money that went in the upkeep of the younger members of the royal family; on the other he deplored the damage that was being done to the kingdom, the advantage that would be given to foreign enemies, and of the dangerous consequences that were to be apprehended from domestic broils. Sir Robert had not been at all confident of winning the day and faced a possibility that he might be delivering his last speech in the House of Commons, but he carried off the situation with his usual mastery, and was plausible, eloquent, informative and moving by turns. The debate continued till half an hour past midnight, when the motion was finally rejected by thirty votes.

George and Caroline were surprised but delighted when they heard the result—all the more surprised, since it had cost the King in purchasing votes less than a thousand pounds, and the sums expended were "only advanced to two men who were to have received them at the end of the session and . . . took this opportunity to solicit prompt payment." Against their son, both the King and Queen were anxious to take stern measures and talked of expelling him then and there from St. James's Palace. Walpole, however, recommended moderation. Frederick was permitted to remain at court, and courtiers soon witnessed the strange spectacle of a family in which the elder son, as far as his parents were concerned, seemed completely to have dematerialized; for, though he came and went and dined in public, and even offered his hand to the Queen on solemn occasions, they neither spoke to him, looked at him, nor acknowledged his greetings. Frederick himself gave no signs of contrition. Though he had failed in the House of Commons, he insisted that the motion should again be brought up in the House of Lords, where it was again rejected and by a considerably larger majority.

On second thoughts, the King and Queen were much dissatisfied. Caroline considered that a majority of only thirty in the House of Commons was not at all reassuring, and they blamed Walpole for having persuaded the King to send Frederick a mes-

FREDERICK, PRINCE OF WALES

Engraving by Picart after Gardner

LORD HERVEY

sage of compromise and conciliation, including engagements from which he now assured them they could not escape. Hervey improved the situation to his own advantage. With the perverse honesty that was characteristic of his ambiguous nature, he admits that the satisfaction he felt in harassing Frederick did not entirely depend upon his partiality for the Queen or Sir Robert but was increased and strengthened by his private hatred for the Prince of Wales. It was typical of Hervey to be so frank and forthright. It was also typical of him to devote such patience and such a degree of delicacy and ingenuity to damaging the prospects of the man he detested. Caroline needed no lessons in disliking her son, but the Vice-Chamberlain saw to it she should not change her attitude; and for the Queen's amusement he drew up a lengthy paper comparing Frederick's character and conduct point by point with that of the Emperor Nero, as described by Tacitus, Suetonius, Dion Cassius and others. Both the Queen (whom Hervey had already compared to Agrippina) and the Princess Caroline (who, gentle to all the world besides, imitated the Queen in her dislike of Frederick) found this paper made remarkably good reading, and the author was asked to read it aloud to them again and again, till he himself grew exceedingly tired of the whole production.

As an indictment, Hervey's *Character of Frederick, Prince of Wales,* seems no longer very forceful or very damaging. It harps upon the theme of the Prince's inconstancy and describes, with the assistance of many antitheses, the contradictory construction of Frederick's mind. In the first place (announces Hervey) he was "both false and sincere. . . . False by principle, and sincere from weakness, trying always to disguise truths he ought not to have concealed, and from levity discovering those he ought never to have suffered to escape him. . . . Another contradiction . . . was that he was at once rash and cowardly, capable of undertaking anything, and of persevering in nothing. . . . He was . . . both lavish and avaricious, and always both in the wrong place. . . .

He was equally addicted to the weakness of making many friends and many enemies, for there was nobody too low or too bad for him to court, nor nobody too great or too good for him to betray. He had all the silly pride of grandeur and all the mean condescension of humility. . . . He was lewd without vigour, would laugh without being pleased, and weep without being grieved, for which reason his mistresses were never fond of him, his companions never pleased with him, and those he seemed to commiserate never relieved by him."

To these general charges, Hervey adds a number of more detailed parallels, drawn between Roman Emperor and English Prince. Nero loved the theatre and had performed in public. Well, had not Frederick championed the Italian opera-singers? Did he not play upon his violoncello at Kensington Palace before an audience composed of servants and underlings? And what of his immoderate addiction to cricket matches? He too had scoured the streets in drunken company, smashed windows, visited taverns and fought the watch. . . . Nero (concludes the paper) had died at thirty-two. Frederick, it was much to be hoped, would not break his record.

In other circumstances Hervey's portrait of his former friend might perhaps be dismissed as a half-serious, half-extravagant satire, thrown off during a period of exasperation. But Hervey's hatred of the Prince had lasting consequences; and it is to his efforts, seconded by those of the Queen and Walpole, that most historians have been indebted for their opinion of Frederick. Few royal personages have been more partially and sternly criticized. But on what grounds? For though his weaknesses were many and his faults were obvious, though he was foolish and inconsistent and vain and headstrong, they hardly justify his condemnation without a hearing. Yes, he has puzzled posterity as he puzzled his parents. And because the evidence produced against him seems insufficient to explain the bad opinion in which he was held both during his lifetime and after his death, historians have assumed some royal mystery—some dark secret, locked away and now forgotten—which, were it known, would elucidate the whole affair. Research would appear to show that there was no such secret— none, at least, whose nature we cannot guess at—and that in the Prince's character there was more inconsequence than downright villainy.

On some occasions his plans were sensible but his timing was wrong; on others he joined wrong timing and unwise action. Thus, having in February 1737 made a perhaps inopportune, but dignified and moderate, appeal to Parliament, some months later he impulsively threw away his entire advantage. During the first week of July, he had written to the Queen informing her that the doctor and the midwife had assured him there was no longer any doubt of the Princess of Wales's being with child. Caroline's reception of this news was cautious, for she had no great belief in the Prince's veracity and was convinced that he would stop at nothing to accomplish his ends. Was Frederick (she wondered) capable of begetting offspring? She had already, in somewhat embarrassing detail, questioned Lord Hervey about any confidences he might have received on this subject from the unfortunate Miss Vane; and, though Hervey replied that Miss Vane had spoken of Frederick's inexperience but never thrown doubts on his physical potency, thick cobwebs of suspicion still clung in her mind. Suppose Frederick were to delude them with a pretended birth? Naturally he wished to cut out his younger brother, her own beloved William, his father's image; and, if he himself were unable to produce an heir, there was no stratagem he would not entertain to spite the family. Children smuggled into royal *accouchements* were not unheard-of, and her mind did not grow any easier when she encountered the Princess. The young woman had apparently received careful schooling and, to all inquiries, merely replied that *she didn't know.* . . .

But Caroline was determined that she would not be "catched," and it was therefore agreed, in concert with Walpole, that the King should send a messenger to the Prince, announcing that he wished the Princess to lie in at Hampton Court, where the royal family and their attendants were passing the summer. Hervey suggested that her husband would keep her travelling back and forth between London and Kew, and at one of those places she would fall ill and her confinement occur as though by accident. If that were so, said Caroline, she could not help it; "but at her labour I positively will be, let her lie in where she will, for she cannot be brought to bed as quick as one can blow one's nose, and I will be sure it is her child." She added that she still doubted whether Augusta were pregnant. . . . To understand the state of Caroline's mind, and the intensity and bitterness of her feelings at the present moment, we have to take into account the King's behaviour. George Augustus appeared to have forgotten Madame de Walmoden—or praised and regretted her with less persistence —but she had been succeeded by another favourite much nearer home. That "pretty fool" Lady Deloraine was in the ascendant; and Lady Deloraine, being neither tactful nor very kindly, made no secret of the violent attacks and passionate protestations to which her virtue was continually being subjected, and intimated that her resistance had begun to crumble. Among others, she confided in the Princess Caroline, who, outwardly sympathetic, was inwardly furious. . . .

Nor had the King's unpopularity yet died down. This summer, "two or three days before the King left Richmond for Hampton Court," an incident occurred which, though in itself sufficiently trivial, showed the emotions he aroused among his British subjects. George Augustus was standing alone on the waterside terrace, when a single waterman happened to row past beneath the terrace wall. Seeing the King there, he shouted up and roundly cursed him, adding curses for "all his Hanover dogs." George

Augustus from above brandished his stick, but, as he was alone, he could not give orders to have him arrested and the waterman drifted out of sight still bawling sedition, while the tiny distant figure of the monarch continued to shake his stick. . . . The Guards themselves, when the King criticized their evolutions and compared them unfavourably with his German foot soldiers, were said to have echoed the rebellious sentiment of the civilian masses.[1]

Meanwhile Frederick and Augusta had arrived at Hampton Court. On Sunday, July 31st, the Prince and Princess dined in public with the royal family and, after dinner, retired to their own apartments. That evening, Augusta's condition suddenly changed. Hervey had been right in supposing that Frederick did not intend that his wife should bear her child under his parents' roof; and he now realized that she had actually begun her labour! The result was a wild access of wrong-headed energy. It was intolerable that he should be defeated by mere ill-luck—unthinkable that he should appear to capitulate at the last moment! And, ignoring his wife's agonies and his servants' dissuasions, he at once directed that his carriage should be brought round to the door. Augusta, in acute pain, could scarcely walk. The more unpleasant preliminaries of childbirth had already manifested themselves; but with Dunoyer, the Prince's favourite and dancing master, "lugging" at one arm, Mr. Bloodworth, an equerry, supporting the other and Lady Archibald Hamilton (who had recently entered the Princess's household) bringing up the rear in a flutter of remonstrances, Augusta was wheedled, dragged and hoisted into the waiting coach. Frederick himself exhorted and encouraged the sufferer, while she protested that her torments were frightful and begged for mercy. *"Courage! courage! ah, quelle sottise!"* responded Frederick as they struggled along passages and down flights of stairs.

---

[1] *Egmont.* July 27th, 1737.

In the coach, besides the Prince and Princess, were Lady Archibald and "Mrs. Clavering and Mrs. Paine, two of the Princess's dressers"; onto the box climbed Vried, the Prince's *valet de chambre* and private surgeon; up behind swung Mr. Bloodworth and several others. Then the equipage set off at full gallop for London, through the darkness, over rutted country roads, Augusta racked with pain stretched on pillows inside, her attendants doing their best to assuage her misery. An hour and a half of jolting brought the coach to London, and they drew up in the deserted courtyard of St. James's Palace.

So pitiful was Augusta's plight that Frederick commanded all lamps should be extinguished. Within the palace nothing had been got ready—there were no warming-pans, napkins or hot water, but these requisites were borrowed from adjacent houses and, in the absence of sheets, Augusta was put to bed between a pair of tablecloths. Two Lords of the Council, the Lord President and Lord Privy Seal, were sent for post-haste; and under their eyes the Princess of Wales was duly delivered. Around eleven she gave birth to "a little rat of a girl," described by Hervey as "about the bigness of a good large toothpick case."

It now remained to acquaint the King and Queen with the birth of their grandchild. A courier was dispatched to Hampton Court; Mrs. Titchburne, the Woman of the Bedchamber, was first aroused, knocked at the bedroom door and woke the Queen, who demanded to know if the house were on fire. Mrs. Titchburne replied that the Prince had sent to inform them that the Princess was in labour. "My God, my nightgown!" said Caroline. "I'll go to her this moment." "Your coaches too," suggested Mrs. Titchburne, "the Princess is at St. James's." ". . . Are you asleep, my good Titchburne?" inquired Caroline, but the Woman of the Bedchamber protested that her story was true, and George Augustus, who had appeared during the interval, flew into one of his usual violent passions, exclaiming in German: "You see, with all your wisdom, how they have outwitted you. This is all your fault. There is a false child will be put upon you, and how will you answer it to all your children? . . ."

The Queen said little, dressed, called her coaches and started for London, accompanied by the two elder Princesses, the Duke of Grafton, Lord Hervey and Lord Essex. Again the road was covered at breakneck speed. But when they arrived at St. James's the palace was dark, and it was some while before a footman could be found with a candle, to light Caroline to her daughter-in-law's apartment. There she met Frederick in nightgown and nightcap. He kissed his mother and led her into Augusta's bedroom. Caroline congratulated her, remarking: *"Apparemment, Madame, vous avez horriblement souffert." "Point du tout,"* responded the Princess, always docile and obedient, from the bed; at which Lady Archibald presented the new-born child, naked except for a red mantle and various napkins. Caroline bent down and kissed the infant. *"Le bon Dieu vous bénisse"* (she murmured), *"pauvre petite créature! Vous voilà arrivée dans un désagreable monde."* [1]

After some further civilities addressed to the Princess and a few words to Frederick (who had waited at the bottom of the stairs to say that he hoped the King and Queen would stand godfather and godmother) warning him not to come to Hampton Court that day, for "to be sure the King is not well pleased with all this bustle you have made . . ." Caroline walked over to Lord Hervey's lodgings, where she wrote George Augustus a brief letter and spent an hour drinking hot chocolate and abusing her son. Was there ever such monstrous conduct, she inquired of her circle. "Such a fool, and such an insolent impertinent fool? And such an impudence, to receive us all with such an ease, as if nothing had happened, and that we were the best friends in the world?" But at least (she said) she was now convinced of the child's paternity.

---

[1] The "little rat of a girl" grew up to be a stout handsome woman and Duchess of Brunswick. She survived till 1813.

". . . I own to you I had my doubts upon the road . . . and if, instead of this poor, little, ugly she-mouse, there had been a brave, large, fat, jolly boy . . . I believe . . . that I should have gone about his house like a madwoman, played the devil, and insisted on knowing what chairman's brat he had bought."

At eight o'clock, after a long conversation with Sir Robert Walpole, who had been summoned to the Palace from his bed, Caroline drove back wearily to Hampton Court. There she found two letters from the Prince of Wales which had crossed her on the road when she set out to London, addressed in terms of exaggerated deference to herself and the King. Frederick's efforts to act the diplomatist did not improve his position. Indeed, he was one of those incurably tactless natures to whom the knowledge that they have behaved badly or decidedly foolishly furnishes at any time a dangerous excitant. The fibs and subterfuges he now employed were of the very flimsiest kind. In these letters, and in various letters by which they were followed, when he had learned from Lord Essex that the King resented his conduct "to the highest degree" and positively refused either to receive him or to enter into correspondence, his excuses and evasions were remarkable for their complete ineptitude. Thus he pretended that he had transported the Princess to St. James's from Hampton Court because at the latter place nothing was prepared for her lying-in, whereas Caroline knew that at St. James's there had been neither fires nor sheets. He also contradicted the previous account he had given his mother of the Princess's symptoms at Hampton Court before she began the journey. . . .

Two embassies were undertaken without success—by Lord Jersey, who waited long and in vain for his reply, on a cold, blustering, wet night, with one foot swollen by gout to the size of his head; and by Lord Carnarvon, who was not asked to stay to dinner. Princess Caroline (who had never esteemed Frederick) sent a message through Dunoyer, the Prince's dancing master, that in her opinion and in the general opinion at Hampton Court, her brother and all his associates deserved to be hanged. But this last reproof Frederick took philosophically, turning away, when he heard the message, to spit in the fire. *"Ah! vous savez la manière de la Caroline; elle est toujours comme ça,"* was his only response.

The Princess Augusta, in the meantime, knew very little of the commotion that circled about her. Frederick, who, profiting by his father's example, used to say that no woman should meddle with politics, had kept her as yet in profound ignorance of the whole affair, and when she at last heard of it she was violently distressed and excited. Nine days after her confinement she received a second formal visit from the Queen, who arrived in company with the two elder Princesses. Frederick did not go down to welcome them and, though "industriously civil and affectedly gay" with the various members of their suite who filled the bedroom, spoke not a single word to his mother and sisters. When they swept out again he accompanied Caroline to the door of her coach. There his eye alighted on the crowd of spectators—that London crowd which had hurrah'd him at the fire in the Temple; and the histrionic impulse became suddenly active. Dropping to his knee on the dirty cobblestones, he seized his mother's hand and kissed it reverently.[1]

Herself a comedian, Caroline had never played to the gallery, and for those who courted the applause of the mob she had a profound repugnance. She found it difficult enough to think of a monarchy as constitutional; that it might become "democratic" and professedly popular she could not foresee; and Frederick's calculating insincerity increased her resentment. As for the King, his opinion of Frederick had passed all words. On August 20th he signified his royal pleasure that the child should be christened, and announced that he and the Queen would stand godparents by proxy. The ceremony took place nine days later. Frederick,

---

[1] Horace Walpole and Hervey both describe this incident; but Walpole makes the mistake of suggesting that it occurred at the Queen's first visit.

whose appetite for making popular gestures had been whetted by
the success of his performance at St. James's Palace, directed that
his daughter should not be called Princess Augusta, "but according to the old English fashion, the Lady Augusta," yet added that
she should bear the title of Royal Highness, which none of his
sisters had received in the same position.

Then, after the christening, came the expected punishment.
There had been deep discussions between the Queen and Walpole
and Hervey as to the form this retaliation ought to take, and Sir
Robert and Hervey in separate and secret conclave had drawn up
a letter of remonstrance from the King to the Prince, which included a definite command that he should quit St. James's, but
added that the little Princess was to be allowed to remain in her
mother's charge. This letter the Cabinet Council reviewed and
decided upon, urged by Walpole, who declared that the King
must conquer before he could be expected to forgive and that a
patched-up peace would be neither lasting nor honourable. . . .
Did his memory fly back to 1720 and to the patched-up peace with
which he himself had returned to office, when he had reconciled
the present monarch and Frederick's grandfather? At least, there
were no such thoughts in the Royal Family: George and Caroline
drew no parallel with their own adventures, and felt no sympathy
for the son and heir who was doomed to retrace them. But the
Queen thanked God that the business was over and uttered a devout hope that she might never see the monster's face again;
Princess Caroline trusted that the Prince might *"crever* . . . that
we may all go about with smiling faces, glad hearts, and crape
and hoods . . ."; while George Augustus summed up the debate
for parents in general: "When one's children behave well to one,
one certainly must be a brute not to behave well to them; but
when they behave ill, they deserve to be worse used than any other
people because the ties they break through are stronger. There
are degrees in all these things. Bad subjects are very provoking;

bad servants are still more provoking; and bad children are the most provoking of all."

On September 10th, a solemn procession, formed by the Duke of Grafton, Lord Chamberlain, the Duke of Richmond, Master of the Horse, and Lord Pembroke, Master of the Stole, left Hampton Court and directed itself towards St. James's. It carried with it the warrant of the Prince's disgrace, in which George Augustus recapitulated Frederick's bad behaviour, rejected his apologies, professions and protestations, accused him of "premeditated defiance" and outrageous contempt of his paternal authority, and concluded that the King could not suffer his palace "to be made the resort of them who, under the appearance of an attachment to you, foment the division which you have made . . . and thereby weaken the common interest of the whole. . . . It is my pleasure that you leave St. James's with all your family, when it can be done without prejudice or inconvenience to the Princess."

While the Duke of Grafton was reading aloud this message, Frederick changed colour once or twice, said that he was extremely sorry for what had happened and maintained an attitude that was "very civil, and very decent." The following day he began to feel the effects of his father's indignation, for the King's notions of vengeance were thorough-going. The Secretaries of State informed foreign ministers that his Majesty trusted they would refrain from visiting the Prince and Princess, and a notice was distributed "to all Peers, Peeresses, Privy Councillors and their Ladies, and other persons in any station under the King and Queen, that whoever goes to pay their court to their Royal Highnesses the Prince and Princess of Wales will not be admitted into his Majesty's presence." The sentinels were removed from the Prince's doors, and (to make sure that no detail had been neglected) instructions were issued to the King's Oilman, who had previously lighted the lamps of the house in Pall Mall, that henceforward he would no longer be expected to do so.

Monday, September 12th, had been fixed for the exodus. A crowd watched Frederick and Augusta leave St. James's Palace, many of those who stood by being dissolved in tears, among others the sentry then on duty, who had been forbidden by the King's orders to present arms. Kew was the destination of the royal equipage; and from the small house where he had spent most of the summer months—too small for his large and rambling household—Frederick conducted his defence and concerted countermeasures. Once again he was in a cautious and pacific mood—wronged but still dutiful, hurt but obedient. All who detested Walpole and distrusted Caroline, despised the King and deplored the association of England and Hanover, saw in Frederick the virtuous victim of a complex tyranny.

The City of London rallied to the support of its favourite Prince. Shortly after the *accouchement* of the Princess, the Lord Mayor and Aldermen had requested Frederick to inform them when it would be convenient for him to receive their congratulations; and, accordingly, during the latter part of September, he went up to accept their homage at Carlton House. The occasion had been cleverly stage-managed. Carteret and Chesterfield gave their assistance. Printed copies of the King's message were handed round, and Carteret made it the text of an impromptu speech, "You see, Gentlemen," he remarked, "how the Prince is threatened if he does not dismiss us; but we are here still, for all that. He is a rock; you may depend upon him, Gentlemen; he is sincere; he is firm." . . . In an age that relied so much upon pamphleteering it was natural that both the King and the Prince should resort to the printing-presses, and Frederick having published the King's message together with a selection of his own letters—the more submissive, slightly touched up in translation—the Queen and Walpole retorted with the entire royal correspondence, translated at Caroline's request by Hervey. Frederick, however, had the last word and perhaps the most damaging—one particularly hurtful to the sovereign's vanity. He resurrected, and gave to the public for purposes of comparison, a similar interchange of letters between his father and grandfather. They anticipated the present quarrel by some two decades.

After all it had proved difficult to get the better of him. Frederick's very irresponsibility made him elusive. Owing to his lack of plan, it was practically impossible to foretell his moves. He provided a problem beyond the grasp of mere intelligence. And then, there was his irrepressible and maddening buoyancy! One might have expected that, disgraced and expelled from the Palace, he would have plunged in deeper and deeper till he had completed his ruin; instead of which his behaviour was cool and moderate. It was important, of course, that he should maintain his dignity, and Cliveden and Norfolk House were selected as rural and urban residences, but he did his best to effect economies and to curtail his household, meanwhile living the simple life of an honest squire. From the high-gabled, red-brick doll's-house in the park at Kew, where he played the harpsichord in a diminutive white-panelled drawing room, he set out on lengthy walks through the surrounding country. Accompanied by the Princess, Lady Archibald and a favourite dancing master, he would stroll innocently for hours at a time through the lanes and fields.

3

*H*E WAS young, vigorous, tolerably self-satisfied. His mother (whom he now regarded as his chief opponent, for his father's temper, he said, was explosive but not vindictive) had few of the physical consolations that her son enjoyed. She was ageing and, though she did not suspect it, her resistance had weakened. The patience of the human organism is not unlimited. Dragooned by the will, goaded by ambition or hope or love, it may support intolerable exactions for a number of years; then, suddenly, it revolts and throws off its burden. Since the birth of her last child in 1724 Caroline had been subject to a variety of ailments—troubled by violent "cholics," tortured by gout, besides another more serious and more painful affection. But none of these maladies was allowed to impede her. George Augustus expected her to go out walking. Very well then, she would plunge her swollen and knotted feet into a bath of ice-cold water till the pain had subsided. Her husband was notoriously impatient of sickness, and it was very seldom and very reluctantly that she retired to bed. Her passionate and selfless absorption in his desires and interests steeled her alike against physical discomfort and spiritual lassitude.

Her life was a martyrdom—yet an enjoyable martyrdom. If power is one of the greatest of human pleasures, and the consciousness of succeeding magnificently in any given role a sufficient recompense for the most strenuous and exhausting efforts, Caroline's reward was all that she had hoped and expected. She commanded fear, admiration, hatred, envy; the authority she exercised she had earned herself—bought at the cost of a deliberate personal sacrifice; the means that she employed were of her own devising. Acquired at this price, her position seemed doubly valuable. The satisfactions of sovereignty had never palled, and in 1737 they were as strong as ever. She was still amiable yet overbearing, good-humoured yet tyrannous. Surrounded by her guards and ladies-in-waiting, her bulky yet majestic person was still to be observed moving at a brisk pace through Kensington Gardens, Richmond or St. James's Park. She kept up her devotion to theology and history, loved to talk of Erasmus or Melanchthon (whose "gentle spirit" she preferred to that of Luther) or discuss a new and learned work on the Council of Trent. To Lord Egmont, a devout and proper churchman, while describing her scheme for commissioning a French translation of Thuanus's *History of His Own Times,* she once admitted having spent twelve years searching for certain suppressed passages by that author ("which she had lately the good fortune to purchase"), and explained that in her own private cabinet she had "papers six foot high from the ground." Historical documents of any kind awoke her interest, and into a large red-and-gold leather-bound volume she pasted remarkable items that came her way, from ancient state papers to modern *jeux d'esprit*.[1] Indeed, she was "curious in everything," Egmont decided, and "read and conversed" on more subjects than the average man, with a breadth of outlook and sureness of judgment that were exceedingly masculine, though her erudition was so lightly carried it never grew tedious. There were occasions, nevertheless, when she concealed her knowledge; it was not permitted to overawe or offend her husband.

She found it less easy to hide her taste for building and gardening. Both at Hampton Court and at Kensington Palace she had made extensive changes; and the construction of "Merlin's Cave," in Richmond Park, was a source of great annoyance to George Augustus, who failed to understand the charm of this romantic vagary and regarded it as a foolish and extravagant whim. Library and waxwork show combined, the small thatched building with pointed Gothic windows enclosed a number of bookcases and, at one end of the room, grouped round a table, six life-sized wax figures, representing Merlin and his secretary, Queen Elizabeth and the Queen of Henry VII, and two personages derived from a poem by Ariosto. The Librarian was Stephen Duck, "the thresher poet," a rustic versifier whose untutored productions were then fashionable and whom Caroline advanced to curacies and rewarded with sinecures. A bust of William Wollaston, the Cam-

---

[1] The Queen, according to Horace Walpole, also collected old plays, both English and French, and, during Lady Suffolk's stay at court, often copied out and read the letters she received from Swift. To the Queen's interest in historical portraits we are indebted for the preservation of the Holbein drawings at Windsor. As a patron of scientific research, she encouraged the early practice of inoculation.

bridge Deist, among other metaphysicians of doubtful orthodoxy, hinted at the daring and speculative character of the Queen's beliefs.

Now she was raising a new library in St. James's Park. Once more William Kent's Palladian niches would be dignified with the busts of famous men; and perhaps in their soothing impassive company, surrounded by solid ramparts of gilt-tooled leather, she designed to build herself a symbolic refuge from the court and world. On the 9th of November she arrived to admire the edifice, but while there was suddenly taken ill and returned home, in great pain and very uneasy. After swallowing, on the advice of Dr. Tessier, Physician to the Household, a dose of a preparation known as "Daffy's Elixir," Caroline gave in and retired to bed. Even her husband realized that she needed rest, but when he offered to dismiss the courtiers and postpone the Drawing Room, she refused the suggestion and declared that she would receive as usual. She therefore rose, entered the state apartments and, when she encountered Lord Hervey, merely observed: "Is it not intolerable at my age to be plagued with a new distemper? Here is this nasty cholic that I had at Hampton Court come again."

Her friend begged that she would go to her own room, but Caroline persisted in the attempt to hide her sufferings, and continued to move about the apartment from group to group. At last she understood that her illness was getting the better of her. "I am not able to entertain people," she told Hervey, apparently a little puzzled at the extent of her weakness. But the King, meanwhile, had become involved in a lengthy argument over the merits of the new burlesque at Covent Garden, and some time passed before he could be prevailed on to dismiss the company. Then, as he was withdrawing, he paused to remind his wife that she had not yet conversed with the Duchess of Norfolk, and Caroline turned back and spoke a civil word. Finally she reached the threshold of her private apartments, and, sick, exhausted and shaken, was hurried to bed.

There her symptoms grew worse as the day went on. Acute pain was accompanied by recurrent attacks of nausea. Towards the approach of evening she became more and more restless, and at seven o'clock, when Hervey appeared at her bedside, she announced that she would take any remedy that he liked to propose. Hervey, himself a sufferer from severe "cholics," had his own idea of the treatment that the case demanded, for he was convinced that her illness "proceeded from a goutish humour in her stomach that should be driven from that dangerous seat into her limbs," and he at once suggested a course of violent medicines. The pharmacopœia of the early eighteenth century was still largely medieval. After consultation with Broxholme, the Prince's physician, and Ranby, the King's house-surgeon, "a sensible fellow," a number of potions were compounded and administered —usquebaugh, a strong spirituous liquor akin to whisky, flavoured with cinnamon, cloves and other spices, snake-root, mint-water and "Sir Walter Raleigh's Cordial," a mysterious nostrum much in favour at royal deathbeds.[1] But the vomiting returned and the pain did not slacken; while an obstinate stoppage which had manifested itself was not relieved. Caroline was bled by Ranby, but remained restless and feverish. George Augustus, thoroughly alarmed, spent the night in the sick-room.

Unfortunately, he elected to lie on the bed itself, so that it was impossible either for him to sleep soundly or for Caroline to toss and turn without embarrassment. Next day, her condition had not improved; but, once she had been bled, her fever appeared to diminish and the King decided that he would hold his levee. The Queen did not share her husband's optimism. To the Princess

---

[1] It had been administered—without effect—to Prince Henry, elder son of James I, and to Charles II.

Caroline she spoke of her approaching death, and added: "Poor Caroline! You are very ill too; we shall soon meet again in another place." Worn out with anxiety and constant weeping the Princess suffered from agonizing rheumatic pains and a copious bleeding at the nose that could not be checked. Even so, she was seldom absent from her mother's pillow, and Hervey kept her company through sleepless nights, drawn to her in the curious intimacy such a scene produces. Nor was the King often far away from his wife's bedside, but roamed helplessly, noisily, unhappily among attendants and doctors.

Only Frederick—and any mention of him—was carefully excluded. Hearing of his mother's illness he drove up to London, and on Friday the 11th, two days after the Queen had fallen ill, he sent a message requesting that he might be allowed to see her. The King was furious at what he considered his son's duplicity. This, he exclaimed, was but another "of the scoundrel's tricks; it is just of a piece with his kneeling down in the dirt before the mob to kiss her hand at the coach door when she came from Hampton Court . . ." Now he had arrived to insult "his poor dying mother. . . . No, no! he shall not come and act any of his silly plays here. . . ." And Hervey was commissioned to inform the messenger, Lord North,[1] that "in the present situation and circumstances his Majesty does not think fit the Prince should see the Queen, and therefore expects he should not come to St. James's."

Caroline, when she heard of the incident, gave her complete approval. Indeed, she repeated her views of the Prince's character, confirmed her detestation of his unfilial conduct and begged that at all costs he might be kept away. Her mind was still lucid in spite of anguish, but physically her decline was very rapid, and during the whole of Friday her condition grew graver. The King's atti-

---

[1] Father of George III's famous minister.

tude was as affectionate as it was inconsiderate. On Saturday morning, when he came into her room after a few hours' rest and saw, no doubt, the change that those hours had made, he was observed to bend down and whisper to her low and urgently. Never had Caroline appeared more agitated; never had she seemed to be closer to peevishness; but George Augustus persisted that he must do his duty and, though she implored him to respect her confidence, he summoned the house-surgeon. Ranby examined her, much against her will and notwithstanding her attempts to misguide his fingers, then turned to speak with the King who stood near the fireplace. The Queen started up furiously from her position in bed. "I am sure now, you lying fool," she cried in her sharpest tones, "you are telling the King I have a rupture."

Ranby answered that it was so, and that time was precious. Caroline did not reply, but she slipped wearily back again and turned her face the other way upon the pillow; for the first and last time during the course of her sufferings, a tear of weakness and humiliation rolled down her cheek. The great secret—the fatal secret—was at length laid bare. Only three living persons, her husband, and her Woman of the Bedchamber, Lady Sundon, and her German nurse, Mrs. Mailbone, knew that at the birth of her last child the Queen had sustained a serious umbilical rupture. To George Augustus she had always made light of the injury, explaining (as he presently told the Vice-Chamberlain) "that it was nothing more than what was common for every woman to have after a hard labour . . ."; and the King had not hesitated to accept her word. In fact for the King alone had she arranged the deception, since she understood that her physical hold on him was all-important and that the strength of his regard might flag once desire was exhausted. Caroline had been long accustomed to arousing passion; no effort was too excruciating if she could retain that faculty.

Now the secret was out and the harm was done. Simultaneously the illness entered on another phase, and new tortures were prepared for the hapless patient. Ranby demanded the support of more experienced doctors; Shipton and the aged Bussière having examined the Queen, both pronounced for an immediate operation. On Saturday evening the swelling was opened, but this, though considerably less drastic than the procedure which Bussière at first proposed, had none of the beneficial results the physicians anticipated. During the small hours of Saturday morning Caroline complained that her wound was becoming extremely painful and begged that they would dress it; when they moved the bandages, they discovered that it had begun to mortify. The Princess Caroline was called, Lord Hervey roused—he had fallen asleep on a mattress in the Queen's ante-chamber—the King awakened by his daughter from a makeshift bed. The assembled doctors announced that they must abandon hope—gangrene or "mortification" was an enemy that always defeated them—and it was impossible that the patient could resist its onslaughts.

All that they could now do was soften the worst of the agony. "Lenient ointments and anodyne preparations" were applied, and they retired, leaving the Queen with her husband and children. Of them she took her leave with tender decorum. To George Augustus, she remarked that she had nothing to say; so close had they been that his thoughts were hers, and their sympathy was so complete there was little she could add to it. With the Princess Amelia her parting was brief, but to the Princess Caroline she entrusted the care of her younger daughters—"Poor Caroline, it is a fine legacy I leave you—the trouble of educating these two young things"—while, "as for you, William" (she continued to the Duke of Cumberland), "you know I have always . . . placed my chief hope in you. . . . Be a support to your father, and double your attention to make up for the disappointment and vexation he must receive from your profligate and worthless brother. It is in you only I hope for keeping up the credit of our family. . . ."

Then, once again, her thoughts swung back to her husband. It was in George Augustus her whole career had been incorporated; his weakness had been her strength, his folly her stepping-stone. Yet any disdain she might ever have felt now vanished in gratitude. Slipping from the finger a ruby ring he had given her at her coronation, she placed it upon his hand. "This is the last thing" (she said) "I have to give you—naked I came to you, and naked I go from you. I had everything I ever possessed from you, and to you whatever I have I return. . . ." While the others wept, Caroline remained almost placid. Calmly she reviewed her husband's prospects, estimated his chances of future happiness and advised him, in the common interest, to take a second wife. At this proof of the solicitude he had so often experienced, the friendly indulgence that had forgiven him so many foibles, George Augustus's grief became even more passionate and, between hoarse sobs, he had some difficulty in producing an answer. *"Non—j'aurai —des—maîtresses,"* he assured her brokenly. *"Ah, mon Dieu! cela n'empêche pas,"* replied the Queen.

Repeatedly the King kissed the dying woman; yet such was the inconsequence of his changes of humour that, when she asked him for her watch which hung by the chimney-piece because she was anxious that he should have the seals, he suddenly reverted to his usual snapping and bullying vein. Then she dozed off and woke, declaring she felt much refreshed. That the reprieve was only temporary she understood, and she wished that her ordeal might have an end—"I cannot recover; but my nasty heart will not break yet"—observing that she believed she would die on a Wednesday, since that day had been memorable throughout her life. She had been born on a Wednesday, had married the King, given birth to her first child and become Queen of England on that day. It was appropriate that Wednesday should complete the pattern and cut short that complex development of pleasure and suffering.

She had not counted on her own tremendous physical fortitude. The following Monday Sir Robert arrived from Houghton,
shedding tears as he knelt down in bulky discomfort to kiss the
King's hand, and she was well enough to receive him at her bedside. Nor did she forget the spirit of their coalition. It was her
desire that Walpole should retain his authority, and to his
guardianship she recommended the King and her children, and
to his wisdom the country they had governed together—a bequest
that was bound to impress itself on her husband's mind, so that
Walpole's power and her own memory would become inseparable.
If she could no longer aid Sir Robert in the royal cabinet her influence should at least assist him from beyond the grave.

So Monday went—and Tuesday, Wednesday, Thursday. On
Monday there had been a further operation, endured by the Queen
without weeping or flinching, and even with certain touches of
sardonic humour. From Ranby, as he dressed her running wound,
she inquired "if he would not be glad to be officiating in the same
manner to his own old cross wife that he hated so much"; and
when Bussière, who stood by holding a candle while Ranby used
his lancet upon her tissues, happened to set fire to the curls of his
wig, she bade the surgeon "stop a while for he must let her
laugh." [1] She also commanded that they should disregard her if
she groaned or whimpered, and submitted to probings and lanc-
ings with the utmost stoicism; her husband considered them necessary and that was reason enough. Beneath the King's irritable exactions, she was always mild and patient, and accepted his turbulent humours with the same equanimity dying as living.

There was no change in her attitude towards her domestic
duties. Equally, there was no alteration in her private beliefs; in
the scepticism she had always adhered to she still persisted. By
Wednesday many of the courtiers were openly scandalized. When

---

[1] *Egmont.* November 22nd, 1737.

would prayers (they demanded) be offered in the Queen's bed-room? Sir Robert Walpole approached the Princess Amelia with a suggestion that they might send for the Archbishop. Personally, he made no secret of his unbelief. "Pray, Madam," he said, in his loud cynical voice, which carried across the ante-room and rever-berated on the ears of an astonished company, "let this farce be played. The Archbishop will act it very well. . . . It will do the Queen no hurt, no more than any good. . . ." Accordingly the Archbishop was called to the Palace and continued to pray at her bedside morning and evening, though the King invariably left as he entered the room and Caroline listened patiently but without enthusiasm. At the same time she spoke to him of Dr. Butler, author of *The Analogy* and one of the modern divines she had most delighted in, and begged the prelate after her death to at-tend to his welfare.

Certainly she did not receive the sacrament; no deathbed con-version transformed her existence, and, like Sophie Charlotte, whom in life she so much resembled, she declined now to capitu-late in the face of death. The Archbishop's ministrations were gently declined. How imperatively he had pressed them on her we do know but, from a diplomatic point of view, his task was invidious. As he left, the courtiers outside the door crowded round him begging for the latest news, and demanding: "My Lord, has the Queen received?" "Her Majesty is in a heavenly disposition" was his only response as he rustled across the ante-room.

In another respect, too, Caroline made no concessions. Her dis-like of the Prince of Wales did not diminish. She neither asked to see him (which she knew would have enraged his father, though George Augustus had allowed her to make her choice) nor ex-pressed herself with any compunction regarding their differences, but sent a vague and general message that she had forgiven his misdeeds. Meanwhile the Prince's behaviour had not been edifying. At first he had put up some pretence of grief and anxiety, but as day succeeded day the pretence grew thinner. "He is very decent," said Lady Archibald Hamilton, laughing, when she was asked if the Prince of Wales was really concerned, and Hervey's spies soon provided him with an atrocious story. The Prince's messengers visited St. James's whenever possible and Frederick sat up all night to receive the reports they furnished, talking excitedly and at endless length of the expected *dénouement*. "Well, sure we shall soon have good news," he was said to have informed his suite; he did not expect that her Majesty could hold out much longer. . . .

But, though hope had disappeared, the Queen lived on. During Thursday the discharge from the wound grew still more offensive —the wall of the gut was thought to have given way—but she remained conscious and more calm and resolute than her husband and daughters. For them the days and nights were now hardly distinguishable. Sleeping in arm-chairs, on couches and improvised pallets, springing up from where they lay at some sudden alarm or to receive a bulletin from the doctors that grew always worse, they passed their time between exhausting vigils and uneasy slumber. Hervey had kept them company since the very beginning (though Sir Robert now kicked his heels in the anteroom), tireless for all his fragility and effeminate graces. He would listen to George Augustus's rambling monologue—in which the King spoke first of the Queen's merits, then of his own equivalent virtues—or attempt to console the grief of the Princess Caroline and sit talking beside her bed or at the foot of her sofa. But, without respite, in the depths of his prodigious memory, the observations he had accumulated were being stored away.

It is improbable he had ever been exposed to a greater strain; no setting could have been worse suited to his fastidious temperament; yet in his *Memoirs* no other episode is more moving and vivid or brings out his peculiar qualities in such strange relief.

Few touches of sentiment or hints of tenderness distinguish his narrative. Indeed there is something almost masochistic in the resolution with which he appears to have determined that not the smallest detail should be allowed to escape his memory, no matter how painful or unpleasing. If he was horrified by the spectacle, he was also fascinated. Between the half-drawn curtains of the Queen's bed, in the fire-lit or candle-lit atmosphere of that overheated room, loud with the noisy whispers of her irascible husband, with the sobs of the Princess Caroline, with the muffled coming and going of anxious attendants, he saw the woman to whose service he had devoted all his wit, all his artistry, all his intelligence, for so many exhilarating, disturbing years, tossed to and fro in the fearful agonies that preceded extinction. Daily and hourly her condition grew worse, till the doctors themselves decided that they must let her alone, for their remedies merely tended to increase her sufferings. Yet the Queen's character was not obliterated by the approach of death—she did not emerge with other and weaker lineaments; its traits were still distinctive, its outline firm.

As before, Hervey's tribute is largely indirect; and his experience of life having taught him that human character is made up of incongruities—and that royal characters are of all the oddest and the least consistent—he was delighted to observe the contrasting behaviour of the persons around him. The Princess Caroline was overwhelmed by grief and anxiety; the King's sorrow was deep, passionate, prolonged and sincere, but he mixed brutality and real tenderness in equal proportions. He would scold the Queen fiercely for refusing food (to which she replied that she knew she was "very silly and very whimsical") or, when he noticed her eyes fixed on a point in the air, observe crossly that she resembled a calf that had just had its throat cut. At other times he would treat her with almost feminine delicacy or launch out into a catalogue of his wife's perfections, declare "that he had never seen her out of humour in his life; that he had passed more hours with her, he believed, than any other two people in the world had ever passed together, and that he had never been tired in her company one minute . . . and that if she had not been his wife, he would rather have had her for his mistress than any woman he had ever been acquainted with. . . ." Then, a little later, he would be describing his escape from shipwreck and the exemplary courage he had himself displayed on that occasion, with a gusto as heart-felt and as unself-conscious.

No less characteristic was the egotism of the Princess Amelia, who, one evening when the King, in nightgown and nightcap, sat talking to Lord Hervey of himself and his courage, appeared to drop into a sound sleep; at which George Augustus, observing that the poor child's dutiful attendance on her mother had left her quite exhausted, rose and went off to the Queen's room, and the Princess suddenly woke up, with the exclamation: "Is he gone? Jesus! How tiresome he is!" and proceeded to expatiate at length on her father's vanity. "In the first place, I am sick to death of hearing of his great courage. . . . In the next place, one thinks now of Mama, and not of him. Who cares for his old storm? I believe, too, it is a great lie, and that he was as much afraid as I should have been. . . ." But, as soon as the King returned, she began to rub her eyes and murmur that she had really slept very heartily, inquiring how long Papa had been out of the room. Hervey, though he understood and mistrusted the Princess, was a little taken aback by this odd mingling of spite and duplicity. . . .

Comic elements were not lacking in the situation, but meanwhile the main tragedy went slowly forward, and by Sunday the 20th its conclusion was already in sight. Caroline herself was impatient to reach the finale. Her sufferings had now continued for ten whole days, and that evening, with her usual calmness and resolution, she asked Dr. Tessier to inform her how long they might last. *"Je crois"* (he said) *"que votre Majesté sera bientôt soulagée."* She had no doubt what kind of relief the doctor promised and replied only: *"Tant mieux,"* with perfect composure, afterwards lapsing into an uneasy sleep. The King lay on the floor at the foot of her bed; the Princess Amelia dozed on a couch in a corner of the apartment; the Princess Caroline and Hervey had both gone to their rooms: when at ten o'clock Mrs. Purcel caught the beginning of the death-rattle. She gave the alarm, and the others gathered at Caroline's bedside—all except Hervey, who arrived too late. "I have now got an asthma," she said, "open the window," and then ejaculated the single syllable: "Pray," at which the Princess Amelia started hurriedly to read from the prayer-book; but, before a dozen words had formed themselves, the Queen was dead. The Princess Caroline held a looking-glass to her mother's lips and took it away without the smallest cloud on its shining surface. " 'Tis over," she cried to her father and sister. But during what remained of the evening she neither wept nor spoke.

In prospect many deaths threaten to create a vacancy: in retrospect there are very few that seem to have left a void. So weak is recollection, so strong is habit. Yet among those who had been most closely acquainted with Caroline, at least four—from motives that were very different—continued to regret her extinction when the struggle was over. The Princess Caroline's grief was deepest and most passionately personal. Hervey, whom she had thought she adored, she could never enjoy; her mother, whom she knew she loved, she had for ever lost; there remained only invalidism, gloom, obscurity—the dim decline of an august but unwanted virgin. Her long vigil at the Queen's bedside had broken her spirit. On Hervey too, equally sensitive if far less tender, his experiences had left a mark that could not be obliterated, and suddenly he impressed beholders as an ageing man, prematurely exhausted, decayed, ridiculous. Soon envy and admiration were replaced by covert sneers, the sneers themselves by irreverent youthful laughter.

It was not that he had attempted to indulge his grief. While Caroline lay in state in the royal Bedchamber, Hervey and his wife held a dinner-party at St. James's Palace, attended by Lady Bristol and various Maids of Honour. During the party he received intelligence of his sister's illness. For Lady Ann he had a real and lasting affection. Provoked by the "indecent gayety" all around him, he left the table and walked angrily away to the fireplace, but not before he had said "a very shocking thing." No doubt this last reminder of human mortality—of time and disease continually eating at the foundations of happiness—had imposed a strain upon his nerves that they could no longer bear.

Cruel commentators noticed Lord Hervey's decadence; it was in the year of the Queen's death, 1737, that the old Duchess of Marlborough made him the subject of her most spiteful portrait —"a painted face and not a tooth in his head!" Of that flagrant, feminine handsomeness there was now little to show. Yet, his teeth loosened or destroyed by the use of mercury, his cheeks wasted by dieting or dissipation—and heavily rouged to conceal their unnatural pallor—Hervey still intrigued and schemed and scribbled. With Caroline his career had lost its focal point. Her personality had supplied the centre his existence needed. He had flattered and striven to amuse her, but his reward was great, for he had had the consoling sense of playing an important part in the affairs of the nation. Once at liberty to follow his own devices, he grew bewildered and began to dwindle into insignificance.

For a time, it is true, his ambitions prospered. Sir Robert, after long pestering, consented to admit him to the Cabinet, in 1739, as Lord Privy Seal; but his admission was deeply resented by Walpole's colleagues. 1742 saw the collapse of Sir Robert's authority;

and Hervey, not resigned to following his master and infuriated by the possibility of enforced retirement, fought an ignominious losing battle to retain his office. Horace Walpole, the Minister's son, was now grown to manhood. "Lord Hervey" (he wrote to a friend during 1742) "is too ill to go to operas; yet, with a coffin face, is as full of his little dirty politics as ever." He "lived shut up with Lord Chesterfield and Mr. Pulteney"—a triumvirate of mutual mistrust and hatred; but these devious combinations served no useful purpose—he was too well known and too ill-liked to return to the government—and he retired, at last, in a storm of embittered invective. At the age of only forty-six, he seemed elderly and brokendown, the once-brilliant, notorious failure of an earlier period.

It was to Lady Mary Wortley Montagu that he addressed his summing up. During their youth they had been distinguished, attractive, fascinating, but now Lady Mary, separated from her husband, had withdrawn into cranky, disreputable exile and was building "a kind of Belvidere" in the South of France, while himself he drifted towards senility in St. James's Square. At all events, he should have the credit of remaining clear-sighted. "The last stages" (he wrote) "of an infirm life are filthy roads; I find the further one goes from the capital the more tedious the miles grow, and the more rough and disagreeable the way. . . ." Hervey continued his exhausting journey some seven weeks longer, reaching its end on the 8th of August 1743.

In 1745, he was followed by Sir Robert Walpole. He, too, had lost much by the Queen's death—the only collaborator with whom he had worked upon equal terms; and with it approached a period of increasing difficulty. Though the Opposition may have included in their ranks few real statesmen—Pitt's qualities had not yet been proved by experience—they commanded the support of unscrupulous publicists and able demagogues, skilled in the development and exploitation of popular feeling. A fresh opportunity came their way when reports reached London of barbarous treatment alleged to have been accorded to certain English adventurers engaged in contraband traffic with the Spanish South American colonies. The city, which hated Walpole and coveted the rich trade of the Southern Seas, was loud in its demands for retaliation; Pulteney, Carteret and their friends increased the uproar—England must fly to arms in defence of her smugglers, now languishing among the verminous straw of Spanish dungeons; Walpole's reasonable remonstrances were swept aside. In 1739 he at length gave way. The motives of the conflict were both commercial and sentimental; Sir Robert, who had no smattering of the new-fangled "patriotism," was equally innocent of modern commercial imperialism; and the great pacifist became an ineffective and reluctant war minister. Ideally, no doubt, he should have resigned his office. But the King, still mindful of his wife's dying recommendation, begged that his old friend would not desert him, and the habit of governing was too strong to be abandoned readily. He had never heard, he remarked, that it was a crime to hope for the best, and once again he expected that he might weather the storm; but for the prosecution of a colonial war he had neither taste nor aptitude. The Duke of Newcastle within the Cabinet grew more and more restive; all around him Walpole heard whispers of intrigue and dissension; even Hervey, his creature and protégé, began secret hagglings.

Walpole's was not a character that could be altered by circumstances. Like Caroline's, his heart was not easily broken; both in his courage and in his cynicism he was monumental—he despised the adversaries he had worsted for twenty years; and he did not fall but was levered earthwards inch by inch. The campaign against him was opened in February 1742, when the Opposition introduced a motion in both Houses that a humble address should be presented to his Majesty begging him to remove Sir Robert from his councils for ever. A long list of supposed misdeeds was produced in debate, varying from his settlement of the South Sea scandal to his recent misdirection of foreign policy; but Walpole carried the day with a magnificent fighting speech. The attack was resumed during the following winter, and meanwhile, though his courage did not decline, there was an unaccustomed weakening of his health and spirits. In his private life he had undergone considerable vicissitudes. Soon after Lady Walpole's death in 1737 he had married Miss Skerrett, that "very clever gentlewoman" about whom the Queen had so often questioned Lord Hervey and with whom he had been living for many years; but only a few months later she died in childbed. Walpole had loved her tenderly, if perhaps not faithfully. . . . Once he had boasted that he put off his cares when he put off his clothes; and, even in moments of greatest anxiety, he would start to snore before his servant could pull the bed-curtains. But now (noted his son) he "never sleeps above an hour without waking; and he, who at dinner always forgot he was minister, and was more gay and thoughtless than all his company, now sits without speaking, and with his eyes fixed for an hour together."

In the House of Commons, however, he revealed no change. A general election took place at midsummer, 1742, and when Parliament reassembled the contest began. To Pulteney's opening attack he retorted with his usual energy. Then the House embarked on the long and wearisome business of adjudging disputed elections—a trial of strength that had little to do with fact or justice. How many of Walpole's nominees could be expelled from their seats? On both sides of the House the excitement was furious and, when Walpole's candidate for the Chairman of Committees was beaten by a narrow margin of four votes, the Opposition lifted their voices in a shout of triumph which welcomed victory and promised no clemency to a defeated minister. Never had the Commons sat so long or so late. As Walpole continued to fight a rearguard action, his opponents hit on the expedient of Saturday sittings that he might miss the week-end exercise he needed and loved. Even so, they found it difficult to break his resistance; in the early hours of the morning, he was still lucid and eloquent; he leaned perilously, but it seemed impossible to drag him down. So massive was the monolith's bulk and so solid its moorings, that stratagem after stratagem was tried and discarded.

But Walpole's pride had always been consistent with conciliation. In a final effort to avert the catastrophe he obtained the King's permission to approach the Prince of Wales with a promise to increase his income to £100,000 a year, pay his debts and raise the ban of his father's displeasure. It was an ill-judged piece of diplomacy, and it did not succeed. Frederick had the double satis-faction of repudiating Walpole's offer and feeling convinced that his repudiation had cost him nothing. Walpole *must* fall, thought Frederick's associates; but the struggle lasted from the first of December to the second of February, and at the end even Pulteney paid him a generous tribute, after a long debate in which his majority had dwindled to three. "Well," he called over from where he sat, "nobody can do what you can." Yonge [1] had done better, Walpole replied. "No," said Pulteney, "it was fine, but not of that weight with what you said."

Walpole was defeated at last, but not dejected. So often accused of the most squalid opportunism, he displayed a stoical dignity as soon as the crisis was over—"a great and an undaunted spirit" (wrote one of his admirers) "and a tranquillity something more than human." George Augustus, when the moment came to part, fell upon his neck, shed tears, kissed him and protested that they must often meet again. On the 9th of February he was created Earl of Orford, while his natural daughter by Miss Sker-rett was raised to the rank of an Earl's daughter as Lady Mary

---

[1] Sir William Yonge, a politician with a reputation for extreme unscrupulous-ness, of whom Walpole had said that "nothing but Yonge's character could keep down his parts, and nothing but his parts support his character."

Walpole. There remained the amusement of watching the discomfiture of Pulteney's friends. Long years of energetic opposition had been a poor apprenticeship for the actual work of government; the confusion that prevailed (according to Pulteney himself at a later time) was so indescribable that he had completely lost his head; and it was with some relief that he retired into the shadow of a peerage. . . . By 1742, the popular clamour against Walpole had died away and, two years later, all attempts to impeach him having come to grief, he was again employing his vast experience of public business for the benefit of Carteret and Henry Pelham. He died in Arlington Street on March 18, 1745, and was buried at Houghton among the generations of Norfolk squires.

George Augustus had survived the Minister as he had survived his wife—he was destined by nine years to outlive his son—and his latter period was passed in solemn, unvarying routine. But as his father grew more royal and immovably regular, so did Frederick's conduct grow more erratic and more harum-scarum. At thirty he was still breaking Dunoyer's windows—merely for the fun of the thing and to frighten the dancing master—or running, disguised, to the bull-ring at Hockley Hole. Other mistresses succeeded Lady Archibald—Lady Middlesex, for example, a woman somewhat older than himself, "short and dark like a winter's day . . . yellow as a November morning"; while he permitted Augusta a mild flirtation with their friend Lord Bute. The tone of his establishment was bohemian and easy-going and, as though to complete the cycle of domestic discord, it was presently removed from St. James's Square to Leicester House—now nicknamed "the Pouting Place of Princes"—whence Caroline and George Augustus had defied his grandfather. They too had been lavish and liberal to annoy the King; they, too, in their own manner, had been democratic; and Frederick, besides patronizing English poets, "walked the streets unattended, to the great delight of the people; was the presiding Apollo at great festivals, conferred the prizes at rowings and racings, and talked familiarly with Thames fishermen on the mysteries of their craft." He still exerted himself for the entertainment of a loyal populace. On the 25th of May 1749, "being the birthday of H.R.H. Prince George . . . the silver cup, value twenty-five guineas, given by the Prince, was rowed for by seven pairs of oars from Whitehall to Putney. Their Royal Highnesses . . . were rowed in their barges ahead of the wager-men, followed by Prince George, the young Princesses, etc., in a magnificent new barge, after the Venetian manner, and the watermen dressed in Chinese habits, which, with the number of galleys attending, made a splendid appearance."

As his life had been irregular, his death was inconsequent. The after effects of a fall from his horse—a bad cold, aggravated by a long windy walk in Kew Gardens—a blow on the chest from a tennis ball he had received at Cliveden—all seem to have contributed to hasten his end. He fell ill on March 6th, 1751; by the 18th he was thought to have almost recovered and sat up in bed, while Dunoyer played to him on the violin. His attendants were at cards in an adjoining room, but the Princess and a physician were both in the bedchamber, when Frederick was attacked by a spasm of coughing and Dunoyer put his arms round him and attempted to raise him. Suddenly he shivered violently, crying *"Je sens la mort!"* slipped from the musician's arms, and fell back dead.

At Kensington Palace the news of Frederick's death created very little stir. It arrived during one of the regular royal card-parties, while George Augustus stood surveying his daughter, his mistress, the Duke of Grafton and the Duchess of Dorset at their usual nightly game. The King merely expressed some surprise because he had been informed that the Prince was better, then leaning over Madame de Walmoden's shoulder (now raised to the English peerage as Lady Yarmouth), "Countess," he remarked mildly, "Fred is gone." Since duty demanded it, he paid a consolatory visit to the Princess: no one could pretend he had not a sense of duty. Indeed, in that singular existence, duty and pleasure were now controlled by the same mechanicism, measured out and strictly regulated by the hours of the clock. His court was exceedingly dull; but it suited the monarch. In 1743 he had been the last English sovereign to appear in person on the field of battle, and at Dettingen had had the stimulating experience of saving his army from a disastrous rout; but, since then, he had reverted to the joys of home life. Madame de Walmoden, brought over from Hanover at Walpole's suggestion, replaced Lady Suffolk; the Princess Amelia took her mother's position as hostess—the Princess Caroline was given up to ill-health and melancholy; while the old courtiers moved placidly in the accustomed treadmill. Every night there was an identical card-party in his daughters' room, attended by Lady Yarmouth, "two or three of the late Queen's ladies" and as many favoured officers of his own Household; and "every Saturday in summer" (according to Horace Walpole) "he carried that uniform party, but without his daughters, to dine at Richmond; they went in coaches and six in the middle of the day with the heavy horse-guards kicking up the dust before them, dined, walked an hour in the garden, returned in the same dusty parade, and his Majesty fancied himself the most lively and gallant Prince in Europe."

Such a nature might seem to have no room for romantic feeling. Yet Caroline's place in the King's emotions was never filled, and to no one else could he expand so freely and passionately. Not long after the Queen's death, early one morning, he summoned Baron Borgman, a Hanoverian officer in his service, and bade him bring a portrait which he heard the Queen had given him and which was said to be a better likeness than any he himself possessed. When he saw it he burst into tears, and ordered that it should be placed on a chair at the foot of the bed and that no one should disturb him until he rang. Two hours went by; then he again summoned the owner. "Take the picture away" (he said), "I never yet saw a woman worthy to buckle her shoe." The sight of a queen dealt him at the card-table was once sufficient to make it impossible for him to continue playing; and for some time the royal family used imperfect packs from which all the queens had been abstracted by the Princess Amelia.

Yet dark fears of the supernatural possessed his mind. On the night of the Queen's death, and several nights afterwards, a page was commanded to sit up in his room. It was on such a haunted night, during the week following the Queen's funeral, that he woke from some hideous dream and "went in a hackney chair through the Horse Guards to Westminster Abbey," where he ordered the vault to be broken open and the lid of the marble sarcophagus to be removed, then "went down into the vault and stood and considered her coffin very attentively a good while," before returning as he had come to a hag-ridden bed.[1] But if he dreaded that Caroline might steal up on him while he still lived, in death he had made special provisions for joining her; and those provisions when the time came were duly honoured. One side of her coffin had been built to slide out, one panel of his was pulled away, and the two were joined, forming the common tomb of the King and his consort. They lie beneath the pavement of Henry VII's Chapel, in a vault that has been reserved for them and their family. The discarded side-panels of their two coffins still lean by the wall.

---

[1] *Wentworth Papers*, p. 538.

INDEX

Index

255

DATE DUE

GAYLORD			PRINTED IN U.S.A.